GROWTH AND DEVELOPMENT
IN AUSTRALIA

THIS book has been written to introduce secondary school students to the study of Australian history. It gives a general picture of social, political and economic changes, with stress on developmental aspects in the nineteenth century and after. Significant examples, biographies of famous people, and excerpts from contemporary sources enrich the narrative throughout.

The book is particularly suited to the new third-form history syllabus in New South Wales secondary schools. This edition continues and consolidates the material which has been found to be valuable in *An Introduction to Australian History*.

By the same authors
AUSTRALIA IN THE TWENTIETH CENTURY

Cover Picture

Circular Quay, Sydney, in the 1870s
(From the *Illustrated Sydney News*, March 1874)

Growth and Development
IN AUSTRALIA

An Introduction to Australian History

A. G. L. SHAW
and
H. D. NICOLSON

ANGUS AND ROBERTSON

First Published in 1966 by
ANGUS & ROBERTSON LTD
89 Castlereagh Street, Sydney
54 Bartholomew Close, London
107 Elizabeth Street, Melbourne

Registered in Australia for transmission by post as a book
PRINTED IN AUSTRALIA BY HALSTEAD PRESS, SYDNEY

PREFACE

Growth and Development in Australia is a combination of two exciting aspects of Australian history. Every beginner in Australian history wants to know how Australia began and how it became what it is today. Even though Australia is only one hundred and seventy-six years old the story is already rich and complicated. A step-by-step Australian history which tries to include all the important factors in something like due proportion must make many general statements with which a beginner would find difficulty. Our aim has been to present a general picture of development, while choosing one or two examples and concentrating on them so as to illustrate the general by the particular. For instance, of the explorers, we have emphasized Sturt, giving an account of his journeys that follow his own as closely as possible; but that is not to say that other explorers did not have equally adventurous individual experiences.

In the latter part of this book we have abandoned the general direction of history in favour of the topical approach. For example, the story of the iron and steel industry illustrates the general field of secondary industry. Politically, our story closes with the creation of the Commonwealth. For those who wish to pursue the later story, *Australia in the Twentieth Century* has been written as a new and separate book.

Selection of significant examples has been our problem throughout. In this volume we have included three short biographies which deal with unusual people and show how some individuals are significant in history. Each biography follows the chapter to which it is most relevant. We have also broken the narrative to describe such matters as inventions, institutions, buildings and meetings, because a beginner must have at least a simple picture of these things to understand history.

For the same reason, we have included as many quotations from the original sources as possible and selected one hundred drawings and illustrations. Our approach has its limitations. Some States are given brief treatment, compared with New South Wales. There are many other people whose lives we could have chosen. But our task was not to satisfy the appetite for history, but to show you the menu and persuade you that the food is digestible. We feel that Australian history is good mental food for Australians and hope that our presentation of growth and development will sharpen your appetite.

A. G. L. SHAW.
H. D. NICOLSON.

THE ILLUSTRATIONS

PICTURES of past events are part of the evidence from which we may draw conclusions about history. When Australia was discovered and first settled, photography had not been invented. Some paintings, drawings and etchings remain, but these have to be carefully examined because the artists were often neither skilled nor accurate. The first photographs in Australia were made in the 1840s. The first illustrated papers appeared in the 1850s. They used wooden blocks carved by engravers, and sometimes lithographs. Photographic process engraving, that is, direct mechanical reproduction of photographs on blocks, came into general use in the 1880s. Thus we have an abundance of pictures to illustrate more recent times.

The collecting of evidence of the past, including illustrations, is most important for history. The best library of early Australian material has grown up around the collection of David Scott Mitchell, who gave his books and pictures in his will to the trustees of the Public Library of New South Wales. The Mitchell Library was opened in 1910.

We would like to thank the Mitchell Library, Sydney; the Commonwealth National Library, Canberra; the Australian News and Information Bureau; the editors of the *Australian Encyclopaedia*, as well as others whose contributions of pictures are acknowledged throughout this book.

CONTENTS

Preface   v
The Illustrations   vi

PART I: GROWTH OF THE COLONIES

1. The Foundation of Australia   3
2. Macquarie and Macarthur—Two Contributors to the
   Growth of the Colony   8
3. Exploring the Rivers   21
4. The Dry Interior and the Squatter's Tracks   30
5. The Squatters   40
6. Immigration   51
   Biography I: Caroline Chisholm   61
7. New Colonies   65
8. Gold   74
9. A Review of the Growth of Colonial Society   83

PART II: DEVELOPMENT OF ASPECTS OF
AUSTRALIAN LIFE

10. The Transformation of Commerce and Industry   95
11. The Development of Steam Transport in Australia   107
12. Primary Industry   112
    Appendix A: Irrigation   133
    Appendix B: The Dairy Industry   135
    Appendix C: The Sugar Industry   138
    Biography II: T. S. Mort   142
13. Secondary Industry   145
    Biography III: G. D. Delprat   158
14. Working Conditions   166
15. The Growth of Sydney   180
16. The Home   194

PART III: ACHIEVEMENTS IN
GOVERNMENT AND SOCIETY 1788-1900

17. The Achievement of Responsible Government   215
18. The Individual Citizen   231
19. The Coming of Federation   241
    Bibliography   251
    Index   255

LIST OF ILLUSTRATIONS

Macquarie's Sydney   12

Some settlements in Macquarie's New South Wales   13

Hyde Park Barracks   16

Sturt's explorations, 1828-30   22

Sturt's exploration of the inland, 1844-6   31

Mitchell's and Cunningham's explorations, 1827-36   35

Mitchell's and Leichhardt's explorations, 1844-6   38

Plan of Adelaide, 1842   70

Developments in the use of steam power   97

The essential parts of Watt's beam engine   99

Parsons's steam turbine   102

Overland Telegraph Line, Stuart and Burke and Wills   105

Railways systems of New South Wales, 1890s   111

Ridley's stripper   119

Change in land use (graph)   131

Basic plan of Snowy Mountains Scheme   134

Sugar industry in Australia, 1959   140

Stages in the Development of foundry practice   150

"Before the Law all Men are Equal"   176

Buildings in George Street, Sydney, in the 1840s   182

Expansion of Sydney, 1788-1950   193

Ground plans of typical Australian houses   208

Bringing the garden into the home   210

Dates lines, 1788-1855   211

Dates lines, 1856-1900   212

Evolution of government in New South Wales   225

Houses of Parliament, New South Wales, 1960   229

LIST OF PLATES

Sydney Cove, 1788   6
"A View of Botany Bay"   6
Conditions of the Aborigines in the early years   7
A convict gang   7
Early artist's depiction of a native funeral   22
Toll gate and asylum, George Street, Sydney   22
Government House about Macquarie's time   23
John Macarthur's residence   23
Portrait of Lachlan Macquarie as a young man   38
Bay whaling in the nineteenth century off Boyd Town Lighthouse   39
The Mutiny on the *Bounty*   39
Her Majesty's Mail   54
The departure of Charles Sturt from Adelaide in August 1844   54
A bushman's hut in the 1850s   55
"Bailed Up"   55
A hut covered with grass   70
Temporary hut formed of a slab of bark   70
A home in the 1850s   70
A pioneer settler's home   70
The Kapunda copper mine, South Australia   70
Klemzig, a Prussian settlement in South Australia   71
Bethany, another Prussian settlement   71
Interior of the electric light tower, Exhibition Grounds   71
The lantern of the Exhibition Dome   71
Shipping wool across a creek in New South Wales   86
Bullock team dragging sledges down an incline   86
Discovery of gold at the diggings   86
A concert at the gold diggings   86
"Off to the Diggings"   87
Gold washing on Summer Hill Creek   87
Cricket in the Domain, Sydney   87
A game like Hockey in Hyde Park, Sydney   87
Punt on the Lachlan River   102
Collision between two paddle steamers on the Parramatta River   102
Cobb's coach crossing a flooded river   103
Glenelg, South Australia   103

Ridley's original stripper 118
Running-in wild horses from the bush 119
Mustering day at a cattle station 119
Sheep shearing in the 1860s 134
Cattle branding in the 1860s 134
Plan of a model dairy 135
O'Meara's homestead 135
Jimbour station, Queensland 150
Victoria River Downs homestead 150
Wheat-breeding and variety plots 151
Depredations of rabbits 151
The Ivel Agricultural Motor 166
Irrigated lands in the Mildura District 166
"The Wayfarer" 167
The Woolloomooloo fish market 167
The swamps on which the Newcastle Steel Works were built 182
The Newcastle Steel Works 182
Sugar cane cutters 183
Stripping sugar cane by machine, 1960 183
The Sydney Post Office in the 1830s 198
In the market 198
Early settler's dwelling 198
A typical nineteenth-century terrace house 198
Brownlow Hill 198
A suburban house in Melbourne 199
An open house 199
Government-built block of 309 flats 199
Opening of the New South Wales Legislative Council 199
Sydney election in the mid-nineteenth century 199
Spring fashions in the 1870s 214
A cooking class in Melbourne, 1875 214
The Melbourne Bicycle club's opening meet, 1878 214
A surgeon's hut in the bush 215
Fishing in Port Jackson, 1878 215
Holtermann's house, North Sydney 215
The School of Industry Ball, 1875 215
Martin Place in 1910 230
Newspaper advertisement showing a shop interior, 1878 231
"Let There Be Light" 246
A Royal Commission's plan for Circular Quay, 1909 247

PART I
GROWTH OF THE COLONIES

CHAPTER 1

THE FOUNDATION OF AUSTRALIA

1. The First Settlement

IN 1786, the British government decided to establish a penal settlement at Botany Bay, in New South Wales. For some years the government had been worried by the over-crowding of the gaols and prison hulks in England, and this seemed a good way to dispose of some of the convicts. Other possible sites, in Africa, had been found unhealthy or barren. Sir Joseph Banks, who had been with Cook when he discovered the east coast of Australia, said he thought this place would do. A few others at home thought it might prove a useful base in the Pacific too, for trade and for the navy. So in May 1787 Captain Arthur Phillip sailed from Portsmouth to Botany Bay with about a thousand men, including 778 convicts, to found the new settlement. When he arrived he moved to Port Jackson, and there on 26th January 1788, which is now celebrated as Australia Day, a party landed in Sydney Cove and unfurled the flag.

2. Conditions in the Early Years

Conditions in the new settlement for some years were very difficult. The newcomers had arrived in a country, which if not a desert, was uninhabited by civilized man. There was no food, except what had been brought out by the ships, or what could be grown in the settlement after clearing some land and then planting and harvesting the crop. There was no shelter except what the convicts could build themselves, without any skilled labour and with primitive equipment and supplies. There was no clothing, except what was sent by ship. There were no markets, no shops, no books to read and no amusements, theatres or entertainments. Above all the settlers, convicts and officers alike, were separated from their old friends and families, if not for ever, at least for many years. The voyage home, should they ever be allowed to undertake it, was long, expensive and dangerous, and in the meantime they were surrounded by natives and by the bush, still unknown and dreaded by town-bred Englishmen, who even fifty years later still thought of it as filled with "a thousand Hob-goblins in the shape of Blacks,

Snakes, flying foxes, Squirels, Mad Bulls and other dreadful animals." These were the typical difficulties which faced the founders of all the Australian settlements, though they were often overlooked by newcomers, who seemed to think that they were coming to a fully settled community (see Chaper 7); but in the years after 1788 they were at their worst, for there were no neighbours to get help from and the nearest white men were at the Cape of Good Hope or in the Dutch East Indies.

3. The Need for Experience and Equipment

For twenty-five years, the infant Colony struggled on; but it grew only slowly, while the English government was more concerned with fighting the war against revolutionary France and Napoleon. During all this time, the problem of how to feed the convicts and their guardians remained a serious one, for supplies of local produce were always uncertain.

In the first place, most of the cultivators, convict or free, were not skilled farmers, and were too poor to buy livestock and tools. The old proverb ran, "Without manure, no crops", and in early New South Wales, with so few animals there was no manure. Much of the soil near Sydney was (and still is) very poor; rainfall was irregular—now a drought, now a flood; clearing land was very hard work, for there was no proper equipment, and the roots of the gum-trees seemed to "spread everywhere". There were only two or three ploughs in the Colony, for only the richest could afford them. The ordinary farming method was the primitive hoe husbandry, with the hoe doing little more than scratching the surface of the ground. Even for the wealthy, farming was difficult; the unskilled ex-convict, without capital to hire labour or bring out tools from England, without any knowledge of good farming practice, found it almost impossible. The wealthier settlers, officers in the government, often had the knowledge and the capital to do well. But horses cost £100, and cows £80; with ten shillings a week the normal unskilled wage, how could the working man save enough money to buy any? In 1803 "as an encouragement to settlers" it was announced that oxen would be issued to those "of good conduct" who had ploughs or could obtain them, but there were so few ploughs that the offer was scarcely taken up. A visiting botanist, George Caley, wrote:

The plough has been tried by some . . . but what appears to me to prevent its coming into frequent use is the want of workmen who know how to use it. . . . I have never seen any people weed their wheat though it is generally over-run with weeds. . . . The wheat is reaped in a slovenly manner. . . . Oats I do not know that they [the colonists] have yet cultivated, even upon trial. . . . Hay is an article I have not seen attempted at. . . . Gardening [i.e., for vegetables] is in an infant state. . . . It is not uncommon to see people in a reputable situation to be without vegetables for some months of the year. . . . Houses in general are nothing more than simple wretched huts, particularly of the farmers. The walls are wattled* and plastered with clay, the roofs thatched. . . . The out-houses, barns etc. of the farmers are miserable-looking sheds, if we except a few that have been built by people who had money.

Hence farming practice was bad. Little attention was paid to manuring. Even on the best farms, there was rarely a proper rotation of crops. Very few farms had threshing and clearing machines. The stumps of trees were a great nuisance, always in the way. There was, it was rightly said, "a want of capital and skill in the majority of settlers."

4. The Social Classes

Of course not everyone in New South Wales was a farmer. There were also the officers, merchants and traders, convicts and emancipists in the little community, and sometimes we find the same man undertaking several occupations.

(a) The officials

At the top of the tree were the local officials, first the governor himself, then the military and naval officers who were stationed in the Colony, and the higher ranking civil officers—the Colonial Secretary, the Treasurer, the legal officers, the chaplains and surgeons and so on. Some of these men received grants of land; as they were intelligent men who possessed enough money to improve their farms, they were usually far more successful than the small cultivator, who was usually an ex-convict. As time went on, some (though for a long time only a few) private persons came out to settle and to cultivate or to trade, and this class was also joined by a few former convicts who had managed to do well in the community.

---

* The word wattle had at that time a different meaning from its present one. It referred to any collection of rods or stakes, interlaced with twigs to make a fence, wall or roof. It was later the popular name given to certain trees of the genus *Acacia,* from the use made of the long pliant branches for making "wattled" fences, etc.

(b) The traders and merchants

The traders and merchants were concerned with bringing goods from Europe to the Colony and selling them there, or with carrying on trade in the Pacific, or with America. Some of this trade, for example in oil and seal-skins, was very profitable, and obviously the merchants importing goods for local consumption were providing things much needed by the colonists. But often they charged very high prices for their goods. Governor King wrote on 28th September 1800:

As the merchants who carry on the whale fishery are now satisfied that the whales are plentiful on this coast, I presume they will continue sending the greater part of their ships here. Much advantage will arise to this colony, not only from the frequent intercourse it will produce between it and England, but also the advantage of bringing convicts and stores out on lower terms than have hitherto been paid. . . . At present the very few things that are brought for sale by these vessels come so exceedingly high that seldom less than 150 per cent is charged by the masters on the English price.

Prices of imported supplies were high, although it was very costly to bring them out to the Colony in the primitive ships of those days, when the voyage took six months and the risks of wreck or loss were great. But the high prices caused complaints (as they do now), and when spirits, especially rum, were imported (and often smuggled) into the Colony, people complained that the importers were making fortunes by encouraging the convicts to drink. Certainly a lot of rum was drunk. Often the promise of a "tot" was an encouragement to work and was added to the day's pay—what else would one expect in a community where other luxuries and amusements barely existed and at a time when drinking was very common among all classes in England as well as in the Colony? Many ex-convicts (and others) were "striking examples of probity, industry, temperance and virtue"; but many of course were not, and their poverty and hardships were often blamed, not on the difficulties of farming, but on their laziness and fondness for rum.

(c) Convicts

The mass of the people were poor and depressed. The bulk of the adults were convicts or ex-convicts. In Sydney, Parramatta and the country, convict gangs could be seen at work. According to a description given to the British Parliament in 1812,

Sydney Cove, 1788.
(Drawn by E. Dayes from a sketch by John Hunter, in Hunter's *Journal*, 1793)

"A View of Botany Bay." H.M.S. *Sirius* and other ships of the First Fleet before the move to Port Jackson.
(From *The Voyage of Governor Phillip to Botany Bay*, 1789)

Conditions of the Aborigines in the early years of Australia.
(From a lithograph by Augustus Earle, 1830 in *Views of New South Wales and Van Diemen's Land*)

A convict gang. Note the variety of clothing and punitive leg-irons.

The convicts in the service of Government, are divided into gangs. . . . They work from six in the morning till three in the afternoon and the remainder of the day is allowed to them, to be spent either in amusement or profitable labour for themselves. They are clothed, fed, and for the most part lodged by the Government; and though in the early periods of the Colony, inconvenience and distress may have arisen from the irregularity of supply from this Country, latterly the food and clothing have been good, and, generally speaking, in sufficient abundance. Should the convicts misconduct themselves at their work, the superintendents have no power of inflicting punishment, but are for that purpose obliged to take them before a magistrate; the sitting magistrate of the week at Sydney, may order a punishment of 25 lashes; a regular Bench, which consists of three, may order as many as 300.

(d) The emancipists

After their sentences had expired, convicts were commonly granted land for a small farm, but then they ran into trouble; for as we have seen, farming was not easy, the ex-convicts were often lazy and would complain that they were being "exploited" by traders.

Governor King wrote in 1802:

It is notorious, that since the time Governor Phillip left the colony in 1792 the utmost licentiousness has prevailed among this class, altho' they have used the most laborious exertions. . . . But unfortunately the produce went to a few monopolising traders . . . and it has often occurred that one night's drinking . . . has eased them off of all their labour had acquired the preceding year.

There was then a conflict between farmers and traders, or rather between the poor ex-convict farmers and their wealthier neighbours, who were traders and large-scale farmers as well. As farmers the latter were more skilful and they often bought the ex-convicts' farms and added them to their own; as traders they lent the small farmer money and sold him goods, but they were usually criticized for charging too much, even after the growth of competition reduced prices. These men could write letters to important friends in England; they were clever men, too, who would try to outwit the naval governors of the settlement, when the latter tried to stop smuggling or to check disputes between the different groups of settlers.

B

CHAPTER 2

MACQUARIE AND MACARTHUR—TWO CONTRIBUTORS TO THE GROWTH OF THE COLONY

1. The Problems

TWENTY years after the foundation, the young Colony was suffering from growing pains. The struggle for survival and a bare existence was over. Instead the settlers began to struggle for social recognition, power, and even wealth. Because farming was so inefficient and industry barely established, the economy of the Colony was weak. The British government still had to pay for the considerable expenses of the Colony. The early governors encouraged the search for some commodity which would help the Colony to pay its way, as an "export staple". Social life in the Colony was low as the different classes feared each other and people lived in quarters which they did not regard as permanent. In addition, there was need for careful and orderly control of government.

In the third decade of its existence, the Colony overcame some of these growing pains. Its governmental, social and economic organization clearly advanced. Two men played large parts in this advance. Strangely, the man who was to help in meeting the economic problems, also helped bring about a crisis in government in 1808.

2. John Macarthur's Ambitions

John Macarthur was an officer in the New South Wales Corps who sought to build a fortune for his family in the new country. He not only took office as Inspector-General of Public Works, but also engaged in trade, and, most importantly, he set up a farm at Parramatta in 1793 next door to the Experiment Farm where James Ruse grew the first successful wheat crop in Australia. He was so successful that in 1794 he was able to write:

Of this year's produce I have sold £400 worth, and have now remaining in my granaries upwards of 1,800 bushels of corn. I have . . . 20 acres of fine wheat growing and 80 acres prepared for Indian corn and potatoes. My stock consists of 2 mares, 2 cows, 130 goats, upwards of 100 hogs. Poultry of all kinds, I have in the greatest abundance.

These things were valuable. Beef was worth 4s. or 5s. the pound, a horse £100, a cow £80; so, as his wife put it, "those persons who took early precautions to raise live-stock have singular advantages".

Though he was very successful, he resented the way that the government interfered in economic affairs by fixing prices and wages, and closely controlling the selling of rum which was so profitable. He did not like the public farms competing with those owned by private individuals. Public farming should be cut down, and private farming encouraged, he urged. This would have suited efficient farmers like himself, but there were not many men of this sort; besides it seemed to the government to be cheaper to produce food itself with the convict labour at its disposal, than to buy what it needed in the market.

As time went on, Macarthur came to think that he could earn greater profits by concentrating on raising sheep. This demanded less labour than growing crops, and, he declared, the "grasses in all seasons are rich and abundant" and the "Native Woods afford a salutary Shelter from the Scorching rays of the Sun in Summer, and from the Chilling Cold of the Wind in Winter". For some years he had been buying sheep, some locally and some from Calcutta and South Africa. He had already been careful with their breeding, and when he went to England in 1802 he took samples of his wool with him. These impressed English manufacturers, and since Napoleon had for the moment cut off their usual wool supplies from the Continent, they strongly backed him. In the end he was given a large grant of 5000 acres at Camden, about fifty miles from Sydney, where he could carry on his grazing activities.

3. Rebellion
When he returned to New South Wales, he soon became engrossed with these; but he was still a farmer and merchant as well, and his trading activities brought him into conflict with that rather hot-tempered martinet, Governor Bligh. The latter was not much interested in the future of sheep-breeding and wool-growing. "What have I to do with your sheep, Sir?" he is said to have burst out. "Are you to have such flocks as no man ever heard of before? No, Sir!" Bligh was more concerned with immediate problems. He wanted to encourage the small wheat farmers; he wanted to curb the sharp practices indulged in by some of the traders of Sydney. When the traders came to believe that such a curb would destroy their livelihood, Macarthur then alleged that Bligh was unjustly interfering with their

property, and his own! Macarthur said that to protect it, Bligh would have to be removed, especially when the Governor was reported to have roared out, "Damn the Secretary of State! He commands at home. I command here."

In the rebellion that followed, Macarthur was certainly the leading spirit. "I have been deeply engaged all this day in contending for the liberties of this unhappy Colony", he scribbled to his wife, after the Governor had been arrested. "The Tyrant is now no doubt gnashing his teeth with vexation at his overthrow." Whether his action was justified is still hotly debated, but it certainly shows that he was determined to overcome all opposition to his plans, just as he was certain that these would benefit the community.

By no means all the merchants agreed with him. For example, Robert Campbell, who had first visited Sydney in 1798 and settled there in 1800, was a strong supporter of the Governor. Between 1803 and 1806 Campbell had imported about 2000 head of cattle, chiefly from Bengal. Their progeny increased rapidly, to the great benefit of the Colony's milk and meat supplies. With others, Campbell developed the building of ships in New South Wales. He promoted seal-fishing, selling their skins and oil; but in this they ran up against the privileges of the East India Company, which had a monopoly of trading anywhere in the Indian and Pacific Oceans. It would not allow "interlopers" to trade, so Campbell could not carry on with this; but he developed an extensive retail business in New South Wales, and this had helped by its competition with visiting ships to reduce the very high prices that had prevailed in the Colony up to 1800. His firm found the importing of rum profitable too, which the government did not altogether approve of; but he did not find it necessary to rebel to further his interests.

The rebellion against Bligh checked the plans of both Macarthur and Campbell, for both had to go to England to take part in the inquiries into the affair—Campbell as a witness for Bligh, Macarthur as a defender of the rebels. Campbell suffered the more by being away, for though Macarthur was not allowed to return until 1817, during all that time his wife, Elizabeth, looked after his affairs in New South Wales very carefully. She controlled and improved his flocks and his farms, and saw to the production of wheat, hay, hogs, cattle and mutton as well as the invaluable wool. As for Governor Bligh, though he was arrested, the British government felt bound to condemn the rebels. They reappointed Bligh for one day, and sent another governor to succeed him, Lachlan Macquarie.

4. Macquarie's Hopes

When Macquarie took over in Sydney, on New Year's Day 1810, he hoped that "all dissensions and jealousies which had unfortunately existed in the Colonies for some time past would now terminate for ever." In this he was optimistic; dissensions and jealousies continued, even though no more governors were deposed. But when he left, twelve years later, he could truly describe the great improvements that had taken place.

I found the colony barely emerging from infantile imbecility, and suffering from various privations and disabilities; the country impenetrable beyond forty miles from Sydney; agriculture in a yet languishing state; commerce in its early dawn; revenue unknown; threatened with famine; distracted by faction; the public buildings in a state of dilapidation and mouldering to decay; the few roads and bridges formerly constructed rendered almost impassable; the population in general depressed by poverty; no public credit nor private confidence; the morals of the great mass of the population in the lowest state of debasement, and religious worship almost totally neglected. . . .
. . . That the colony has, under my orders and regulations, greatly improved in agriculture, trade, increase of flocks and herds, and wealth of every kind; that the people build better dwelling-houses, and live more comfortably; that they are in a very considerable degree reformed in their moral and religious habits; that they are now less prone to drunkenness, and more industrious; and that crimes have decreased, making due allowance for the late great increase of convict population; every candid, liberal minded man, at all acquainted with the history of the colony for the last twelve years, will readily attest.

5. Sydney Under Macquarie

Sydney itself was changed almost out of recognition. Where no streets, in the true sense of the word, had existed, but only straggling paths, crooked, muddy, full of ruts and stumps, Macquarie laid out and built thoroughfares which still exist. He insisted that houses and gardens should not encroach on them, that pigs should no longer roam in them, that ashes and rubbish should not be thrown into them. Other improvements to the city followed—a police establishment, a new general hospital, and a military hospital, a lighthouse at South Head, a highroad to it and to Parramatta, a dockyard, a new stone wharf on Sydney Cove, government stables, four military barracks, a new church, Hyde Park, a market, a courthouse, four convict barracks, a gaol, a fort on Benelong's Point—in fact "everything in his power that can in the least degree contribute to the ornament and regularity of the town of Sydney, as well as to the convenience and safety of the inhabitants thereof!"—for which Macquarie "felt both pride and exultation."

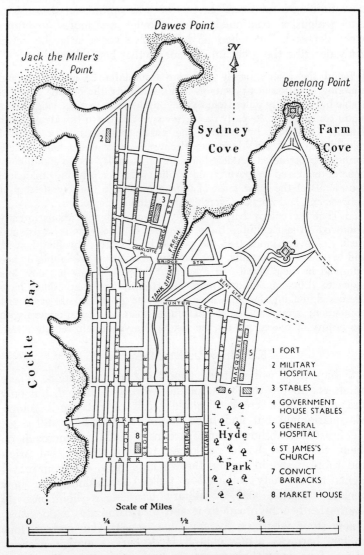

Plan of Sydney showing Macquarie's influence

6. New Roads and Towns

It was not only Sydney that received Macquarie's attention. Soon after his arrival, work began on developments in the "interior"—at least as far as it was then known. Eighty miles of turnpike roads and eighty miles of carriage roads were linking the various townships by 1822, not to mention the 100-mile road over the Blue Mountains to Bathurst. To the townships of Parramatta and Sydney were added Liverpool, Windsor, Richmond, Castlereagh, Pitt Town and Wilberforce, the latter christened in 1810 with the governor "drinking a bumper to the success of each". By the time he left, new churches with their rectories graced these country towns, there was a court-house at Windsor and hospitals at Parramatta, Windsor and

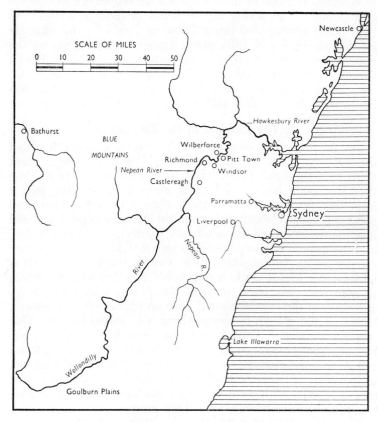

*Some of the settlements in New South Wales when Mac-
quarie was governor*

Liverpool; nine military and ten convict barracks had been built in the Colony and the penal station at Newcastle had grown into a flourishing settlement. With the crossing of the Blue Mountains, the exploration of the Goulburn Plains, and the spread of settlement behind Sydney, New South Wales as a whole was no longer entirely a penal station, and other things than convicts were beginning to be important for its welfare.

7. Farming

Macquarie, like the previous governors, wanted to encourage farming in order to ensure the food supplies for the Colony. He advanced livestock to some of the settlers, and he tried to persuade them to move from lands that were especially liable to flooding. But few of these settlers were skilled farmers. Moreover, while a bad season due to floods or drought would send food prices soaring and bring threats of famine, as for example in 1811 or 1815 and 1816, good seasons brought gluts on the market and very low prices to cultivators, as in 1812-13. Floods caused great damage to the farms, but there were also grubs, caterpillars, rust, smut and weevils to contend with, and no one really knew how to deal with them.

8. The Problem of the Emancipists

But the expansion of wool-growing raised a difficulty about the convicts. Until this time official policy had been to grant them land for small farms when their sentences expired. True they had often been bad farmers and sold their land; but at least this gave to the convicts a chance to settle down and become respectable citizens again. But sheep-farming demanded much more land than the small scale grants given to ex-convicts, and the growth of sheep-farming made it difficult for the former convict to become anything more than a shepherd—a landless labourer for life; it made it impossible, in other words, for him to own his own farm, so that Macquarie, who was always anxious that the convict should have an opportunity for reform, looked at the growth of sheep-raising with mixed feelings. This was a pity, for it helped to make more bitter the quarrels between the emancipists, as the ex-convicts were coming to be called, and the exclusives or "pure merinos", that is, the officers and wealthy settlers who tended to despise the convicts, who had little sympathy with them and regarded them as fit for nothing except to work as labourers for their "betters".

Macquarie tried to introduce into "society" a small number of the better-educated convicts, feeling that after their sentence was finished they should be "restored to society". In a few cases his attempts were justified, for a small number had been transported, especially before 1815, for political offences rather than any serious crime;* but Macquarie's attempt, though only applied in a very few cases, helped to stir up the feeling of ill will between the two sections of the community, and it was something for which the governor was later on reprimanded by the English government.

9. The Convict System

After the Napoleonic wars there was a great increase in crime in England. This was probably due to unemployment and the economic difficulties that followed the end of the war. Many people argued that criminals were not being punished severely enough. They thought that conditions in New South Wales were too attractive and therefore that many men committed a crime in order to get a free journey to Botany Bay, where, it was said, they would live in luxury for the rest of their lives. So Macquarie was blamed for being too lenient and so encouraging crime in England.

"The settlements in New Holland," wrote the British Secretary of State, "not having been established with any view to Territorial or commercial advantages, must chiefly be considered as Receptacles for Offenders. . . . Their Growth as Colonies must be a Secondary Consideration. . . . Transportation to New South Wales is intended as a severe Punishment, and as such must be rendered an object of real Terror."

In fact, transportation was a severe punishment. The number of "gentlemen" convicts whom Macquarie tried to introduce into colonial society was barely a dozen; they were men of good education, whose offences were often political rather than criminal. Macquarie certainly argued that "once a Convict has become a Free Man . . . he should in All Respects be Considered on a Footing with every Other Man in the Colony, according to his Rank in Life and Character." For this reason he hoped the emancipist would become a good farmer settler. But the lot of the convict was always a hard one. When he arrived in New South Wales he might either be employed by government or assigned to a settler. Under Macquarie, most worked for government for he wanted a great number of men for the numerous

* The number of these "politicals" has commonly been exaggerated in the Australian tradition; they were in fact very few indeed—but so were the emancipists whom Macquarie "received" at Government House.

public works. He was particularly anxious to keep skilled tradesmen working for government. But the settlers wanted to employ
these men themselves, and so they began to criticize the governor.
When the British government received the bills for all Macquarie's buildings they began to complain too, forgetting that as
the Colony grew, and more convicts kept arriving, more public
buildings were necessary. One of these buildings was the new
convict barracks. This description gives an idea of the accommodation the convicts were given:

Hyde Park Barracks, Sydney, before alteration
(Drawing by Morton Herman)

The convict barrack is built at the north-east end of a large open
space of ground called Hyde Park, and is inclosed by a wall of 10 and
a half feet high, that separates it on the north from the hospital
ground; and the pleasure grounds attached to the government house,

and towards the south and west from Hyde Park. On each side of the entrance, that is towards the west, are two small lodges 12 feet square, occupied by a clerk and constable; and in the centre of an area, not sufficiently large for the numerous buildings and offices that range along the interior of the walls, is the principal barrack. It is a handsome brick structure, 130 feet in length and 50 in breadth, and contains three stories, that are each divided by a lofty passage, separating one range of sleeping rooms from the other. There are four rooms on each floor, and of these six are 35 feet by 19, and the six others are 65 feet by 19. In each room, rows of hammocks are slung to strong wooden rails, supported by upright stauncheons fixed to the floor and roofs. Twenty inches, or two feet in breadth and seven feet in length are allowed for each hammock; and the two rows are separated from each other by a small passage of three feet. Seventy men sleep in each of the long rooms, and thirty-five in the small ones.

Macquarie was the first governor to provide barracks. Previously the convicts had "lived out" in the town, and although this privilege was still given to those who were well-behaved and some who were married (for the barracks did not have enough room for all) the Governor was in fact trying to improve convict discipline in the Colony. But although as the governor of a penal settlement, Macquarie had necessarily to look after his convict charges, he was always thoughtful of their reformation after their sentences had expired and would reward good conduct with some shortening of their sentences.

10. Macquarie's Achievement

He tried to develop the Colony as a whole, and when he left New South Wales he felt that he had done a great deal. "I left it," he wrote, "reaping incalculable advantages from my extensive and important discoveries in all directions . . . and in all respects enjoying a state of private comfort and public prosperity."

He had reduced the threat of famine, encouraged farming, distributed livestock among the settlers, encouraged religion and morals, built schools, dockyards, wharves, roads, bridges, a hospital, churches and other public buildings, established a bank (the Bank of New South Wales), encouraged trade and local manufactures, looked after the Aborigines, the paupers and the orphans, established a police system in Sydney, and so helped to create a remarkable degree of law and order in the community.

His farewell tours in 1820 and 1821 throughout the Colony showed him that he had worked well; today his name records his achievements in city and country alike, and even the British

Secretary of State, Lord Bathurst, admitted that "the great increase of population and the advances . . . made in agriculture, trade and wealth of every kind, cannot but be highly creditable to your administration. If, as a place of punishment, it has not answered all the purposes for which it was intended, this is certainly not owing to any deficiency . . . on your part."

11. The Want of a Staple

In the matter of finding a suitable staple for the Colony Macquarie had not been personally successful. In 1813, many settlers had sent a memorial to Macquarie lamenting "the want of a staple commodity, by the exportation of which we may be enabled to procure such articles of import as are absolutely indispensable to civilised life."

Many suggestions and experiments were made—hemp and flax, for example; but would they grow? And what of the cost of sending them to Europe? Would the English government buy them for the navy? Macquarie

pledged himself to all such Persons as may engage in the Pursuit [of growing flax] that he will furnish them with the Produce of Manufacture in return . . . and they will be indulged with his further Patronage and Support.

But it was no good. In 1820 only enough was grown to "supply the shoemakers". The tobacco plant was tried, and so were tea, sugar and cotton; but the early settlement was too far to the south for these tropical crops. A few skilled farmers had some success growing the vine and the olive; but this was rare. Whaling, as we have seen, had been successful and profitable; but a whaling fleet was expensive to fit out, and the risk of loss was considerable. There was some trade with the Pacific Islands, especially New Zealand and Tahiti, in coconut oil, pork, bêche-de-mer (sea-slugs of tasty varieties) and pearl-shells, but traders were apt to seek profit by supplying firearms to the natives and their brutality caused trouble. In short, as time went on, only one possible staple had been discovered, and that was wool.

12. John Macarthur and the Wool Trade

When Macquarie arrived in Australia, John Macarthur was in "exile" in England. He used the time to study the London wool market, to find out the types most wanted, and to learn how it should be prepared for sale. The pastoral industry, even when helped by huge free land grants, demanded a heavy

investment in stock and a long waiting period before returns
began to come in. Some pastoralists could accumulate this
capital from the profits they made in their farming and mercantile enterprises, and others were quite well-to-do when they
arrived, but they could not earn good profits from their wool
until they developed the market for it. Macarthur's genius lay
even more in his work in developing this market, as a salesman,
than in his technical skill as a grazier, which was shared by
other colonists.

In 1819, he converted to his views J. T. Bigge, the commissioner sent out from London to inquire into the affairs of the
Colony. At first Macarthur suggested that he be given a
monopoly to supply pure-bred rams to all the graziers in the
Colony, and another huge land-grant to keep them on, which
was further evidence of his grand designs; but though Bigge
naturally refused this proposal, he wrote that "on the expediency
of promoting in the Colony the growth of fine wool no doubt
can be entertained", for he was sure that sheep-grazing offered
great prospects to New South Wales. Its temperate climate, its
extensive unoccupied land, its supply of convict labour for
shepherding, combined with a demand for wool in England
which now began to grow rapidly as a result of this improvement
in wool manufacture brought by the Industrial Revolution, made
the prosperous development of wool-growing a certainty.

13. The Beginning of Pastoral Expansion

Macquarie had hesitated to allow expansion of the pastoralists
outside the coastal region because he feared that the convicts
would be able to escape. He allowed eight men to graze stock
at Bathurst while sheep were dying on the coastal plain. Bigge
wrote to Macquarie in 1820:

Every encouragement should be held out to those who possess sheep
and cattle to repair to the grazing districts either at Bathurst or in the
New Country beyond the Cowpastures . . . the very exhausted and
insufficient state of the pastures in this part of the Colony, and the
difficulty that is felt by most of the settlers in sending their flocks and
herds to such a distance as Bathurst and incurring the risk and
expense of erecting temporary stockyards for their protection, upon a
mere temporary permissive occupancy liable to be withdrawn or
narrowed upon the approach of new settlers made it imperative that
grants and purchases of land should be allowed at Bathurst and
Argyle.

Macquarie took no official steps to implement this, but the settlers started to explore for new lands and some even sent their sheep without finding a new run for them. Thus in 1820, the pastoral expansion started.

In the same year John Macarthur showed thirty-nine sheep at the Parramatta Fair which was attended by Governor Macquarie. He sold thirty-six rams for £510/16/6. At the same time his merinos were beginning to produce, as a result of pastoral care and breeding, a longer stapled wool than was customary. Other families were not far behind, and in many aspects the Riley family were ahead of the Macarthurs. Between 1809 and 1825 exports rose from 74,284 pounds to 323,995 pounds, and Australia's staple export was established.

CHAPTER 3

EXPLORING THE RIVERS

1. Reasons for Exploration

FOR the thirty years after Macquarie left Sydney, the most important thing in the life of Australia was wool. Wool became the principal export. It brought great wealth to graziers; it caused men who had insufficient land to try to find more, so that it was largely responsible for exploring and opening up the interior. The need for huge grazing properties caused the sheep-owner to occupy vast tracts of land and to fight against anyone else who wanted to try to settle there; the profits from sheep-raising led to much speculation, and also to the improvement of living conditions and the building of town mansions by the wool-kings; it caused the purchase of much land from the Crown to turn into parts of sheep-runs. The demand for labour caused many migrants to come to Australia; their arrival and the increasing wealth of the community eventually made it impossible for the British government to continue transporting its convicted criminals to a Colony which was so prosperous and flourishing.

But before we see how the development of squatting affected the community in all these ways, we must first notice how it spurred men on to explore more of the continent. By 1820 it was being realized how profitable wool-growing was. For the next generation men were always seeking more land for their flocks, looking for "good land further out"; for as Governor Gipps wrote in a despatch in 1840, "as well attempt to confine an Arab within a circle traced on sand, as to confine the graziers or wool-growers of New South Wales within bounds that can possibly be assigned to them." From Sydney they went south-west to the Riverina, the Murray and Port Phillip (later Victoria), and north to the Liverpool Plains, New England, the Darling Downs and the Northern Districts (Queensland); from Van Diemen's Land (Tasmania) they crossed Bass Strait and landed stock at Port Phillip and Portland.

As soon as the colonists had discovered a route across the Blue Mountains, behind Sydney, in 1813, they faced the challenge of the "new country". They needed the land; Macquarie

was right when he forecast that it would soon "prove a source
of infinite benefit to the colony", though the settlers had to
adapt themselves to its oddities—its relative dryness and its occasional floods. But the interior was not only profitable; it also
aroused curiosity because of what men called the "problem"
of the rivers—they all seemed to be flowing *inland*, to the west.
Where did they go to? Did they flow to an inland sea, or across
the continent to the north-west, where they might open up
settlement and trade with Asia? For more than ten years stockmen and explorers found no answer to this problem, though in
the meantime many more streams were discovered—the Macquarie, Lachlan, Murrumbidgee, Murray, Condamine, Dumaresq, Gwydir and others.

2. Sturt's First Journey

In 1828 Captain Charles Sturt, an officer on service in New
South Wales, but bored by the idleness of garrison life, took

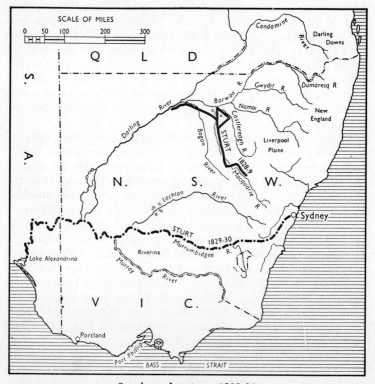

Sturt's explorations, 1828-30

An early artist's depiction of a native funeral. It shows the interest in the
life of the Aborigines displayed by the early settlers; also an inability to
observe exact details of their crafts and manners.

(Engraved by P. Slager, published by A. West, 1814)

Toll gate and benevolent asylum at the end of George Street, Sydney.
(From "A Series of Lithographic Drawings of Sydney and its Environs",
by courtesy of the Mitchell Library, Sydney)

Government House about Macquarie's time.

John Macarthur's residence, near Parramatta.
(Section taken from J. Lycett's sketches, by courtesy of the Mitchell Library, Sydney)

charge of an exploring expedition to the north-west. It was
a year of drought, and he hoped that this might have dried up
the swamps on the Lachlan and Macquarie which had stopped
earlier expeditions in this direction. It had; the river was a
mere trickle; but the drought brought other difficulties. There
was little feed for the party's cattle, and the general effect was
disheartening: "it was lamentable to see the state of vegetation
upon the plains from want of moisture," he reported afterwards, and though he thought much of the soil was "far from
poor", yet "the space I traversed is unlikely to become the
haunt of civilized man."

He explored the course of the Macquarie; then on New
Year's Day, 1829, he discovered the Bogan, which he called
New Year's Creek, and he followed it until he came to its
junction with a "noble river", which he called the Darling, after
the Governor. But the effects of the drought were serious.

We passed hollow after hollow that had successively dried up,
although originally of considerable depth; and when we at length
found water . . . sometimes it was so bitter as to be quite unpalatable.
. . . There was scarcely a living creature, even of the feathered race,
to be seen to break the stillness of the forest . . . though we passed
some considerable plains, lying to the westward, on parts of which the
grass, though growing in tufts was of luxuriant growth.

The Darling itself, when they found it, was salt, and when
the men rushed to drink from it, Sturt wrote, "Never shall I
forget the cry of amazement that following their doing so, or
their looks of disappointment. . . . The cup of joy was dashed
out of our hands before we had time to raise it to our lips."
Sturt thought that though "this remarkable and central stream"
might be valuable, he feared that "the country through which
it flows holds out but little prospect of advantage." Back at his
camp at Mt Harris on the Macquarie, he found nearly all the
vegetation "perished", though rather to his surprise, the animals
were in better condition.

It might, therefore, be reasonably presumed that herbage affording
such nourishment in so unfavourable a season, would be of the richest
quality, if fresh and vigorous under the influence of seasonable, and
not excessive, rains. . . . The appearance of the country was, however,
truly melancholy; there was not a flower in bloom, nor a green object
to be seen.

They went eastward to the Castlereagh; there the situation
was little better. It was terribly hot and the river was only a

C

series of water-holes. From time to time they found spots where there was still a little grass; all the same, the natives here were "dying fast, not from disease, but from the scarcity of food." At last they reached the junction of the Darling, ninety miles above the spot where they had struck the river before; it was exactly the same—heavily timbered, filled with fish, and still too brackish to drink. Reluctantly, Sturt decided they would have to go back to Sydney. The drought was too much for them.

During the short interval I had been out, I had seen rivers cease to flow before me, and sheets of water disappear. . . . The vegetable kingdom was almost annihilated. . . . The largest forest trees were drooping, and many were dead. The emus, with outstretched necks, gasping for breath, searched the channels of the rivers for water, in vain; and the native dog, so thin that it could hardly walk, seemed to implore some merciful hand to despatch it.

Such was the result of two years when it appeared "as if the Australian sky was never again to be traversed by a cloud."

This journey showed some of the difficulties of outback life in this new continent, which would arise, as Sturt foresaw, from the "droughts to which we have reason to believe the climate of New South Wales is periodically subject." Even in districts where usually there was sufficient rainfall, stock would die in such a season; the top-soil would blow away; there would be loss or disaster for the cultivator. Much of the soil seemed poor. Despite some good grazing land, there seemed an "undue preponderance" of "barren tracts" between all the principal streams, though Sturt admitted that it was "impossible for me to have formed a correct opinion under the present melancholy circumstances"; but he hoped that Governor Darling was wrong when he wrote off the whole area as being "from the total absence of water altogether unavailable for the purpose of tillage or pasture", for Sturt himself realized that in the areas of good soil and in good seasons, conditions would be very different:

it has borne the appearance of barrenness, where in even moderate rain, it might have shewn very differently. . . . Our animals, on the whole, have thriven on the food they have had, which would argue favourably for the herbage.

Such was the country that Sturt had found. And, as far as the rivers were concerned, he had solved one problem and raised another. He had cleared up the mystery of the marshes, and had found that the Macquarie, Bogan and Castlereagh (and presumbly also the Gwydir, Namoi, Condamine, Dumaresq and Lachlan) were all tributaries of the Darling. But whither did the Darling flow?

3. Sturt's Second Journey

We know now where the Murray reaches the sea, and that its mouth is blocked by sand bars; but in 1829 this was still a mystery. When Matthew Flinders, in 1802, had sailed across the south of Australia, charting the coastline from Cape Leeuwin to Encounter Bay, he had not reported any great river mouth; so some people thought that the Darling river system ran to the north-west, or even to some inland lake. At all events, in 1829 Sturt set out along the Murrumbidgee to try to discover what happened to it. "As the Mirambidgee is a River of some magnitude," reported Governor Darling, "it will be satisfactory to be assured of its course and termination, as well as of the nature of the country through which it runs. Should it unite with the Darling and proceed to any part of the Southern Coast within reasonable distance, it might in the event of the Land being of a good quality, prove an inducement to . . . Settlement, as . . . there can be little doubt . . . of these Rivers being navigable . . . which might be the means of opening a direct and perhaps an easy communication between Sydney and that part of the Colony."

Sturt left Sydney in early November. He soon reached the river and found the country very good; the river flats "for richness of soil, and for abundance of pasture can nowhere be excelled". He only regretted that it was "at such a distance from the capital as to be unavailable". It would not always be so.

Further downstream he found it difficult to travel along the banks of the winding stream, constantly crossing and recrossing it, and often having trouble with the mud, so he decided to take to the whale-boat which he had brought in sections by land from Sydney. On 7th January, with seven companions, three soldiers, three convicts, and George MacLeay, the 20-year-old son of the Colonial Secretary, he set off. But the very next day their casks of salted meat sank, and though they were recovered they were spoiled by fresh water getting mixed with the brine, and so the party ran very short of meat before their journey ended.

For four days the journey was uneventful through country "as flat as it is possible to imagine". Then suddenly

the channel contracted, and became almost blocked up with huge trees, that must have found their way into it down the creeks or junctions we had passed. The rapidity of the current increasing at the same time, rendered the navigation perplexing and dangerous. . . . In every reach we had to encounter fresh difficulties. In some places huge trees lay athwart the stream, under whose arched branches we were obliged to pass; but, generally speaking, they had been carried, roots foremost, by the current, and, had we struck full upon any one of them, it would have gone through and through the boat. . . . The river . . . swept round to every point of the compass with the greatest irregularity. We were carried at a fearful rate . . . [until] we were hurried into a broad and noble river. . . . I can only compare the relief we experienced to that which the seaman feels on weathering the rock upon which he expected his vessel would have struck—to the calm which succeeds moments of feverish anxiety, when the dread of danger is succeeded by the certainty of escape.

They had reached the junction of the Murray, "of noble breadth and splendid appearance". Progress now was easier, despite occasional rapids. They met several parties of natives "undoubtedly a brave and confiding people" and "by no means wanting in natural affection", but "the most loathsome diseases prevailed amongst them. Several were disabled by leprosy, and two or three had entirely lost their sight." The travellers always succeeded in making friends with them, with more or less difficulty, until after about ten days "a vast concourse of natives" came in view, singing their war song, and painted and armed for combat.

The river was shoaling; the aborigines rushed out on to a sand-bank, and covered it in a dense mass. They flung themselves into the most extravagant attitudes and worked themselves into a state of frenzy by loud and vehement shouting. I foresaw it would be impossible to avoid an engagement, yet with such fearful numbers against us, I was doubtful of the result.

Sturt handed arms to his men, and took up his gun.

A few seconds more would have closed the life of the nearest of the savages. . . . I was determined to take deadly aim, in hopes that the fall of one man might save the lives of many. But at the very moment when my hand was on the trigger, and my eye was along the barrel, my purpose was checked.

Four natives with whom the travellers had made friends the day before suddenly appeared on the scene. One dived into the water and after struggling across the channel to the sand-bank, stood in front of the savage at whom Sturt had been aiming. It was not long before the mob were pacified.

Curiosity took the place of anger. . . . In less than a quarter of an hour from the moment when it appeared that we were on the point of commencing a bloody fray, which, independently of its own disastrous consequences, would have blasted the success of the expedition, we were peacefully surrounded by the hundreds who had so lately threatened us with destruction.

At this point another river, one hundred yards wide and more than twelve feet deep, with sloping grassy banks over-hung by magnificent trees, flowed in from the north. Sturt felt sure it was the Darling, though he had last seen it three hundred miles away, its waters "saline and useless, in the midst of drought and desolation".

An irresistible conviction impressed me that we were now sailing on the bosom of that very stream from whose banks I had been twice forced to retire. I directed the Union Jack to be hoisted, and giving way to our satisfaction, we all stood up in the boat and gave three distinct cheers.

The going down the Murray now became easier. But Sturt was continually worried about the return journey and anxious about his men, "who had borne their fatigues and trials so cheerfully, and had behaved so well." Provisions were already running low. The salt meat was spoiled; they had seen few wild-fowl. There was little other than flour to eat. And this was the easiest part of the journey, downstream. On the way back they would be fighting the current. Would their strength hold out? At least for the moment they were having less trouble with the Aborigines, for they were introduced from tribe to tribe as they passed along. But all the same the natives were a great nuisance. Diseased and filthy, they insisted on trying to talk to the explorers, whom they could not understand, and on pulling their beards and touching their clothes. No wonder their presence was "disagreeable". Yet thinking of their return journey, they had to remain friendly, "to keep up the chain of communication, to ensure our own safety"—and apart from this, Sturt always prided himself on avoiding conflict with the Aborigines.

A fortnight after leaving the junction of the Darling, they arrived at Lake Alexandrina, at the mouth of the Murray, thirty-three days after leaving the depot on the Murrumbidgee. The river problem was solved. It only remained for them to try to find out whether there was a channel to the ocean. There was none. The way to the sea was "barred by shoals and sand-hills, and the mouth of what channel did exist was defended by a double line of breakers, amidst which, it would be dangerous to venture, except in calm summer weather."

Now the party had to face the journey back. The men were tired and weak from lack of proper food, yet they had to row nearly a thousand miles, up-stream, past possibly hostile natives, in the middle of a hot summer. Rations were reduced to ¾ lb flour a day for each man. Any delay or accident, however slight, might bring disaster. The river had fallen and was now so shallow that the boat had to be hauled over a number of bad spots. One particular set of rapids, just above the junction of the Murray and the Darling caused great trouble.

We were up to our armpits in the water. Rain was falling as if we were in a tropical shower, and the force of the current was such that if we had relaxed for an instant, we should have lost all the ground we had gained. Just at this moment, a large tribe of natives, with their spears, lined the bank and took us most completely by surprise. At no time during this anxious journey were we ever in so defenceless a situation. It had rained so hard, that our firelocks would have been of no use, and had they attacked us, we must necessarily have been slaughtered.

Fortunately no attack was made, and they finally got over the rapids by tying ropes "upon the large rock that formed the left buttress as it were to this sluice", and pulling upon them. When, after thirty-one days, they reached the Murrumbidgee again, they

began to experience the effects of the rain that had fallen in the mountains. The river rose upon us six feet in one night, and poured along its turbid waters with proportionate violence. For seventeen days we pulled against them with determined perseverance, but human efforts, under privations such as ours, tend to weaken themselves. . . . Our daily journeys were short and the head we made against the stream but trifling. The men's arms appeared to be nerveless; their faces haggard, . . . and their spirits wholly sunk; from mere exhaustion they frequently fell asleep during their painful and almost ceaseless exertions. . . . Our provisions were nearly consumed and would have been wholly exhausted, if we had not been so fortunate as to kill several swans.

One night, Sturt heard one of his men whispering, "I must tell the Captain to-morrow I can pull no more." But the next day he went on just the same. It was not until 11th April, a month after entering the Murrumbidgee, that they reached their camp, having rowed, since 6th January, more than 1700 miles. Sturt himself was disappointed and returned to Sydney "disheartened and dissatisfied", thinking he had found

no country likely to be of present or remote advantage to the Government; the noble river on whose buoyant waters we were hurried along, seemed to have been misplaced, through such an extent of desert did it pass, as if it were destined thus never to be of service to civilized man; and for a short time the honour of a successful undertaking, as far as human exertion could ensure it, was all that remained to us after its fatigues and its dangers had terminated.

This was perhaps natural; but it was unjustified. He had solved the problem of the drainage of south-eastern Australia, and the lands he had discovered were more valuable than he thought. True, the Murray Valley, when it was found not to be navigable to the sea, could not be thickly settled until railways could be built. Parts of it needed to be irrigated. But he had discovered one of the richest areas of Australia, as he himself realized; the only difficulty was its situation. "If its hundreds of thousands of acres were practically available," he wrote, "I should not hesitate to pronounce it one of the richest spots of equal extent on earth, and highly favoured in other respects." Even so, the expedition was not without result. When Sturt returned to England and published an account of his experiences, the high praise he gave to the land in the valley of the lower Murray and around St Vincent's Gulf was important to the plans then being made in England for founding another settlement in South Australia.

CHAPTER 4

THE DRY INTERIOR AND THE SQUATTER'S TRACKS

1. Sturt's Third Expedition

BY ABOUT 1840 most of the grazing land in eastern Australia had been discovered and occupied, as we shall see in the next chapter; but the centre of the continent was still unknown. Sturt was convinced there must be fertile land there. He had tried to settle as a grazier in New South Wales, but he had not been very successful, so he moved to Adelaide. Here he was employed first in the survey department, then as Registrar-General; but he did not enjoy this work, so he proposed, in 1843, to undertake another exploring expedition, this time to Central Australia, to solve "the most important and the most interesting geographical problem in the world". He recalled that when he was on the Darling he had noticed cockatoos and parrots, which liked the "richest and best watered valleys", flying "in countless numbers" to the north-west. Now he was living in South Australia and he saw them flying "directly from the north". He argued that where these two lines of flight met, "a little to the northward of the tropic", there ought to be fertile country, or even perhaps, an inland sea; at all events, he was determined to try to find out.

Unfortunately he overlooked the fact that it was easier for birds to fly quickly over the desert than for man to toil wearily across it. He confessed afterwards that he had not expected the intervening country to be quite so barren and waterless as it actually was. But he proposed to avoid the route due north, which another explorer, Edward John Eyre, had already discovered was blocked by the barrier of Lake Torrens; he would travel up the Darling to Menindie, and from there would strike out north-west into the unknown. On 15th August 1844, with twelve men, three carts, two hundred sheep, eleven horses and thirty bullocks, he set out on the great adventure; it was to last nearly eighteen months.

The journey up the Murray and Darling rivers to Menindie was easy; but there Sturt was disappointed to find that the River Williora, which he had hoped to follow to the north-

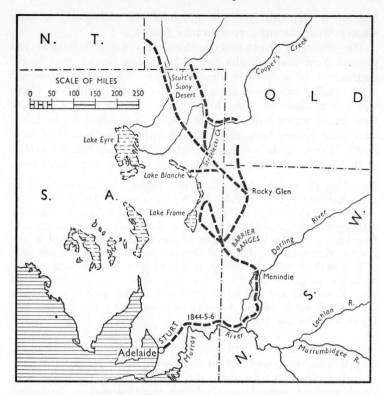

Sturt's exploration of the inland, 1844-6

west, was nothing but a back-water of the Darling. If he wanted to carry out his plan of travelling north-west, he would not be able to follow any regular water-course. The natives warned him how inhospitable the country was, with ranges covered with sharp-pointed stones and great rocks that would fall on us and crush us to death", intense heat, and neither "water nor grass, nor wood to light a fire with".

Nevertheless, in October the party set out in the direction of the Barrier Ranges (near the present Broken Hill); when they reached them, they travelled to the north along the western slopes. The ground was covered with quartz, iron-stone and granite, so that "it appeared as if McAdam had emptied every stone he ever broke to be strewed over this metalled region". Sturt, and later his second-in-command, Poole, crossed the ranges to the north-west; Poole even reached the salty Lake Frome; but both were forced to return by heat and lack of water. Sturt thought much of the soil good; "it only wanted water to enjoy comparative luxury"!

The explorers continued northwards along a line near the present New South Wales-South Australian border, and found themselves in a "perfect desert" where "sand ridges covered with spinifex succeeded each other like waves of the sea. There was not a blade of grass to be seen." At the end of January they found water and shelter at a spot they called Rocky Glen, near what is now Milparinka, in the extreme north-west of New South Wales, "little imagining that we were destined to remain at that lonely spot for six weary months". They were marooned,

locked up in that desolate and heated region . . . as effectually as if we had wintered at the Pole. The heat was terrific. The thermometer reached 132 degrees in the shade; the average for three months was 103 degrees; the ground was thoroughly heated to a depth of three or four feet. . . . The horn handles of our instruments, as well as our combs, were split. . . . The lead dropped out of our pencils; our hair, as well as the wool on the sheep, ceased to grow, and our nails became as brittle as glass. The Flour lost more than eight per cent of its original weight, and the other provisions in still greater proportion. . . . We found it difficult to write or draw, so rapidly did the fluid dry in our pens and brushes.

Some of the men got scurvy; eventually one died of it. Expeditions were sent out to the north, the west and the east; but all were driven back by the desert, where "the stillness of death reigned around us, no living creature was to be heard; nothing visible inhabited that dreary desolation but the ant— even the fly shunned it."

Not until the end of July did a fall of rain let them go on—once more to the north-west, on across the desert. They made an excursion due west which brought them to the salty waters of Lake Blanche; they crossed Strzelecki Creek and Cooper's Creek, and then ran into Sturt's Stony Desert, "a gloomy stone-clad plain", with rows of sand ridges on both sides, "running in parallel lines into the very heart of the interior, as if they absolutely were never to terminate". On 8th September they reached their most northerly point, at latitude 24° 40′ S., just south of the tropic of Capricorn, near the present Queensland-Northern Territory border. But they had to turn back.

Water and feed had both failed. Spinifex and a new species of *mesembryanthemum*, with light pink flowers on a slender stalk, were the only plants growing in that wilderness. . . . From the summit of a sandy undulation . . . we saw that the ridges extended northwards in parallel lines beyond the range of vision, and appeared as if interminable. To the eastward and westward they succeeded each other like the waves of the sea. . . . Familiar as we had been to such scenes, my companion involuntarily uttered an exclamation of amazement when he first glanced his eye over it. "Good heavens," said he, "did ever man see such a country!"

The return was a race against the onset of scurvy and the drought. A dry year meant that there was little or no water in the pools which had been filled the season before. On 17th November they reached Rocky Glen, where they had spent the previous summer amid "ripe grass and shrubs, and quantities of birds"; now they found that "not a herb had sprung from the ground, not a bud had swelled, and where the feathered tribes had swarmed in hundreds, not a bird was now to be seen". And they were still 270 miles from the Darling! A party went ahead to Flood's Creek to find if there was still water there. It brought back the answer: "There is still water; but it is black as ink and in a week it will be all gone." So they had to push on. Sturt himself was by now too ill to walk; but a fortnight later they reached the Darling safely, and on 19th January 1846 arrived back in Adelaide.

Sturt had failed to cross the continent, or even to reach its centre. He did not find an inland sea, nor the good country that he thought was shown by the flight of birds. All the same he had suggested the solution of the geographical problem of Central Australia. "I have torn down the dark curtain which hung over the interior," he wrote. He discovered "the greatest unknown river system which the interior still contained", with its "outlet" in the salt lakes of the interior.

Sturt's expeditions did not open up very valuable territory excepting the lower Murray and St Vincent's Gulf, but he had accomplished great feats of exploration and suffered unparalleled hardships; and he showed, and this was important, that sheep-raising and cattle-grazing could not be carried on everywhere in Australia, because much of it was too dry.

2. Cunningham

Meanwhile, during all this time other explorers had been at work too. Some were sent out at the head of official parties; some were simply squatters looking for new land. Allan Cunningham, a botanist, who found he could "blend discovery with botanical research tolerably well" in 1823 found a way through the Liverpool ranges opening a road from Bathurst to the Liverpool Plains. Later on, in 1827, Governor Darling asked him to lead another expedition northwards, on which he discovered the Darling Downs, and the pass (Cunningham's Gap) over the ranges down to Moreton Bay.

3. Mitchell's Discoveries

Major Thomas Mitchell was another successful explorer. A "most indefatigable person", he had joined the New South Wales Survey Department and quickly became Surveyor-General. In 1831 he made his first expedition to the upper Darling, and four years later he was on the river again, tracing its course for three hundred miles to the south-west. But he did not discover where it finally flowed to and in 1836 Governor Bourke sent him to western New South Wales again, to settle the Darling question for good.

His party, with one Aboriginal and twenty-two volunteer convicts, promised an absolute pardon if the expedition were successful, had an almost military appearance. The major in scarlet jacket and the convicts in new grey trousers and red woollen shirts made quite a procession, with some leading the packhorses, some driving the sheep and cattle—food for the next few months—and some walking beside carts filled with instruments, tools, tents and stores. Two men, we are told, had to carry the barometers, taking care to hold them upright so as not to disturb the mercury. Then came the boat carriage, bearing two whale-boats, which might be useful if the Darling or the Murray proved navigable. And so the carriage, with its boats, carts, cattle, sheep, horses and men set out from Parramatta, over the Blue Mountains, across the hot dry plains of New South Wales.

Shortage of water prevented the party from travelling due west; they had to keep to the waterholes left in the beds of the rivers. Sometimes they made up to fifteen miles, but on bad days, when the cart-wheels sank into cracks or when rocks were blocking the way, they travelled barely half this distance; meanwhile Mitchell wrote down all he saw of the Aborigines, the soil, plants, and flowers, the marsupials and the birds, parrots and cockatoos. At last he reached the Murray, a magnificent stream even in this year of drought, and noted its junction with the Darling, which Sturt had found seven years before.

When he reached the Murray, Mitchell should, if he had followed his instructions, have turned for home. Instead, he went on south and soon saw open grassy plains, a land so inviting and still without inhabitants! As I stood, the first European intruder on the sublime solitude of those verdant plains, as yet untouched by flocks or herds; I felt conscious of being the harbinger of mighty changes; and that our steps would soon be followed by the men and animals for which it seemed to have been prepared.

With understandable delight, he wrote that they had

at length discovered a country ready for the immediate reception of civilized man; and destined to become eventually a portion of a great empire. . . . Of this Eden I was the first European to explore its mountains and streams—to behold its scenery—to investigate its geological character and, by my survey, to develop those natural advantages, certain to become at no distant date, of vast importance to a new people.

He travelled on, southward to the sea, now crossing rivers and swamps, now climbing mountains, now moving "merrily

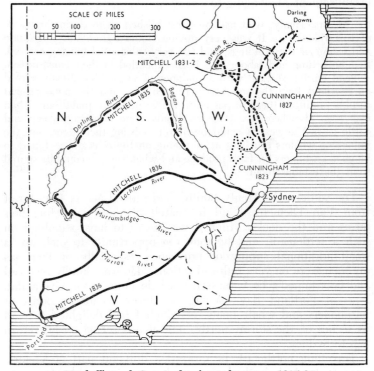

Mitchell's and Cunningham's explorations, 1827-36

over hill and dale", through forest land or grassy plains. There were plenty of difficulties—mud, short rations, rain, gales, cold, Aborigines. In compensation, he found "most beautiful" valleys with "peculiar and romantic features", which "contained excellent soil and grass, surpassing in quality any I had seen in the present colony of New South Wales", and a host of new types of plants and flowers. He finally discovered a fine river which seemed to be flowing south to the sea. On this, which he called the Glenelg, the boats were launched, and the party rowed on to discover its mouth; but "there was scarcely sufficient water to float the boats, and thus our hopes of finding a port . . . were at an end."

When he reached the coast Mitchell was surprised to find "the fresh marks of cattle . . . and the shoe marks of a white man. . . . That whaling vessels occasionally touched there, I was aware . . . but how cattle could have been brought there, I did not understand." He found "a considerable farming establishment", belonging to

the Messrs. Henty, who had been established there during upwards of two years. . . . It was very obvious indeed from the magnitude and extent of the buildings, and the very substantial fencing erected, that both time and labour had been expended in their construction. A good garden stocked with abundance of vegetables already smiled on Portland Bay; the soil was very rich . . . and the potatoes and turnips produced there surpassed in magnitude and quality any I had ever seen elsewhere. . . . Messrs. Henty were importing sheep and cattle as fast as vessels could be found to bring them over, and the numerous whalers touching at or fishing on the coast, were found to be good customers for farm produce and whatever else could be spared from the establishment.

The settlers, the Henty family, had moved across Bass Strait from Van Diemen's Land in search of more land for their farms and the flocks. Mitchell was lucky to have stumbled on such a settlement, and he took the opportunity to pick up "a small additional supply of provisions, especially of flour, as my men were on very reduced rations". He was "kindly received and entertained"; he witnessed a whale hunt "from a verandah . . . at Portland Bay", seeing "all those wondrous perils of harpooners and whale boats, of which I had delighted to read as scenes of 'the stormy north'," and finally set off on his return trip to Sydney.

Travelling north-east, he crossed a different part of Victoria from that which he had seen on his way from the Murray to the coast. He climbed Mt Macedon and from its summit saw Port Phillip Bay, and "a mass of white objects which might have been either tents or vessels"—the signs of yet another new settlement of squatters—and then went home, back to the Murray and to Sydney. He had discovered on his journey wonderfully rich and extensive lands for the squatters—temperate, well-watered and accessible. His route, the "Major's line", soon became the route of "overlanders" driving sheep and cattle, the centre of the squatting occupation of a new Colony, the region Mitchell named "Australia Felix, the better to distinguish it from the parched deserts of the interior, where we had wandered so unprofitably and so long".

The "Major's line" was soon a booming track, with many mobs of sheep and cattle plodding southwards, driven by their owners "crowding one after another to the newly-opened and rich pasturages of the south". In a few years, the best land between the Murrumbidgee and the Victorian ranges was occupied, while other settlers pushed out from Port Phillip Bay to occupy the newly discovered lands. Other overlanders, including both Eyre and Sturt themselves, took their stock to the new province of South Australia, until such journeys—really remarkable achievements, across trackless and unsettled country —came to be barely noticed or recorded.

4. Opening up the North

By this time the search for good pastoral country was going on in Queensland. We have noticed Cunningham's discovery of the Darling Downs, but while they could get them most graziers preferred the lands to the south. As these filled up, interest turned to the north again, though mountains, heat and hostile natives were all obstacles to easy and swift occupation. The Prussian explorer, Leichhardt, made four expeditions to the north and west between 1843 and 1848, on the last of which he and his party disappeared without trace.

In 1845-6 Mitchell led another expedition to the north-west. This was another large-scale affair—thirty-two men, eleven carts and drays, two boats, eighty bullocks and 250 sheep. They discovered the Warrego River, and then, to the west, "the realisation of my long cherished hopes, an interior river falling to the N.W. . . . Balboa's delight at the first view of the Pacific could not have surpassed mine on this occasion . . . which . . . seemed like a reward direct from Heaven for perseverance, and as a compensation for the many sacrifices I had made." This he thought would flow into the Gulf of Carpentaria, "typical of God's providence in conveying living waters into a dry parched land, and thus affording access to open and extensive pastoral regions, likely to be soon peopled by civilized inhabitants". He named it, "with sentiments of devotion, zeal and loyalty", the Victoria—but it did not behave as he expected. Soon afterwards, E. B. Kennedy found that it turned to the south-west; it was none other than the upper part of Cooper's Creek, found lower down by Sturt, and was later re-named the Barcoo.

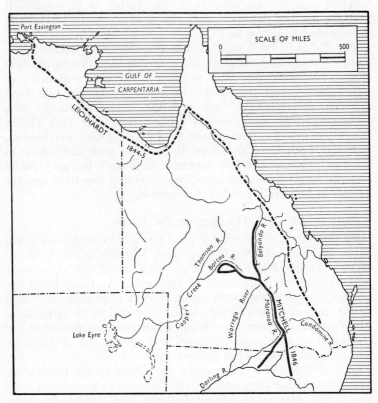

Mitchell's and Leichhardt's explorations, 1844-6

However, if Mitchell failed in his main object of discovering a river system flowing north, he had opened up more good pastoral country in the Maranoa district and around the Barcoo. For wherever the explorers went, if they discovered fertile land the squatters were quick to follow. Here is an advertisement from a Sydney newspaper, the *Australian*, of 4th February 1848:

Portrait of Lachlan Macquarie as a young man.
(From the portrait by John Opie, R.A., in the possession of the Trustees of the Mitchell Library, Sydney)

BAY WHALING
off the Boyd Town Light House. Twofold Bay. N.S.W.

Bay whaling in the nineteenth century off Boyd Town Lighthouse, Twofold
Bay, N.S.W. When Sydney was first settled, British whalers were entering
the Pacific Ocean. Deep-sea whalers used Sydney as a base in the 1790s and
bay whaling began early in the 1800s. The industry grew until about 1850.
Boyd Town and East Boyd at Twofold Bay were built by Ben Boyd in the
1840s, but the settlements were abandoned when Boyd's schemes proved too
costly.

The Mutiny on the *Bounty*—setting Bligh adrift.

SIR T. L. MITCHELL'S EXPEDITION
May be had at this office, and of the principal Booksellers in the City, a Map of the Explorations of the above Expedition, combined with the travels of Dr. Leichhardt. With the descriptive matter. Price, 3s. 6d. Map alone 2s. 6d. This Map is of the highest importance to the Squatting interests.

The south-east of Australia had already been occupied; northern New South Wales and parts of Queensland were filling up. The "pastoral occupation" of the country, if thinly spread, seemed almost complete.

CHAPTER 5

THE SQUATTERS

1. Land

In the early days, when a grazier had found good land, he had usually been able to get a land grant from the government. But in 1831 such grants were stopped; after this, if the grazier wanted Crown land, he had to buy it. There were two reasons for this. First, land sales brought the government money which it could use to help bring free immigrants to the Colony, which it badly wanted to do (see page 53); secondly, the British government thought that if settlers had to buy land they would not try to occupy more than they could cultivate, and so they would not try to settle all over the Colony.

It was soon found to be impossible to stop this "dispersion". The grazier needed land for his flocks, and for this he wanted thousands of acres. When he could not get his land free, by a grant, he simply "squatted" on it (hence the name), and soon the governors had to recognize this. The squatters were granted licences of occupation; they could "occupy" their stations for grazing, though the land still belonged to the Crown. "There was a tacit understanding that no one was to take up a station nearer than three miles to another person", wrote one squatter, but he had "no security of tenure". Since he was only "squatting" on "Crown land", he might be turned out if the government ever put up "his" land for sale and someone else bought it; and as long as he had no security the squatting-grazier was reluctant to improve his property by putting up fences or dams or buildings, or even a comfortable homestead. Sometimes he might buy a bit of his "run"; but he could not afford to buy it all, and it was not until 1847 that he was allowed to "lease" it for a fairly long term. These "long leases", though desirable for the squatter, caused disputes between him and men who wanted to turn part of the runs into farms, as we shall see later on.

2. Provisions

Meanwhile, if the squatter did not have to buy his run, he had to buy his sheep and all his supplies. Alfred Joyce, a pioneer squatter in Victoria, describes in *A Homestead History*, how he started off in 1844:

The taking up of a new far-off run was out of the question, the initial expenses of settling on it and effecting the necessary improvements being quite beyond our power. . . . Runs of various capabilities were occasionally offered for sale, the usual practice being to sell the sheep as so much a head with the run given in. Finishing up the purchase of the run and completing the purchase of the dray and bullocks and stores took up a good portion of the succeeding month as well as a considerable portion of our £150.

Stores were necessary. Here is a list of those sent up to a station in New South Wales in 1831:

40 lbs tobacco	1 lb twine
2 lbs corrosive sublimate	1 lb thread
1 lb sulphur	5 gals of Gin
1 lb blue-stone	1 jack plane
12 gals turpentine	15 wool-packs
1 lb tar	1 wool press
6 pr shears	1 table for sorting wool
1 cwt soap	1000 Hurdle rails
2 cwt salt	6 sickles
24 lbs tea & 137 lbs sugar	1 cask
2 spades	1 tent
1 straw gimblet	1 matrass
70 yds of parramatta cloth	1 pillow
14 sheets	4 blankets
7 blankets	1 carpet bag
5 beds	

Station life up-country was primitive in the early days. Another squatter, E. M. Curr, in his *Recollections of Squatting in Victoria*, writes:

The overseer's hut . . . consisted of three rooms, one of which was a store, in which were kept the flour, tea, sugar, meat-cask, etc. of the establishment; another was the bedroom of the overseer's female servant; whilst the principal apartment did duty as kitchen, dining room, and overseer's bedroom, and was arranged in this way: On one side, and close to the fireplace, stood a rough bedstead, an opossum-rug spread over, which concealed the bedclothes beneath. In the centre of the room there was a large sea-chest, which served as a table; and at the fireplace, which occupied the whole of one end of the building, and was almost as large as one of the smaller rooms, the supper was being cooked—to the no small increase of a heat already excessive. Against the walls, around which were hung a pair or two of horse-hobbles, a gun, a stockwhip, some tin dishes, pannikins, a rickety-looking-glass, and other odds and ends appertaining to the gentle craft of squatting, were set three rough stools. . . . In one of the walls of the hut there was an aperture of about a foot square, cut through the slabs as a window, before which was drawn, on strings, a little curtain of white calico. The outer door, which always stood open by day, was secured at night by a bar; and a couple of wool-packs, nailed to the tie-beams and reaching to the ground, supplied the place of doors to the two smaller apartments.

It was clean in its way, but very comfortless as I thought then; later on I got used to things still rougher. . . . "You'll find everything very comfortable and dry," said the overseer. "A grand thing, sir, a dry hut; a grand thing! My old one in Western Port used to leak like a sieve, and we were always wet." . . . The atmosphere of the room, the fire, the vapour, the odour of the "fat lamp", the scalding hot tea and reeking mutton, were neither pleasant nor inviting; but as there was no preferable alternative, we did "sit in" to the edge of the sea-chest on our three-legged stools, and, setting to work manfully, acquitted ourselves as well as could have been expected of novices under the circumstances.

3. Life and Work

The work was strenuous enough, in the days before fencing, when the flocks were mustered every night; even so, less labour was needed than for growing crops. P. Cunningham, in his book *Two Years in New South Wales*, describes how the sheep were looked after:

The sheep here are divided into flocks of about three hundred breeding ewes, or four hundred wethers, in each. Every flock has a shepherd, who takes his sheep out to graze before sunrise in the morning, and brings them in after sun-set at night. He keeps always before the flock, to check the forward among them from running onwards and wearing out the old, sick, and lame; making all thus feed quietly, so as to keep them in good condition. In summer, he sees too that they have water during the heat of the day; and in drawing up under a tree for shade when it is too hot for feeding, he passes occasionally gently among them, spreads them out, and makes them take a fresh position in as small groups as possible under another tree, because, when they remain crowded too long together in one place, they are apt to become broken-winded. . . .

The shepherd takes out his victuals with him, and is required to be on the alert all day long, to prevent the sheep from being lost in the woods, or the native dogs from pouncing in among them. They must always be driven slowly to pasture, and if you perceive that the shepherd can walk quietly among them without disturbing them, you may set him down as a gentle and careful man; for if he uses his flock harshly, they will be naturally terrified by him. Three flocks are always penned together in contiguous hurdles under the charge of a watchman, who counts each regularly in at night, and the shepherds again count them out in the morning;—so that they form a regular check upon each other, and prevent losses from carelessness or depredation.

Many shepherds in New South Wales were convicts; though bond or free, the work was the same. Alexander Harris, an "emigrant mechanic", who worked for sixteen years in the Australian backwoods, complained in his book of reminiscences, *Settlers and Convicts*:

The master grumbles if the flock is not allowed to spread; he says the shepherd must be keeping them together by severe dogging, and that running so close they cannot fill their bellies; for this, if the shepherd is a free man, he will often refuse to pay him his wages; if he is a prisoner, he takes him before some other sheep-holding settler in the commission of the peace and flogs him. On the other hand, if the shepherd suffers the flock to spread, in these mountainous runs especially, they get into creeks and hollows; and he loses sight of them and leaves them behind; or a native dog sneaks in among them, and, as it is the habit of these animals to bite as many as they can before beginning to prey, 20, 30, 50 get bitten, most of them mortally, before the shepherd sees or hears the stir and comes to their rescue. By this time the whole flock perhaps is scattered in all directions by the panic to which sheep are so liable. For these mishaps again, if the shepherd is free, the master refuses to pay his wages, and tells him to go to law and get them if he can; which he knows, in nine cases out of ten, the man will not do from want of confidence in the administration of justice: if he is a prisoner, he flogs him.

Life was lonely and often cheerless. Accidents were serious when help was difficult to get; and the squatter always ran the risk of being attacked by Aborigines or bushrangers. His flocks might be attacked by dingoes; his hopes of gain could be blasted by trade depression or by flood or drought. Here is a letter written in 1849:

We are all in the greatest state of alarm about the dry weather —we have had no rain to speak of for the last 12 mos. The water holes are all drying up, and the feed is failing. Unless the windows of heaven open this month we shall have a fearful winter. The effect upon us will be this—that the autumn lambs which are now dropping will not be worth picking up, and our fat sheep instead of yielding the average of last year will not give 20 lbs of fat and instead of being worth 8/- they will not realize 5/-. This is a terrible prospect and so fearful am I of its realization that I watch the weather —the sun at dawn and set and the moon till I go to bed with intense anxiety.

Although in good times, good profits were made, the work was hard and losses frequent. One squatter told a committee of the New South Wales Legislative Council in 1842, that

the profit on sheep farming, after deducting 10 per cent interest, is from 10 to 13 per cent per annum. These calculations are made without any reference to the casualties of the diseases of sheep, so dreadful in their consequences, and which even the best management cannot entirely ward off. Many are only applicable to districts where the sheep farmer can grow his own wheat. The profit I have spoken of can only be obtained by the very best of management; and I think I am within the mark of stating that it is not obtained in one case out of twenty.

4. The Aborigines

The squatters, pioneering in unsettled country, had many encounters with the Aborigines. Some were friendly, for the Australian native rarely attacked the white man and from the first settlements was ready to live with him, to help him in need, to share his food and water, and so on. But sometimes, unknowingly, the white man might interfere with some place or some emblem which was sacred to the black; or the black in need of food might steal and kill a sheep or interfere with the squatter's other stores. Sometimes there would be trouble over women, or the white man might have taken over lands on which some black tribes had been used to hunt or gather food. This is what M. M. Banks, a Queensland squatter's daughter, had to say, in her *Memories of Pioneer Days in Queensland*, of the tribe that originally lived near her father's run.

This tribe never molested our cattle or our sheep. Its rights to camp in the old haunts, to hunt kangaroos, opossums and fish, and to hold the Bunya-nut feast on the hills were respected, and it respected my father's property in return. If a tribe were chased away from its native district, its own place on the river, or among the hills, there was no place for it anywhere else. The surrounding country belonged to other tribes, who allowed no trespasser on their preserves; the displaced tribe became outcast and homeless, and often died miserably. The first settler knew nothing of these tribal laws, of the totem's home, or of the virtue pertaining to certain

places. . . . He found fires started from a camp raging through his
grass in a dry season, when there was no hope of rain to set it
growing again, and this meant heavy loss of stock. He thought it
quite reasonable to rule the blacks out of the station boundaries,
since he imagined the blacks to have the freedom of all Australia,
and might as well look for Bunya-nuts on one hill as another. When
the black man refused to give up his old camping ground, grew
revengeful, and speared cattle, or even men, he was driven away as
an enemy and, in some places, shot. . . . This I know, that there
were very many places where the natives were treated with kind-
ness and affection, and that much of the harshness was due to
ignorance and misunderstanding. But for actual cruelty, which unfortunately cannot be denied, no excuse is possible.

A Victorian pioneer, in a letter to Governor La Trobe in 1853,
told of his difficult experiences:

During my residence at the Glenelg, [in 1843-4] the aboriginal
natives were very troublesome, constantly taking sheep in large
lots by force from the shepherds or stealing them from the fold
at night. I had to follow them three different times driving my
sheep away, but each time overtook them, after several days'
harassing tracking, and took from them all the sheep they had not
eaten or destroyed; but not without running considerable risk in
doing so, and having received several wounds from their spears
and boomerangs. The last time in particular they broke the legs
of about sixty of my sheep, leaving the poor animals to die in a
heap in a small yard, in, of course, the greatest agony; and whilst
I was examining them my horse and I were both severely wounded
by a discharge of spears from a body of natives in ambush.

But in another letter to La Trobe, we read of an attack on the
natives in 1845:

Some white men on one side of the Murrabit called out to some
blacks on the other side to come to them; the latter inquired who
they were, and were told they were Mr. Curlewis' men, shooting
ducks. The unsuspecting blacks were crossing in a canoe, when one
or two of them were shot by the whites.

The whites of this period even when they had the best of
intentions, had little knowledge of Aboriginal life, and no
sympathy with them. The blacks seemed dirty, smelly, often
diseased, lazy, superstitious, and without any desire to become
"civilized" or to abandon their unsettled and roving life. To
try to do much for them would be a "useless expenditure of
a large amount of money in a hopeless cause", wrote a corres-
pondent of the Bishop of Melbourne, in 1853, and so, without

understanding or caring much, the colonists slowly forced the natives from the best parts of Australia, even when the authorities were able to prevent their being attacked, ill-treated or killed.

5. Labour Conditions

Sheep-farming demanded labour. For this, the natives were found quite unreliable, so that there did not grow up the practice of employing coloured workmen, as was the case in colonies in some other parts of the world. The place of "native" labour in the economy was taken by convicts; but one important drawback to this system was that the men were not "skilled" labourers, and were usually not used to working on farms or in the country. On farms this was serious; "the difficulty of obtaining good farming servants and especially good ploughmen" was considerable, and since the masters themselves often had little more practical knowledge, they frequently could not teach their servants their work. However, the work of a shepherd was more easily learned, and despite complaints of idleness or negligence, convict servants were, over the years, in charge of flocks worth many millions of pounds.

Many shepherds were free men, but the great majority were prisoners or assigned servants. The practice of assignment had grown with the settlement, and by 1830, with the heavy demand for labour, it was the normal fate of convicts who were not doing hard labour as punishment (in the road gangs, chain gangs or penal settlements). Three-quarters of the convicts were working for private masters in the 1830s. Government service became less important; public works were frowned on as being too expensive, and it was widely believed that assignment was a better punishment. It dispersed the convicts instead of herding them together, and it taught them "useful labour"; the private employer was thought likely to be a good task-master—fair but firm, and free from the favouritism or the brutality sometimes found in government overseers. In most cases, assigned servants were reasonably treated, as it was profitable for an employer to look after his men, but there were always some masters who were brutal, severe or thoughtless. Government laid down minimum rations and clothing, and "luxuries" (tea, sugar or tobacco especially) were often given as rewards for good behaviour. A letter written by a convict in 1835 describes his experiences:

I have a place at a farm-house, and I have got a good master, where I am a great deal more comfortable than I expected. I work the same as I were at home; I have plenty to eat and drink, thank

God for it. I am allowed two ounces of tea, one pound of sugar,
12 pounds of meat, 10 pounds and a half of flour, two ounces of
tobacco, the week; three pairs of shoes, two suits of clothes, four
shirts a year; that is the allowance from Government. But we have
as much to eat as we like, as some masters are a great deal better
than others. All a man has got to mind, is to keep a still tongue
in his head, and do his master's duty, and then he is looked upon
as if he were at home; but if he don't he may as well be hung at
once, for they would take you to the magistrates and get 100 of
lashes, and then get sent to a place called Port Arthur to work
in irons for two or three years, and then he is disliked by everyone.
I hope you will study these few lines which I have wrote to you,
my dear mother and father, brothers and sisters and all my friends
belonging to me in that country; this country is far before England
in everything, both for work and money. Of a night, after I have
done my work, I have a chance to make a few shillings; I can go
out hunting or shooting of Kangaroo, that is about the size of a
sheep, or ducks or swans, tigers, tiger-cats or native cats.

If well-behaved, the convict was entitled to obtain a ticket-
of-leave after serving about half his sentence. This became
a regular practice after about 1825 and allowed the convict
to work for himself, to earn wages and to save money. This
was an incentive to the prisoners to good behaviour and to
reform themselves; and in fact, despite criticism and a number
of failures, most ex-convicts did quite well in the Colony, where
they were nearly always able to find work. They were not usually
successful farmers, as we have seen, but they were often good
labourers or craftsmen.

Some never did well. "Of the numerous crimes committed
in the Colony", it was said, "the greater part are perpetrated
by this class. Among the emancipists and ticket-of-leave men
are to be found cattle-stealers, receivers of stolen goods, keepers
of illicit spirit-shops." These men carried on in Australia the
career of crime which they had begun in England. Most of
the convicts sent to Australia were criminals of the English
city slums, to be pitied, certainly, because of the way they had
to live in England, badly housed, over-crowded, unemployed,
illiterate, but following a life of constant petty crime and theft
until transported.[*]

---

[*] It is a common mistake to regard all the convicts as sentenced for
trivial offences or for "political" offences. Although a few were of this
type the great bulk were the products of slum life, and were professional
criminals.

There is little doubt that transportation was a severe punishment. Doubtless in many cases the convict was materially better off than in England. He lived in a good climate, had regular work and good food. But he was separated from his family and his friends, lost his freedom to go where he wished and do what he wanted, and was always subject to a tiresome and often harsh discipline. Colonel Arthur, Governor of Van Diemen's Land for twelve years, considered it a hard punishment when

an offender was stripped of all his property—deprived of his liberty—shut out from intercourse with his family, totally separated from them—denied every comfort . . . placed on board a transport —subjected there to the most summary discipline—exposed to ill usage from criminals still worse than himself—conveyed to a distant country in the condition of a slave—then assigned to an unknown master, whose disposition, temper, and even caprice he must consult at every turn and submit to every moment, or incur the risk of being charged with insubordination, which, if proved before the magistrate, will be followed by corporal punishment, or removal to the service of the Crown, where his lot will be still more severe according to the degree and nature of his offences. He has indeed, by the regulations of the Government, sufficient food and clothing, but the dread of his master's frown is to him what the drawn sword was, over the head of Dionysius's courtier!

6. The Bushrangers

Certainly, the convicts provided the bulk of the bushrangers in the colonies. Many of these had simply "bolted", that is, absconded or escaped from either their assigned masters or government service. Absconding was not difficult, as the prisoners worked in the open, were often not locked up at night and were frequently sent on long journeys, unguarded, for their masters or for the government. But once they had taken to the bush, they had to live, and this was most easily done by stealing stock and holding up country homes or travellers. Here is an extract from a letter written in 1839:

Besides the unfavourable seasons, the country was overrun with bushrangers. Neither life nor property was safe, not even in villages. When travelling with the mail, I found at every inn horsemen and gigs waiting to accompany the mail for protection. I saw the corpse at Gray's inn of one who had been shot while in charge of a dray. I saw another near Goulburn.

In his *Homestead History*, Alfred Joyce tells us of a "visit and bailing up from the notorious bushranger Captain Melville":

He brought round a double-barrelled gun from the far side of him and presented it at me, at the same time informing me who he was and what he wanted and warning me to make no resistance as he was fully armed and that he supposed I was not. If I submitted quietly to his demands, no violence would be offered to me; he said the police were after him and he wanted a fresh good horse in place of the one he was riding, which was a small and jaded hack. . . . The few horses that were in the paddock were quietly followed into the stockyard where he quickly selected my own special riding hack, with a bit of breeding in her. The horse selected, the next thing was a saddle and bridle to suit, for which purpose I was marched up to the store and directed to take the best I had and put them on my horse. That done the mare was led out and fastened up to the fence, and another visit made to the store for a supply of tea and sugar and some tobacco, and to see if there was any drink to be had; fortunately there was not, or he might have been a bit reckless.

The next thing was, had I a gun? Yes, there was one in the kitchen. Seeing that it was better than the one he had got, he decided to take it. . . . As soon as he got into the house . . . he took down my riding whip and spurs, then my meerschaum pipe. . . . He caught sight of my writing desk. Tapping it with the whip, he directed me to open it to see if there was any money in it. The six sovereigns it contained were at once appropriated, and then he caught sight of the bedroom, the door of which was half open. This must also be examined. . . . My best riding suit of clothes, boots and sundry other apparel was selected and rolled up ready to strap on to the saddle. When he required to do anything himself, he laid his gun down in front of him, between himself and me, ready to take up in a moment if he saw occasion. Seeing I was wearing a watch, he directed me to show it to him. As it was one presented to me by my father on leaving home, I did what I could to persuade him on that account not to take it, but the only satisfaction I got was that he would see.

To try to deal with these people a special organization, the mounted police, was created in New South Wales. Moreover, by the Bushrangers Act, all travellers had to carry a pass to show they were neither bushrangers nor absconding convicts; if the pass was lost, the travellers could be arrested on the spot. Many free workers suffered from this rather arbitrary system, and sometimes unscrupulous employers would try to detain a free labourer who might want to change his job, by improperly keeping his "pass". In his reminiscences, *Settlers and Convicts*, Alexander Harris gives many examples of the abuses of this law; this is only one:

A lad once told me he had some time before passed seven weeks out of three months marching in handcuffs under the Bushranging Act. . . . Some busy constable . . . arrested him, on suspicion of being a bushranger, at one of the farthest stations of Hunter's River, where he was looking for work. After being taken in handcuffs to Sydney, full 250 miles, and discharged, he went to the Morrumbidgee on the same errand, where he was again taken into custody . . . and forwarded in handcuffs to headquarters under the same law.

7. Squatters and Convicts

Squatters and convicts—together these were the pioneers of Australia. The former produced a valuable commodity for export —wool. In their search for pastures they had stimulated exploration and occupied the vacant lands of eastern Australia, which were fertile enough for their flocks, if often too dry for the wheat-farmer. The squatters founded new settlements, far away from Sydney (see Chapter 13); they fought against and overcame most of the obstacles of the bush—its loneliness, its climate, its native people—and, persevering in good times and in bad, they were, by about 1850, beginning to be able to enjoy the profits their industry was earning and to live in greater luxury, even in the outback—if with luck and hard work, they had been successful. But many failed through ignorance or laziness or were dogged by misfortune; for in the early days, squatting provided no royal road to fortune.

But although the capital and the enterprise of the squatter were essential, he would have been helpless without labour. This the convict supplied—and to government as well as grazier. Nearly all the early public works—public buildings, docks, roads and so on—were built by convict labour. After about 1820, if well behaved, convicts were assigned to work for the settler; but if undergoing punishment, they worked in a government road-gang, often in irons, but working—and little other labour was available. Even if they were sentenced to further punishment at a penal settlement, their labour was usually not wasted. Convict labour at Newcastle, Port Macquarie or Moreton Bay prepared the way for settlement there. Only on Norfolk Island or at Port Arthur in Van Diemen's Land was their work of little use except for their own subsistence; there, everything was subordinated to punishment, and the economic value of the convict was virtually nil.

As time went on, many of the colonists began to dislike the presence of the convicts, as we shall see in the next chapter. Eventually transportation to eastern Australia was stopped—to New South Wales in 1840 and to Tasmania in 1852. But before this, there can be no doubt of the value of their services as Australian pioneers.

CHAPTER 6

IMMIGRATION

1. Free Settlers

By 1840 there were many free labourers in Australia. For nearly twenty years there had been a very large demand for workmen of any description. Some were ex-convicts; others were Australian-born, the children either of convicts or free settlers in the Colony; others again were immigrants from Great Britain. There were very many of these, for after 1830 the British government began to assist migrants to come out to Australia, both to satisfy the demand for labour there, and to reduce the number of what was regarded as surplus population in the mother country.

2. Conditions in the United Kingdom

Conditions in the United Kingdom were hard at that time. The population was growing so rapidly that it was not easy for all to find work. In Ireland, most people were peasant farmers; but there was not enough fertile land for all to have a farm which was big enough to produce a living. Younger sons had to migrate or starve. Some went to cities like London, Liverpool or Glasgow, some to America, and a few to far-off and little-known Australia. The Roman Catholic Bishop of Limerick put it this way:

Now, though it be true that emigration could not at once take away all that may be burthensome to the country, though it could not even finally do so, it would give relief to many, and hope to all. At present they are in a state of hopeless, despairing recklessness; therefore they scruple not the worst. Give them hope, and they will endure; particularly if it is known that good character will be a recommendation.

In Scotland, many small farms were being enclosed for grazing; this conversion of the land to pastures turned out the crofters who often could not find any other work.

Even in England the industries which were growing rapidly because of the technical inventions of the Industrial Revolution could not provide work for all; the unskilled manual workers especially were often unemployed and therefore poverty-stricken. They might be relieved in the poor-house; in the country districts they usually were, but this was unpleasant and degrading as well as expensive. In the rapidly growing towns many lost their jobs in times of bad trade and they had no hope of keeping alive except through crime or charity; and though wages were higher than in the country, living conditions were very bad, for the towns were badly drained and dirty and housing accommodation was overcrowded.

Governments did not realize the need for control over the growth of towns; they did not realize how rapidly they would grow or what problems they would bring in the future. They did not know that dirt was a cause of disease; and so they did not worry about drainage or the providing of pure water or the clearing of slums; such things seemed to be expensive and to interfere with the liberty of the people. In any event, when there was no public transport, no means of getting to work except by walking, people had to live close to their jobs; crowding was inevitable, especially round the docks or the markets, and the low-lying districts of the cities, near rivers like the Thames in London or the Mersey in Liverpool, were particularly unhealthy. Moreover, as the workman could not afford to pay a high rent, houses (or flats, rooms or even cellars) had to be cheap—and this they were, even if they were too often cheap and nasty. Here is an 1840 description of some housing in Stockton, an industrial city in the north of England:

Shepherd's Buildings consist of two rows of houses with a street seven yards wide between them; each row consists of what are styled back and front houses; that is two houses placed back to back. There are no yards or out-conveniences, . . . each house contains two rooms, viz., a house place and sleeping room above; each room is about three yards wide and four long. In one of these houses there are nine persons belonging to one family. . . . There are 44 houses in the two rows, and 22 cellars all of the same size. The cellars are let off as separate dwellings; these are dark, damp, and very low, not more than six feet between the ceiling and the floor.

Conditions like this, the poverty in the countryside, the dirt, disease and squalor, the overcrowding, cellar-dwelling and unemployment in the towns, made people in England willing to think of emigrating. But how could they afford to go? Where was the money to pay for the passage to come from? Emigrants, in any event, preferred to go to North America; it was closer and therefore the journey did not cost so much. Australia was

a "funny" country, with hobgoblins and blacks and snakes and
a terrible bush, and in any case there were a lot of convicts being
sent there, so surely it was a good place to keep away from.

3. Australia's Need for Workers

But there was something to be said on the other side. In
Australia there was a great demand for labour. As the wool
industry developed and the various settlements grew, the convicts
were not nearly enough and more and more free workmen were
wanted in the Colony. As a result, regular employment was easy
to find, and wages were very good for the time—far higher than
they were in England, and there were many stories told of men
who had been able to make their fortunes very quickly. Also the
climate was good, and although there might be plenty of dirt
and crowding in Sydney, some, at least, were not afraid to go
to the bush, and found there a good chance of earning a
comfortable living. The question of the cost of a passage
remained; but here the government could take a hand. What if
it were to pay the migrants' passage money? After 1831 it agreed
to do this. A despatch from the British Colonial Office, sent to
Governor Darling, emphasized the advantages, to both Britain
and Australia, of assisted emigration.

Considering Emigration as a means of relieving the Mother Country
. . . it is the emigration of the unemployed British Labourers, which
would be of real and essential service; while I think it also appears
that this would be the most useful class of Emigrants, as regards the
colony, from the extreme difficulty which is now complained of in
obtaining labourers.

Two types of migrants were helped to travel out. First, there
were "females"; for there were too many men in Australia
owing to the numbers of male convicts transported, and the
government wanted both to "supply the deficiency of females"
and so help the building up of family life, and to provide women
servants for the settlers and their families. Again, according to
the British Colonial Secretary:

There are, in England and especially in the Agricultural Counties,
many young women, who, having been brought up in such a manner
as to qualify them to discharge the duties of Servants in the families
of a farmer, are unable in this country to procure such situations or
to gain an honest livelihood, and who would, therefore, gladly avail
themselves of an opportunity of emigrating to a Colony in which they
could rely upon finding the means of doing so. In New South Wales
and Van Diemen's Land, all accounts concur in stating that such

persons would without difficulty find eligible situations, and that their arrival would be very acceptable to the Settlers, who seem to be almost entirely unprovided with Female Servants.

Hence the government agreed to pay the fares of selected female migrants, and it appointed a commission to supervise the work of choosing migrants, arranging their passages, hiring ships and looking after them on the voyage to Australia. Here is an advertisement for female migrants in 1833:

NOTICE TO YOUNG WOMEN

Desirous of bettering their condition by an Emigration to New South Wales.

In New South Wales and Van Diemen's Land there are very few women compared with the whole number of people, so that it is impossible to get women enough as Female Servants or for other Female Employments. The consequence is, that desirable situations, with good wages, are easily obtained by Females in those Countries; but the Passage is so long that few can pay the expense of it without help. There is now, however, the following favourable opportunity of going to New South Wales.

The Committee has been formed in London for the purpose of facilitating Emigration, which intends to send out a ship in the course of the Spring, expressly for the conveyance of Female Emigrants, under an experienced and respectable Man and his Wife, who have been engaged as Superintendents. The parties who go in that Vessel must be Unmarried Women or Widows; must be between the ages of 18 and 30; and must be of good health and character. . . .

Every arrangement will be made for the comfort of the Emigrants during the voyage; and Medical Assistance provided: they will also be taken care of on their first landing in the Colonies. . . .

Persons who, on reading this Notice, may desire to emigrate in the manner pointed out, should apply by Letter to the "Emigration Committee, 18 Aldermanbury, London". . . .

All applications made in the foregoing manner, will be answered; and it is requested that Parties will apply without delay, as the fine teak-built ship, "Bussorah Merchant", 530 tons burthen, now in the London Docks, is appointed to sail on the 13th April next expressly with Female Emigrants selected by the Committee.

There was also a demand for agricultural labourers and mechanics, and the government agreed to assist these to migrate too. Some were selected by the Emigration Commissioners under much the same arrangements as for the females. Local authorities in England advertised for people willing to emigrate; their passages were paid and when arrangements for their

Her Majesty's Mail.
(From the Newbold sketches, by courtesy of the Mitchell Library, Sydney)

The departure of Charles Sturt from Adelaide in August 1844.
(From a lithograph after S. T. Gill in *South Australia Illustrated*, 1847, by G. F. Angas)

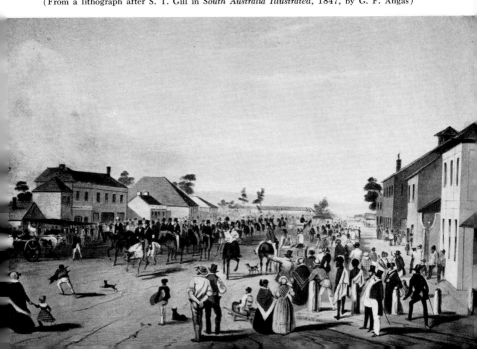

A bushman's hut in the 1850s.
(From *The Australian Sketch Book*, by S. T. Gill)

Bushrangers in action—an oil painting by Tom Roberts entitled "Bailed Up".

voyage had been made they set sail to seek their fortunes in a
new country.

Other migrants were chosen by the settlers themselves, who
were given a bounty to pay their passage money. Here is a
government notice published in Sydney in 1835, giving details
of the scheme:

The sum of £30 will be granted as a bounty towards defraying
the expense of the passage of every married man, whether mechanic
or farm servant, and his wife, neither of whose ages shall exceed,
on embarkation, 30 years; and the sum of £5 for each of their children
whose age shall exceed 12 months. A sum of £15 will also be allowed
for every unmarried female whose age shall not be below 15 nor
above 30 years, who shall come out with the consent of the settler
or his agent, under the protection of the married couple, as forming
part of the family, and destined to remain with it until such female
be otherwise provided for. A bounty of £10 will also be allowed for
every unmarried male mechanic or farm servant, above the age of
18 and not exceeding 25 years, brought out by a settler, who at the
same time brings out an equal number of females, accompanying and
attached to a family, as hereinafter described.

Of course not all the immigrants were quite what people
wanted. The British government told the Emigration Commissioners to be careful whom they chose:

Every exertion is to be made to procure them of good character,
and industrious and respectable habits, for which purpose you will
seek information from their Religious Ministers or former employers,
or any other source you may find available. It is particularly essential
to avoid the selection of persons who have been at all addicted to
intemperance, as the temptations to that vice are much greater in
New South Wales.

The colonists often complained that they received only "the
outcasts of the United Kingdom", but it was difficult always to
find good migrants. Those in good jobs in England did not want
to leave them, and the Commissioners had to send those they
could get. As they said in 1840, in reply to criticism,

The Remarks made on this subject [selection] in the Colony are
somewhat too apt to assume that there is an unlimited command of
Emigrants in the Country. It may be natural for an officer at Sydney
to point out that the persons who arrive are not the best that could
be desired; but the duty, to which the officers at home must attend,
is to send the best who can be procured, and it may be questioned
how they should otherwise have succeeded in doubling and Quad-
rupling the emigration to Sydney within the last three years.

E

4. The Problems of Settling

However, the results were that people came out and, despite employers' complaints, they did help to reduce the labour shortage in the Colony. As we have seen, many of the squatters employed free shepherds as well as convicts; and indeed, without the arrival of so many free immigrants, squatting and wool-growing could not have spread as quickly as it did.

Despite the migration, there was still a shortage of labour. This meant that workmen could earn good wages; employers often resented this and criticized what they thought to be the too independent attitude of their employees. One employer, a bank director, told a Committee of the New South Wales Legislative Council in 1843:

The high rates of wages, which prevailed during the last five or six years, have spoiled these people, have injured alike master and man; for the exorbitant wages to which they were accustomed, were expended in dissipation and other hurtful enjoyments; a labouring man, in the country, would be as well off at £10 a year, as he would have been with £40, to dissipate in town. Further, the little work done here, by the labouring classes, is ruinous for their employers. . . . It will be recollected also, that the general rate of wages in Bedfordshire, and Bucks, is only 7s. or 8s. a week, and in Ireland 5s. without food. There is ample employment in this Colony, at remunerative wages.

Of course, this was the employer's picture. The working man himself had another tale to tell: for example that of Alexander Harris, the "emigrant mechanic", in his book, *Settlers and Convicts.*

The fact is, the upper classes of New South Wales settlers have so long been used to deal with the poor wretched convicts, and to tell them they have no rights, and to taunt and mock them if they talk about seeking redress for any ill treatment, that the habit and the feeling at the bottom of it have become rooted in their very nature; and they would wish to treat free people in the same way. "Is not the free labourer here for our convenience—as a substitute for convicts who can no longer be found in sufficient numbers to supply us? What more profit is one to us than the other? Why should we treat one better than the other?" Such is positively the feeling. . . . Supercilious intolerance pervades the whole feeling with which the upper class in New South Wales generally regards the lower, and is the cause of such grievous injuries to the free labourer as often entirely to counterbalance the advantages which emigration otherwise offers.

Despite such complaints, many immigrants seem to have been

able to do very well. Here are two statements made in Sydney in 1845:

Arrived in 1841; had no money on landing; was engaged as farm servant nine days after my arrival, at the following wages; £20 a year, and a weekly ration of 12 lbs. flour, 10 lbs. meat, 2 lbs. sugar, quarter lb. tea. I have now eight head of cattle, and am worth in cash £30; the highest wages I ever received before I emigrated to this Colony was £3 10s. a year; I am well known to . . . and to . . .; I subscribe to a school, and the Colonial Observer; since in this Colony I was out of employment about three months, but I must say it was nearly my own fault. I refused £15 a year, and rations; I am now receiving 20s. a week, and board myself; have a nice house, free of rent.

Came to this country in 1839; on landing, my money and property were worth about £30; was engaged two days after my arrival, at 24s. per week, afterwards 30s.—out of this I got my own food; when I had been three months in service, was engaged as overseer; commenced for myself with the sum of £40, on a clearing lease of ten acres, rent £10 a year; this land I have since purchased for £70; have about half the sum paid; I have 3 horses, 2 carts, and a dray, 10 goats, a number of poultry, and have a tolerable house of my own; I employ two labourers, giving them board and lodgings, and 8s. a week; if I had the capital I could employ more with profit to myself; my young children I send to school, and pay 6d. per week each.

All the same, some resented the difficulty they had in becoming farmers. They could not afford to buy land, for its price had been deliberately raised by the government to £1 an acre when it began to sell land after 1831, instead of granting it for nothing. This high price was a grievance to many who thought they should be able to get a farm easily; but in fact, as we have seen, poor soil and lack of skill and of machinery made cultivation difficult in any case; and the bad roads in the Colony were another obstacle. There were no navigable rivers, and it cost more to carry grain 100 miles in New South Wales than to bring it all the way from Van Diemen's Land. This led New South Wales farmers to go in more for grazing than for agriculture, but grazing was an occupation more suited to the man with capital than to the poor immigrant.

5. Results of Free Immigration

The most important result of the migration was to change New South Wales from a convict to a free settlement. The percentage of convicts in the population fell from 46 per cent in 1828 to 29 per cent in 1840; even in Van Diemen's Land, where free immigration was much less, the convicts amounted to only 38 per cent of the people in 1840; and in other parts of Australia there were hardly any convicts at all. As the number of free settlers increased, they demanded greater political freedom; the methods of governing a gaol population were no longer suitable for the ruling of a free settlement. Hence many colonists demanded trial by jury and a free press; later on they demanded some say in the control of their own affairs; they demanded a local assembly which might be elected by the people and which could enforce its will on the governor if his policy was unpopular, and which could limit the taxation which the government imposed.

Some civil rights were granted—trial by jury was introduced in 1824 and after 1828 in New South Wales there was no censorship of the press. But the English government and colonial conservatives were always afraid of granting too much political freedom to a Colony where convicts and ex-convicts were so numerous: the Legislative Council, which was set up in 1824, was nominated by the Governor. Many complained of the injustice of this form of government, and a petition from the popular party, in 1836, declared that "the Legislative Council as at present constituted . . . has no hold upon the public confidence . . . (and) . . . that the only safe and effectual remedy for (its) admitted defects . . . consists in the establishment of a Representative Legislature upon a wide and liberal basis."

We shall see how responsible government was granted later on; but apart from this, the people of New South Wales, and of Sydney in particular, became more and more opposed to the transportation of convicts. A penal settlement was not, and could not be, a free colony. Although a few squatters welcomed the cheap labour of the convicts, most Australians thought they were undesirable. Some of them were badly behaved; they were a blot on the Colony; harsh laws were necessary to control them, and the competition of their labour tended to keep wages down. Thus many wanted to see the end of transportation, and when, after it had been stopped for a few years, the British government between 1846 and 1850 tried to revive it, there was a tremendous outburst of opposition in Sydney and Melbourne. Protest meetings were held in both cities, and the views of the people can be seen from the tremendous applause which greeted this speech made in Sydney in 1849 when the convict ship, *Hashemy*, arrived in the harbour.

The time for discussion on the principle of the convict question was past. They were not met to exclaim against the proposals of the English Government. The threat of degradation has been fulfilled. The stately presence of their city, the beautiful waters of their harbour, were this day again polluted with the presence of that floating hell—a convict ship. (*Immense cheers.*) They had lived again to behold the cargo of crime borne across the waves to them. In their port they behold a ship freighted, not with the comforts of life, not with luxuries of civilized nations, not with the commodities of commerce, in exchange for our produce; but with the moral degradation of a community—the picked and selected criminals of Great Britain.

This was not a question of the injury which the 250 felons on board the *Hashemy* could do to the Colony. They would perhaps cause but little evil—but it was a question—a question in which they had a right to be heard in protest—whether the inhabitants of this Colony should be subjected to the contamination of trebly convicted felons. . . . (*Cheers*) . . . Those who branded the people of the Colony with mere worldly selfishness in the part they had taken on this question did them injustice. It was not the mere fear of competition amongst operatives that now united them on this question; it was not a mere breeches pocket question with the labouring classes, though it might be with the employers. It was a struggle for liberty—a struggle against a system which had in every country where it had prevailed been destructive of freedom.

Many of the radicals who opposed transportation also demanded other reforms. They wanted a reform of the land laws which would make it easier for settlers to buy small farms, forgetting how great were the obstacles to small-scale farming. They also wanted to amend the Masters and Servants Act which often made a "servant" liable to breach of contract if he left his job, no matter how unreasonable his "master" might have been. Free immigration certainly helped all this political and social agitation; it also helped Sydney to grow.

Many newcomers preferred to stay in town rather than to go bush, and as the population increased, simple manufactures began—first brewing and milling, then household commodities like soap and candles, salt, leather goods, boots and saddlery; soon there were woollen mills and cheap clothing, and the beginning of sugar refining. But by far the biggest activity in Sydney, apart from the government services, was commerce—with drays carrying goods up country and down to the sea, stores for retail trade, ships to be loaded, unloaded and repaired, porters, boatmen on the harbour and all the activities of a busy port in the days when there was no machinery and all carriage of goods and people had to be done by horse wagon, ox-dray or by hand.

By 1850 Sydney had become quite a large town. Unfortunately in some ways it was beginning to resemble the insanitary and overcrowded towns of England—except that it was sunnier.

The house accommodation of the working classes of Sydney is admitted on all hands to be deplorably bad; even in the more recently erected dwellings the means of drainage and ventilation are almost entirely neglected, and many of the older tenements are so unfit for the occupation of human beings that one witness declares them to be "past remedy without a general fire".

Very much the same applied to Melbourne, when it was said in 1848, that much disease arose from "the want of sufficient drainage, the filthy condition of the narrow streets, courts, alleys and backyards; the slaughtering of sheep and pigs on the premises of butchers within the city without adequate means of cleansing." But this was part of the cost of growth; and if Sydney began its life as the centre for administrating a convict population, by 1850 it was a port and commercial town, with the beginning of industry; it contained more than a quarter of the population of New South Wales, it had lively political organizations and was the centre of a working-class movement and of opposition to the "squattocracy".

Caroline Chisholm: Humanitarian and Social Worker

IN the nineteenth century, there was a shortage of labour in Australia, just like that of today; so, in 1831, the British government began to "assist" poor migrants to go to Australia. It hoped that this policy would relieve poverty and unemployment at home; it would certainly provide free labourers in New South Wales and South Australia. Between 1831 and 1842 more than 70,000 migrants landed at Sydney; but few people thought it necessary to look after them when they arrived. They might stay on board ship for a few days, or in old convict barracks up to a month, while looking for work and lodging; apart from this they had to fend for themselves. Then in 1841 came an economic depression. Migrants who had embarked with high hopes, long before news of it had reached England, now found themselves in Sydney in great distress. Those who suffered most were men with large families, and the many young women who were then being sent out among the migrants, to offset the surplus of males among the convicts. The girls' plight aroused the compassion of Caroline Chisholm.

She was the daughter of an English yeoman, and like many women of her time had been taught that philanthropic work among the needy was an important duty in her life. After she married an officer of the East India Company, and went out to Madras with him, she organized there a "Female School of Industry for the Daughters of European Soldiers". Then Captain Chisholm came to Australia on sick leave. He and his wife arrived in 1838, but when he returned to service in 1840, Caroline stayed behind. Worried by the distress she saw around her, she determined to try to help the destitute immigrant girls. As she wrote later:

On Easter Sunday, 1841, I was enabled at the Altar of our Lord, to make an offering of my talents to the God who gave them. I promised to know neither country nor creed, but to serve all justly and impartially. I asked only to be enabled to keep these poor girls from being tempted by their need to mortal sin, and resolved that to accomplish this, I would in every way sacrifice my feelings, surrender all comfort, nor in fact consider my own wishes and feelings, but wholly devote myself to the work I had in hand.

She appealed to the public, the Press and the clergy. She wrote to Lady Gipps, the Governor's wife. After some difficulty she even gained an interview with the Governor himself, who said,

I expected to have seen an old lady in white cap and spectacles who would have talked to me about my soul. I was amazed when my aide introduced a handsome, stately young woman, who proceeded to reason the question as if she thought her reason, and experience, were worth as much as mine.

Gipps allowed her to use part of an old wooden barracks for her "home"—provided the Government would be put to no expense. It was very draughty. There was no fire-place; she could not even heat water. She soon found there were rats everywhere. But here she organized her home of refuge and labour exchange. She began with about ninety girls, brought in from the streets, from Hyde Park, from the notorious "Rocks" district. She realized, "having a very fair knowledge of human nature, that to be able to do good, I must be prepared to encounter certain disagreeables". She found some positions for girls in Sydney, but she wanted to send as many of them as possible into the country, where more suitable work was easier to find. She sent out circulars to all types of settlers in the country asking about the prospects of employment for women, married couples with children, and how they could best make the journey to the interior. These the government agreed to carry post free. She was able to charge employers £1 when she placed any of her "clients", to cover the cost of sending them to their workplaces up country. She used to send off parties in bullock drays, though when the time came, the first load, dreading "blacks, bushrangers, and bunyips", refused to go—"their fears overcame their good resolutions"—and she had to set off with them herself.

In the first year she found situations for more than seven hundred young women, and gradually her success won more support among the public and in the press. She organized branch homes in several country towns, which, like the parent institution in Sydney, provided shelter for women and acted as a labour-exchange for all. She travelled all over the Colony. She took parties of women to places as far afield as Campbelltown, Maitland, Liverpool, Port Macquarie, Yass, Gundagai, Goulburn and Bathurst. She went from farm to farm, finding out the characters of residents before entrusting "her children" to them, always bargaining for fair conditions and good wages, and keeping a copy of the terms of the contract so that she could see that it was not broken.

She also wanted to settle migrants on the land in groups, but she could not obtain land for them, nor could they buy it themselves, when the minimum price was £1 an acre. She forgot that it was more profitable to graze sheep than to lease land to peasant tenants. She tried one such settlement in the Illawarra district, but it was not a success. She wanted to promote family life, to save men from "the demoralising state of bachelorism". This would reduce crime. "For all the clergy you can despatch, all the school-masters you can appoint, all the churches you can build . . . will never do without God's police-wives and little children." But she seemed to think farming a very simple operation, and she never realized the difficulties that faced the small farmer in Australia. For all that, when she left Sydney in April 1846 she was given a testimonial and an address thanking her for her "active and zealous exertions", which had enabled her to help 10,000 immigrants, or more than a quarter of those who had arrived in the Colony.

When she reached England, she wanted to promote more emigration. She had collected nearly seven hundred "voluntary statements" from settlers, describing how they were faring in New South Wales.

I arrived in 1840 with seven children, wrote James Reed to Wiltshire; my wife died on the passage out. I was engaged by a Mr. Suttor as a smith; my three daughters were in the service of Mrs. Suttor, two are now well married. I get £30 a year wages, plus rations. I am well off and have several privileges . . . I have thirty head of cattle, a horse and cart and a very good garden.

W. Thompson of Norfolk told a very similar story:

I came to New South Wales in 1837 . . . with my wife and six children; I rent 20 acres for £20. I run fifty cattle, and keep a mare, thirty pigs and poultry, I have 50 bushels of wheat in store . . . Thank God, I don't want for anything, I have meat 3 times a day, and butter milk and eggs. I have a team of 10 bullocks and a dray and go to Sydney four times a year.

Armed with this evidence, she tried to promote what she called "a national system of colonization". She tried to persuade the government to send five hundred unmarried women to Australia "to relieve the forlorn state of Australian bachelors". In 1849 she formed the Family Colonization Loan Society, to lend money to families who wanted to migrate. When added to their savings these loans would enable them to go; once in Australia, the migrants would soon be able to pay back what they had borrowed, or so she thought. Unfortunately her faith was not justified. Many of the loans were not repaid. All the same the Society sent eight shiploads of migrants to Australia.

In 1854 Mrs Chisholm herself came back, landing in Melbourne in July. She did not carry on work with the Family Colonization Loan Society, but instead began to concern herself with the troubles of the gold-miners, the unsuccessful diggers, and the unemployed. Again she wanted to settle families on the land in small farms; but first she decided to visit the diggings and look at the conditions there for herself.

The roads were shocking, but she was used to bad roads. She visited Bendigo, Castlemaine, Maryborough, Avoca and Ballarat. She saw the tents or log-huts of the miners and she thought highly of the men; but she disapproved of the break in their family life, for naturally many of the diggers had left wives behind them, so that they "entered their blankets at night more like dogs than men". One of the greatest obstacles to women living on the gold-fields was the difficulty of getting there—the bad roads and the lack of accommodation on the way. Mrs Chisholm at once proposed that accommodation houses should be built at various points on the roads, which would make it easier for families to get inland to the gold-fields; they would be "the first link in the chain of country dispersion". By the middle of March 1855, her plans for "Shelter Sheds" were completed. By the end of the year, ten sheds on the road to Castlemaine had been built. She must have contributed a considerable amount to the cost of building and maintaining them.

Next year she joined the campaign "to unlock the lands"; but before it was successful, she had to retire from the fray sick and tired after her years of hard work. In 1862 she opened a girls' school, but it lasted only two years. In 1866 she returned to England for a visit, but she never came back to Australia again, and her death in 1877 was scarcely noticed.

Much of her economic thinking was very muddled; but her work as a practical philanthropist was magnificent. We must think of her leading parties of "her children" through New South Wales, "making forced marches at the head of armies of emigrants, as far as three hundred miles into the far interior, sometimes sleeping at the stations of wealthy settlers, sometimes in the huts of poor immigrants or prisoners; sometimes camping out in the bush, teaching the timid awkward peasantry of England, Ireland and Scotland how to 'bush' it; comforting the women, nursing the children, and putting down any discontented or forward spirits among the men; now taking a few weary children into her covered tandem-cart, now mounting upon horse-back and galloping over a short-cut through the hills to meet her weary caravan, with supper foraged from the hospitable settlers". It was her great achievement so to help the poor, bewildered and needy immigrants at the time of their greatest distress—this it was that earned her the title—the "Immigrants' Friend".

CHAPTER 7

NEW COLONIES

1. Norfolk Island

WHEN Governor Phillip founded the first settlement in Australia at Sydney Cove in 1788, he quickly followed this up by occupying Norfolk Island. He wanted to get more food for Sydney and to reduce the number of convicts there, and he hoped that the soil of this island in the Pacific might be more fertile than that near Sydney; he also hoped that the settlers on the island might be able to grow flax, for this was something urgently wanted in England which the British government had ordered him to provide if he could.

2. Tasmania

Fifteen years later the first settlements were begun in Tasmania, then called Van Diemen's Land, on the River Derwent in the south and the Tamar River in the north. This was done in order to forestall any attempt by the French to found a Colony; for French explorers were sailing in Australian waters and Governor King was afraid they might want to stay. This was a time when the English and French were very jealous of each other, even when they were not actually fighting, and the British government did not want any French colonies, which could be used as enemy bases in time of war, to be established in this part of the world.

3. Western Australia

The same fear of the French caused the establishment of settlements in Western Australia—first at Melville Island in the north-west, then at King George's Sound (Albany) and a little later on the Swan River, near the present site of Perth. Of these, the first had to be abandoned; it was too remote and too hot; the soil was poor and there was no trade with the East Indies as had been hoped for. The two settlements in the south were eventually successful; but they had a hard struggle to survive at first.

It was more difficult than most settlers thought to establish a new Colony. They arrived, if not in a wilderness, at least in completely uninhabited land. There was no shelter. There were no hotels or inns, no houses except what the settlers built with their own hands; there were no shops, no food and no live-stock except what they brought with them or grew themselves; there was no equipment except what was brought; the land had to be cleared before any crops could be grown; there were no amusements, no hospitals, no services—not even an assured water supply—no drainage or lighting, no roads to carry supplies to the farms, not even any wharves or docks where they could be unloaded. Moreover, the newcomers knew nothing about the country where they were to settle—where water supplies were, where there was good soil or good timber and so forth. Nothing could be achieved except by hard work—and those who disliked this suffered intensely. One settler wrote from the Swan River in 1830:

If I were coming again I should content myself with grubbing hoes, felling axes (mine are too long and narrow), spades, some kitchen utensils, plenty of provisions and a hammock; these would do to begin with. Those who brought great apparatus and stock were sadly burdened with the first and did not know what to do with the second. Many of their cattle ran into the bush and were lost, and some of the more delicate died from want of care and fodder on shipboard or on landing.

Some seemed to imagine they would at once live in luxury, bringing out shoe-blacking and olive oil,

as though men employed in felling trees, digging the ground and other laborious occupations would consider it necessary to see their faces reflected from their shoes . . . or that their stomachs were so fastidious that they could not eat their fish or salads without oil to give them a relish . . . and . . . who expected to have again commenced a career of idleness and dissipation depending on their labourers to cultivate their land. . . . The master was to amuse himself in shooting, catching fish, or hunting kangaroos. And his wife (should he have one) was to enjoy herself in visiting, card parties, assemblies, etc. These are the persons whose cry is the loudest against the Colony.

Here is Governor James Stirling's opinion of the first settlement near Perth:

People came out expecting to find the Garden of Eden and some . . . were astonished at finding hard work an indispensable pre-liminary to meat and drink. All were in fact in a state of disappoint-ment. . . .

The plan which was adopted in the Formation of this Settlement may be viewed as an Experiment in Colonization on a new Principle. The Expenses incurred in the Transport of Settlers to their Place of Destination, in the Operations of Agriculture, and in every other Branch of Industry, were to be defrayed out of their own Funds, the Government having given no other Pledge than that a small Civil and Military Establishment should be provided for Protection, and for the Despatch of Public Business, and that Land should be distributed on the most liberal Terms. It so happened that these Inducements, co-operating with the Novelty of the undertaking and the Misrepresentations, and Amplifications of interested Individuals, were quite sufficient to attract a large Body of Emigrants to the Shores of the New Colony. Of those who came, a certain Portion were efficient People of Respectability and Means, but many were Adventurers without Conduct, Capital or Industry, and a large number of indigent Families were induced to embark for a Settlement where no Provision had been made for their Maintenance by those who were interested in getting them out of England.

. . . Had the settlers been all equally industrious and well provided, as the best of them, there were enough to have accomplished rapidly and successfully the Establishment of a Colony. . . . But so small a Proportion of the Community being fit for the Task which they had undertaken, it has been only partially successful, the Credit of which is due alone to those whose Industry, Intelligence and Means have enabled them at this moment to consider themselves not only established but secure in a great Measure of the Reward of their Exertions. All others except that Class have suffered severely.

. . . The Truth is that very few Persons can imagine previously the Difficulties, and irretrievable Losses which are met with in all such Enterprises. But even where there is Spirit and Resolution to overcome all these, there is incurred in establishing an Emigrant in a New Country a long continued Outlay before any Return can be looked for, during which Period if the Settler's means fail, all his Exertions are lost and his Property ruined. His unfinished House, or half-cultivated Grounds cannot be sold, for the Want of Capital is the pervading Want of the Community, and while the Necessaries of Life and Labour are high, all that is not absolutely necessary has no marketable value.

Gradually these difficulties were overcome, and the Colony of Western Australia prospered.

4. South Australia: A Planned Colony

Some people in England wondered whether a new Colony, in which careful planning might prevent these hardships, might not be founded somewhere else. This was the idea of "systematic colonization", and in 1834 a group of men persuaded the British

government to allow them to try out their theories in a new
Colony to be founded in South Australia, in the land recently
explored and praised by Captain Sturt. In 1836 the first settlers
arrived.

The promoters of the South Australian Company had argued
that what was needed in a successful Colony was a combination
of land for cultivation, men to cultivate it, and capital (tools
to work with, seed to plant, livestock, and the means of providing
temporary shelter, food and so on). Land certainly was present;
but nothing else. So one idea of the "systematic colonizers" was
that the land should only be sold to capitalists for a "sufficient
price". The money could then be used to bring out labourers
to work it, that is, for assisted migration.

The price was also important because it stopped men buying
more land than they could clear and cultivate; it was intended
to keep a balance between the amount of land being used
and the labour and capital available to use it. The price, too,
meant that only "men of substance", men possessing capital,
would be able to buy land; there would be no poor land-
owners, who knew nothing of farming and had no means of
buying tools or paying for clearing, ploughing and so on.

This plan would make sure that there was a labour supply
for the new settlement; it would provide for a regular allotment
of land; it would ensure that there was enough capital for cultivation and temporary equipment.

In the case of South Australia the plan included some other
things. There were to be no convicts; for by this time, despite
the value of convict labour, men had begun to think that
prisoners were morally undesirable as settlers. Also, although
the governor would be appointed by the English government,
there were to be commissioners to look after the selling of
land and the bringing out of migrants on the principles of
the plan.

But even the planned Colony of South Australia had its
difficulties. First it was difficult to get the support of the
capitalists who were necessary to start the ball rolling—to buy
the land and provide capital to cultivate and bring out settlers.
The capitalist wanted his profit; it would come, if at all, from
cultivation, from the sale of crops and so forth, and, if the
Colony was a success, from the chance of selling land at a
profit later on, when trade would increase and the Colony
begin to thrive. But there was a risk of failure; at best the
Colony might be a long time thriving, and meanwhile, what
profit would the investor earn? It was only after much trouble

that G. F. Angas eventually succeeded in floating the South Australian Company, with a capital of £320,000 to invest in buying land, bringing out labourers and providing other services to help the trade of the new Colony. This is what Angas hoped to do:

The object of the Company in the first instance was to assist . . . in carrying out the establishment of the Colony . . . first of all by purchasing land. . . . The next operation was to provide shipping for the purpose of supplying the Colony with the necessary means of planting an institution of that kind in a distant land, also for the purpose of establishing a whale fishery, because we felt that unless we established a colonial trade, there would be no means of providing employment . . . and if we could not obtain money for the purpose of employing the men on shore as well as at sea, the Colony was not likely to progress. . . . And in addition . . . we thought it our duty to cultivate land to the utmost extent of our means. . . . We established a bank. . . . We sent out coasting vessels, of from 100 to 200 tons, to import provisions from the neighbouring colonies, feeling confident that the emigrants could not raise provisions immediately. . . . We felt that in the establishment of a new Colony there ought to be extensive flocks and herds, therefore . . . some of our vessels [proceeded] to import cattle and sheep from Van Diemen's Land and New South Wales.

Despite these hopes, the early years of the new Colony were difficult. The Company had tried to take great care in choosing migrants; but some were unsatisfactory. "We are grieved at the Commissioner's emigrants", wrote one settler. "It is a sad selection. . . . We have been astounded at the spectacles of vice and debauchery . . .", and another grumbled that "almost all our people have turned out idle, impudent and worthless".

Some of the many complaints were exaggerated, as is nearly always the case; but it is clear that the settlers to the new Colony included a fair share of those who were not willing to face the hardships involved. And, despite planning, there were hardships. The first farmers, though eventually successful, had many difficulties to encounter. Angas wrote in a letter to a friend,

Our agricultural operations go on very slowly . . . it is such immense labour to clear the land. . . . As soon as the rains set in I hope to get the ground broken up, but at present no plough will touch it. . . . I took a very powerful implement, which . . . was to break up any ground; this has broken twice, in only trying a few furrows. . . .

Plan of Adelaide, 1842

The dots indicate buildings and the dark lines show the supply lanes which Colonel Light's original plan did not provide, but which the settlers found to be necessary.

(From *Centenary History of South Australia*)

The whaling industry ran into trouble, because "the persons sent out from England were with a few exceptions totally unacquainted with the system of whaling . . . and had little idea of managing operations or selecting men. These faults resulted in poor catches and serious shipwrecks."

Then there were the personal quarrels which seem to be

Australian natives' huts. A hut
covered with grass, with a small
entrance that can be closed to
keep out mosquitoes, Normanton,
Queensland.

A temporary hut formed of a slab
of bark folded in the middle, Jardine
River, Queensland.

A brick-built veranda cottage of the 1850s. "The apartments
consist of a sitting-room, dining-room, two bed-rooms, and a good
kitchen and pantry, above which are two other bed-rooms. The
veranda is 29 feet long and 6 feet in width. This cottage would
readily let for £4 per week."

(From an advertisement for an auction sale in the *Illustrated Sydney News*, July 1854)

A pioneer settler's home.

(By courtesy of the Mitchell Library, Sydney)

The Kapunda copper mine, South Australia.

(From the Angas collection, by courtesy of the Mitchell Library, Sydney)

Klemzig, a Prussian settlement in South Australia.
(From the Angas collection, by courtesy of the Mitchell Library, Sydney)

Bethany, another Prussian settlement.
(From the Angas collection, by courtesy of the Mitchell Library, Sydney)

Interior of the electric light tower, Sydney Exhibition Grounds.

(From the *Illustrated Sydney News*, April 1879)

The lantern of the Exhibition Dome. View looking over Sydney towards Darling Harbour.

(From the *Illustrated Sydney News*, August 1879)

inevitable in a small community, so largely cut off from outside, and disputes between the governor and the commissioners in charge of land and migration. There were not enough trained surveyors to plot the land sold for farms, and though the first Surveyor-General, William Light, laid out a magnificent city on a plan which South Australians are justly grateful for today, he had not enough assistants to survey the farm lands which the settlers wanted. Hence they tended to crowd into the town; but here building was held up because the local timber was so difficult to obtain—not because of any lack of trees, but because there was no skilled labour available for felling and splitting. This made it impossible even to fence off little garden plots for growing vegetables to exclude the "armies of marauding pigs". Some of the settlers bought more land than they could cultivate, despite the high price charged for it (which was meant to prevent this). These immigrants preferred the hope of selling their land again to new settlers at a profit rather than the hard work of clearing it for farming. So there was not enough land cultivated—in 1839 only 443 acres out of 170,000 acres sold. Many of the population of 5000 could not find work, and food and other supplies had to be bought from the older colonies.

In 1838, Governor Hindmarsh was recalled and replaced by Colonel George Gawler. His first task was to solve the survey problem which was so seriously holding up farming settlement. He persuaded Sturt to come to his help, gave him four new assistants, and engaged private surveyors whenever he could. The services of every efficient surveyor of good character were accepted, he reported afterwards; and he soon had nine good officers in the field. Despite the need of finding tools, tents, carts, horses and the like, 620,000 acres had been surveyed by June 1841, more than enough to meet even the great demand for land in the boom years of 1839-40, when the news of rebellion in Canada turned British emigrants towards Australia, which seemed then to be so prosperous, before the drought in New South Wales and the fall in wool prices caused anxiety and loss.

Gawler's surveys naturally helped settlers to take up farms. Throughout 1839 and 1840, some 4400 people moved to the country, at the rate of 180 per month, "in shoals, cultivating and sheep-farming in every possible direction," according to the manager of the South Australian Company, in March 1841. At the end of the year, over 7000 acres were planted with crops, and there were 250,000 sheep in the Colony. Angas could now rejoice at the farmers' prospects:

I have seen as fine crops of wheat and barley grown here as I ever beheld in England. All the land which I have seen cultivated with anything like ordinary management produced abundantly. . . . The crops raised here I should say will vary from twenty to thirty bushels per acre, but the cultivation is often of the most slovenly character. My opinion is that there is a numerous class of persons in England whose circumstances in life would be materially bettered by emigrating to this or one of the Australian Colonies.

. . . I will just conclude by saying that Sheep farming is considered much more profitable than the cultivation of the soil, and in this Colony there are many extensive districts of unoccupied land where sheep or cattle stations may be formed without any danger of interfering with or being interfered with by neighbours.

Unfortunately Gawler's activity, necessary as it was to put the Colony on its feet and to cope with the stream of immigrants, was expensive. Public buildings in Adelaide, a wharf, customs house and sheds at the "Port", roads to Encounter Bay, the Murray mouth, and Mount Barker, a police force, a gaol, an immigration depot, not to mention the very important surveying work, all cost money. By 1840 the expenditure was running at about the rate of £140,000 a year. To Gawler this seemed reasonable. "The Colony was founded to prosper," he wrote in April 1841, and it was his duty to look to "its reasonable prosperity."

But already, by the end of 1840 there were signs of depression, "due to a sudden and unexpected check in immigration". The sale of land fell off, and so, correspondingly did government revenue. Despite this, Gawler thought that he could only prevent unemployment and distress "by a large Government expenditure". But to English ministers, such an expenditure seemed intolerable. They overlooked (as they had in Macquarie's time with regard to New South Wales) the needs of a growing Colony; they only saw financial demands on the mother country. They had been assured that the South Australian settlement would be "self-supporting"; its cost would be met by the sale of land. If land was for the moment not being sold, then the Government must economize.

Gawler was replaced by Captain George Grey, who was to enforce this economy, even if he carried with him the depression then prevailing in England and, by cutting down public works, caused unemployment in South Australia. In fact, though perhaps Gawler could have economized in minor details, he laid the foundations of the prosperity of the Colony by solving the survey problem, and by his necessary public works. This expenditure only went to prove that the carefully laid plans for

South Australia were not faultless in practice; and the sale of
land at a fixed price did not provide enough revenue *both*
for assisting migration at a time when so many were anxious
to leave England *and* for providing the means to settle the
migrants on farms in a new Colony.

The immediate result of Grey's economy was a sudden and
violent crisis, with much unemployment, bankruptcy and distress. In November 1841, 2427 persons were being supported
by the government, though "in exactly the same manner that
they would have been provided for in an English workhouse.
. . . I will grant no single indulgence to them, but I will not
suffer them to starve." Gradually primary industry expanded
enough to reduce the number of unemployed; no new immigrants arrived and many people moved from Adelaide to the
country. By 1845 there were 500,000 sheep in the Colony and
the difficulties facing the wheat industry were slowly overcome.
Exports of grain to the other Australian colonies had to wait until
the discoveries of gold increased their population and therefore
their demand for food; but costs began to fall as some of the
better farmers became interested in scientific farming, in the use
of guano and lime to fertilize the soil and in the invention of
John Ridley's machine for reaping wheat. Finally, when the
recovery had already begun, the discovery of copper at Kapunda
and the Burra increased the prosperity of the Colony, and
brought fortunes to the lucky mine owners, as celebrated in a
popular song:

> I'll sing you a song by a youthful pate,
> Of the Burra Burra shareholders who had a fine estate,
> Which to them came by luck, not aim, most wondrous to relate,
> And little men unknown till then suddenly grew great
> As Burra Burra proprietors, lords of the Monster Mine.

Though this might be true, by 1850 the value of mineral
exports was greater than that of wool and wheat put together,
and the mines provided more employment than any other part
of the Colony's economy.

CHAPTER 8

GOLD

1. Discovery

GOLD was an important subject in the Australian Colonies about 1850. There had been rumours of discoveries in the past; in fact these rumours were true, but the news of these finds had been kept quiet. In a convict Colony, such a thing might be dangerous. "Transportation would . . . cease to be a punishment," said Governor Gipps once, though it is not true that later he told an enthusiastic amateur geologist who found a specimen of gold, "Put it away, or we shall all have our throats cut."

But in 1848 the gold rush to California began, and a number of men left Australia to seek their fortunes. One of the diggers, Edward Hargraves, who had little luck in America, noticed that the gold-bearing rocks he saw there seemed very like some of the country he knew in New South Wales. He returned to test his ideas, and he was quite right. This is his story.

It was with an anxious heart that I again landed at Sydney, in the month of January, 1851. On my passage [i.e., from California] thither and immediately on my arrival, I made known to my friends and companions my confident expectations on the subject; one and all, however, derided me, and treated my views and opinions as those of a madman. Still undaunted, on the 5th February [1851] I set out from Sydney on horseback alone.

. . . I found myself in the country that I was so anxiously longing to behold again. My recollection of it had not deceived me. The resemblance of its formation to that of California could not be doubted or mistaken. I felt myself surrounded by gold; and with tremulous anxiety panted for the moment of trial, when my magician's wand should transform this trackless wilderness into a region of countless wealth.

. . . I took the pick and scratched the gravel . . . which ran across the creek at right angles with its side; and, with the trowel I dug a panful of earth, which I washed in the water-hole. The first trial produced a little piece of gold. "Here it is!" I exclaimed; and I then washed five pan-fuls in succession, obtaining gold from all but one.

2. The First Gold Rush

Hargraves told his news to the government officers at Sydney. This time it was not kept secret. The effect was electrical. By May there were four hundred people on the field, and thousands more followed. Many fortunes were made, especially by speculators and traders. Prices more than doubled. Carriers put up their charges. In Sydney shops

wares suited to the wants and tastes of general purchasers were thrust ignominiously out of sight, and articles of outfit for gold-mining only were displayed. Blue and red serge shirts, Californian hats, leathern belts, "real gold-digging gloves", mining-boots, blankets white and scarlet, became the show-goods in the fashionable streets. The pavements were lumbered with picks, pans and pots; and the gold-washing machine, or Virginian "cradle", hitherto a stranger to our eyes, became in two days a familiar household utensil, for scores of them were paraded for purchase, "from 25s. to 40s." in front of stores and stalls, so that a stranger or an absent-minded person, who had not yet heard the gathering cry of "Gold, gold!" might have imagined that a sudden and miraculous influx—a plague, in short—of babies had been poured upon the devoted city.

Many were afraid there would be an outburst of crime, disorder and lynch law, and the squatters feared they would be unable to hire labourers to tend their sheep, as fresh discoveries brought new excitement. So many men came to New South Wales that the authorities in Victoria, just separated from the parent Colony, began to worry over their loss of population. In Melbourne, in June, a Gold Discovery Committee was formed and the government offered a reward to anyone who found gold within 200 miles of the city. It was quickly claimed. By the end of the year there were extensive diggings at Ballarat, Bendigo, and many places between the two—Creswick, Clunes, Daylesford and Castlemaine.

As in the case of Hargraves at Bathurst, a letter from a Victorian squatter written long before had suggested that there might be gold near Castlemaine. As he said later on,

I wrote [in 1838] a long rigmarole account of all my journeys through the ranges to an old friend of mine who was a gold-refiner. . . . John Betts of Birmingham, in answer to my description of the country, [replied]: "John, look closely into all the streams; dig and wash the earth; search diligently for gold, for I am sure your feet are passing over immense wealth every day".

3. The Victorian Fields

These Victorian fields, now they had been proved, were richer than those in New South Wales, and they were much easier to reach. At once there was a rush—far greater than that from Sydney to Bathurst. The effects were tremendous; here is part of the report of the Governor, Charles La Trobe, to the British government:

It is quite impossible for me to describe the effect which these discoveries have had upon the whole community, and the influence which their consequences exercise at this time upon the position and prospects of every one, high and low. The discoveries early in the year in the Bathurst district of New South Wales unsettled the public mind of the labouring classes of all the Australian colonies to a certain extent, and had a marked and immediate influence upon the labour market, and the price of provisions in this colony; still both the distance from the scene of the discovery and the approach of winter were in our favour, a journey to the Bathurst district requiring a degree of decision and preparation which few comparatively of the labouring classes were in a position to meet. The discoveries within our bounds, coming as they do at the close of the wet season, in localities in comparative proximity to our towns, exercise a far wider influence upon our excitable population than did the discoveries in New South Wales upon that colony, under the advantages of a larger population and the greater remoteness of the gold field. Within the last three weeks the towns of Melbourne and Geelong and their large suburbs have been in appearance almost emptied of many classes of their male inhabitants; the streets which for a week or ten days were crowded by drays loading with the outfit for the workings are now seemingly deserted. Not only have the idlers to be found in every community, and day labourers in town and the adjacent country, shopmen, artisans, and mechanics of every description thrown up their employments, and in most cases, leaving their employers and their wives and families to take care of themselves, run off to the workings, but responsible tradesmen, farmers, clerks of every grade, and not a few of the superior classes have followed. . . . Cottages are deserted, houses to let, business is at a standstill, and even schools are closed. In some suburbs not a man is left, and the women are known for self-protection to group together to keep house. The ships in the harbour are, in a great measure, deserted; and we hear of instances, where not only farmers and respectable agriculturists have found that the only way, as those employed by them deserted, was to leave their farms, join them, and form a band, and go shares, but even masters of vessels, foreseeing the impossibility of maintaining any control over their men otherwise, have made up parties among them to do the same. Fortunate the family, whatever its position, which retains its servants at any sacrifice, and can further secure the wonted supplies for their households from the few tradesmen who remain, and retain the means of supplying their customers at any augmentation of price. Drained of its labouring population, the price of provisions in the towns is naturally on the increase. . . . Both here and at Geelong all buildings and contract works, public and private, almost without exception, are at a standstill.

4. The Diggers

All this naturally posed a problem for the government, suddenly faced with a large number of eager gold-seekers and the need to keep law and order on the diggings. Where could it find police, magistrates and soldiers? How could it build roads to the goldfields, and protect the gold when it was being sent to town? Even when the police pay was raised, it was hard to keep the men, and meanwhile ex-convicts coming from Tasmania seemed a threat to orderly society; even though some stories were exaggerated, La Trobe wrote in February 1852 that the

number of thoroughly dissolute characters . . . has increased . . . and this fact, taken into account with the great increase . . . of the illicit sale of spirits . . . is sufficient to account for any amount of . . . disorder. . . . Violent quarrels, thefts amongst the huts, tents and workings have been . . . common.

This was one side of the picture. But despite the swindlers, cheats, petty thieves and sly-grog sellers on the fields (and it would have been very surprising if they had not been there), many observers and visitors were surprised at the order and good behaviour of the majority. "Judge Lynch" did not haunt the Australian diggings; "Sunday" reported La Trobe, "continues to be observed . . . as a day of repose and however little the majority may be disposed to attend to religious duties . . . decency is rarely openly outraged." An English visitor to Bendigo in 1850 found that the police commissioner in charge of the district, collecting fees, guarding the gold and punishing offences, "had as his only coffer a tin box secured by a sixpenny padlock; and his coercive force consists of three policemen, two carbines and a sword. Yet his tent has never been robbed nor his authority resisted."

The diggings were in some ways like an army camp, with thousands at work beside the streams, washing their dirt for gold. The size of each claim was only 12 feet square and the finding of gold on it was a matter of luck. There were two kinds of digging—surface digging or "the simple process of skimming off a thin layer of gravel to the depth of a foot or so," and hole-digging. The important operation was cradling; this is how it was done:

The instrument itself is about six or eight feet long, with its head covered with a coarse sieve, and its foot perforated with a hole. To work this machine close to a stream or a water hole requires four men—one to dig, another to wheel, a third to rock, and a fourth to keep dashing water on the earth to effect the sifting process. The sieve prevents the coarse stones from falling into the cradle, whilst the water gradually softens and washes away the earth . . . leaving the particles of gold mixed with sand behind some small cleats. . . . When all the earth is washed away, the rocker and the washer cast their longing eyes into the sieve to see if there be a "nugget" too large to get through the holes, and if not, the sieve is displaced, and the stones are thrown away. This is the process carried on "from morn till dewy eve".

The average earnings of a party were round about one ounce of gold a day, though of course some got a lot more, and some got nothing at all.

On the fields the diggers lived in bark huts, or more often tents—"a few poles and a stick athwart, overstretched with a few yards of calico"—with a couple of tree stumps for chairs and an old box or tree chest for a table. No one shaved, of course; "soaping a chin might lose a nugget". The stores, even, were only large tents, though here,

everything required by a digger can be obtained, from sugar candy to potted anchovies; from East India pickles to Bass' pale ale; from ankle jack-boots to a pair of stays; from a baby's cap to a cradle; and every apparatus for mining, from a pick to a needle. But the confusion—the din—the medley—what a scene for a shop walker! Here lies a pair of herrings dripping into a bag of sugar, or a box of raisins; there a gay-looking bundle of ribbons beneath two tumblers, and a half-finished bottle of ale. Cheese and butter, bread and yellow soap, pork and currants, saddles and frocks, wide-awakes and blue serge shirts, green veils and shovels, baby linen and tallow candles, are all heaped indiscriminately together; added to which, there are children bawling, men swearing, store-keeper sulky, and last, not least, women's tongues going nineteen to the dozen.

Most of the store-keepers are purchasers of gold either for cash or in exchange for goods, and many are the tricks from which unsuspecting diggers suffer.

These "tricks" sometimes caused trouble. So did sly-grog, very common on the diggings, where spirit-selling was strictly forbidden:

The result has been the opposite of that which it was intended to produce. There is more drinking and rioting on the diggings than elsewhere, the privacy and the risk gives the obtaining it an excitement which the diggers enjoy as much as the spirit itself; and wherever grog is sold on the sly, it will sooner or later be the scene of a riot, or perhaps murder. Intemperance is succeeded by quarrelling and fighting, the neighbouring tents report to the police, and the offenders are lodged in the lock-up; whilst the grog-tent, spirits, wine, etc. are seized and taken to the Commissioners.

5. The Miners' Grievances

The greatest cause of discontent was the miners' licence. Of course, the government needed more revenue to pay for its increased costs of administration. Expense arose from the enormous number of migrants—more than 100,000 in Victoria in the eighteen months after the first gold was discovered—from the need to maintain law and order, and from higher wages and prices. To provide revenue to meet these costs, the diggers had to buy a mining licence, for 30s. a month, to get permission to dig for gold. This taxed the unsuccessful miner as well as the lucky one; but it was a heavy tax for any one and it immediately aroused opposition. As early as August 1851 there was a protest meeting at Buninyong, on the Ballarat fields—a "solemn protest of labour against oppression", reported the *Geelong Advertiser*—but the tax remained (though it was reduced to £8 per annum in 1853) and complaints grew more bitter as the yield of gold (at least near the surface) began to fall off.

The diggers had other grievances too. Some, weary of the goldfields, wanted to buy land for farms; but they could not, as it was very dear and the graziers who owned it were unwilling to sell. They wanted political rights; but though Victoria had been promised self-government, its constitution had not yet been finally drawn up (see Chapter 17) and the government policy in the Colony was still determined by a governor responsible to the English authorities.

Perhaps the greatest grievance of all was "inspection". To see that every miner had a current licence, any policeman could ask him to show it at any time, and some of them at least, were rough and tactless. This is what was said to have happened in June 1854 at a place called Campbell's Creek.

Nearly every person walking on the Queen's highway was stopped, and a licence demanded; tents were entered, and the inmates dragged out, if not in the possession of licences, as if they were the vilest criminals; all the stores were called at, and the storekeepers required, in the most insulting manner, to produce their licences. In one case, a schoolmaster, teaching his scholars, was taken from his school; men were taken from their employment; diggers who had licences at their tents were taken away in custody; and Englishmen marched along the highway in charge of the mounted police, exposed to the gaze of the populace. . . . The diggers and storekeepers are greatly exasperated. Here and there, little knots of diggers may be heard murmuring that in California this state of things would soon be altered.

6. Eureka Stockade

Discontent with this sort of treatment grew. Then, in October 1854, a Ballarat hotel-keeper, Bentley, and his wife, accused of murdering a miner, were acquitted of this charge by the magistrates. So furious were the miners at what they thought to be a corrupt and wrong verdict that they attacked and burned down the hotel. Bentley was retried and was now found guilty, but the leading rioters were arrested and sentenced to imprisonment. The diggers then formed the Ballarat Reform League. They demanded that their comrades should be released at once, that the licences should be abolished and that a democratic form of government should be introduced into Victoria immediately. When the Governor, Sir Charles Hotham, refused these demands, some of the miners began to organize armed resistance. They built a crude stockade at Eureka; but this was quickly attacked and destroyed by the police, with military reinforcements. On that December day, four soldiers and thirty rebels were killed, one hundred and twenty prisoners were taken and a legend was born.

The affair started as a justified protest against bad administration and tactless, if not corrupt, police and magistrates. It should never have developed into a riot; but the governor's rigidity stopped him giving concessions to the men in time. But all was soon over. After two days martial law was withdrawn; next year, the "miner's right", for £1 per annum, replaced the licence and gave its possessor a vote; revenue was raised by an export duty on gold instead; special courts were set up on the goldfields to settle disputes; the administration was improved and responsible government came into operation in Victoria.

7. Later Gold-mining

As time went on, the character of gold-mining changed. Alluvial mining (near the surface) became unprofitable; the day of the individual digger was over and he was replaced by the mining company, sinking its shafts deep below the surface and crushing, with expensive machinery, the quartz brought up.

8. Consequences of the Gold Rushes

But the gold rushes brought great changes to Australian society, even though some of these were only a speeding up of developments already under way. In 1850 there were 400,000 people in the Australian Colonies; by 1861 there were very nearly three times as many. Gold raised was worth £124,000,000; what a lot of imported goods could be bought with that money!

The squatter or grazier no longer ruled the economic roost alone; and he often had to change his way of life. He found it hard to get shepherds to look after his flocks; so he began to fence his runs, and a few boundary-riders took the place of four or five times as many shepherds. Wages rose, and so did the cost of producing wool; but so did the value of meat, and many graziers now began to think of beef and mutton (not to mention milk and vegetables) as well as wool. The number of cattle in Victoria and New South Wales rose from 1,750,000 to 2,900,000.

Wheat-growing, like sheep-farming, suffered from the first attack of gold fever, when all able-bodied men left the farms to go to the diggings. But after the first check the increased demand for goods caused more land to be cultivated, and the area under crop more than doubled—480,000 acres in 1850, over 1,000,000 in 1860.

For the first time in fifty years there was a large local demand for food. This caused some difficulties. Many ex-diggers wanted to go on the land; the hostility to squatters grew with the demand to "unlock the land" (see Chapter 12), and the government surveyors were often unable to survey land quickly enough to satisfy all eager buyers. Even if they did, there were still plenty of problems for the farmer, (see Chapter 12). Other diggers settled in the cities. Melbourne and Sydney grew, so did their slums; people did not yet know much about how to keep the cities clean and healthy (see Chapter 15). Trade grew —imports and exports, shipping, shops and warehouses. Public works, especially on the docks and roads, gave work to many former miners, and there was even a beginning of railway building.

In all these ways, living in Australia was changed—chiefly owing to the very great increase in the population. But two other changes—not material ones—came as well. The gold discoveries put an end to the transportation of convicts. In 1851 they were still being sent to Tasmania; but the Tasmanians were strongly objecting and so did those who disliked the ex-convicts crossing Bass Strait to settle on the mainland. "If this is a gold country, it will stop the Home Government from sending us any more convicts," the Chief Secretary of New South Wales had remarked when he learned of Hargraves's discovery. He was quite right. "There are few English criminals who would not regard a free passage to the gold-fields . . . as a great boon", so, except to Western Australia, transportation was abolished. Soon after this came responsible government (see Chapter 17). It was true that there was a large free population in eastern Australia before 1850, and free Australia does not date merely from the gold rushes and the arrival of the diggers. But no country can have its population trebled in ten years without important consequences; and by 1860 the south-eastern States had changed in a way little dreamed of years before.

CHAPTER 9

A REVIEW OF THE GROWTH OF COLONIAL SOCIETY

1. Transplanting

LOOKING back to another age, even one hundred years ago, is very difficult. Nevertheless, it is important to see how people saw themselves in another age. The Australians of 1850 were, with few exceptions, British people transplanted to a new land. Although they were in Australia they still tended to see the country through the eyes of the British peoples from whom they came. They were very conscious of the manner in which they or their parents had come to Australia. Some had come under sentence; they were bond. Others had come to serve the government or as private persons; they were the free. The native Australians, the Aborigines, were regarded as "savages", and their country was a "wilderness".

The settlers tried to create in their new home conditions of living like those they had left behind. One woman pioneer in Western Australia wrote of her new home:

It is a sweet place and improvements are daily springing up around us. The house we now occupy would strike you at a distance as a comfortable substantial-looking mansion. As you approach it, the garden, well fenced and productive in all English vegetables, would almost make you forget you were in Australia.

Most early settlers tried to forget that they "were in Australia", and around their homes they cut down the native Australian trees and planted tidy formal gardens and left a bare paved street. In their homes and buildings they behaved as they had learnt to behave in Britain.

2. Manners

High society was very formal in the late eighteenth and the early nineteenth centuries. For example, ladies and gentlemen bowed to each other on meeting, wrote letters with long introductions, and men even learnt to wrestle and box according to rules. The lower classes copied as much as they could understand or afford, but the lowest classes were crude indeed.

"Manners" were supposed "to make the man" but, on the whole, manners were put on to suit the situation or class in which a man found himself. Sea-captains assumed commanding tones, and those beneath were expected to say "Sir"; parsons intoned from their pulpits; common soldiers had to salute officers; young people were expected to be respectful to elders; and so on through all the positions and situations of everyday life. Some of these special manners are kept today, either because they suit the situation or because they help us to show regard for others.

3. The Classes

When Australia was first settled, every man had his special position or status in society. The differences between higher and lower status were very marked, as everyone was careful not to mix with his or her inferiors. In England, society was a pyramid of classes. At the top of the social pyramid were the king and the royal family; close to him were noblemen and gentlemen, wealthy and well-educated, who firmly believed they had a right and duty to rule over their inferiors. The gentry were superior to bankers and doctors. The middle classes were thought superior to working classes, and skilled tradesmen did not mix with labourers or homeless paupers. The special term used for such a pyramidal arrangement is *hierarchical*. The groups in society were hierarchically organized as well; the Church from archbishop down to curate, the army from general to private, the workshops which had owners, factors to manage for them, foremen to look after the workers, skilled workmen divided into grades, and unskilled workmen and children to do rough or tiresome work.

4. The Gentry

The gentry, almost alone, had political rights. They were the backbone of rural society. As landlords they were anxious to cultivate their estates along the lines of modern scientific agriculture. They were interested in other "improvements", in communications, in roads and canals. They supported the Church of England, that is, the Established Church. They were anxious to relieve the poverty and hardships of the poor when they thought they could, but they looked on this as "charity" for which the poor should be duly grateful; never was poor relief thought to be a "right" by those who received it. The squire, whether a nobleman or not, stood with the parson at the centre of English rural life, as any contemporary novel shows, and though sometimes these people might become petty tyrants, they did, as a rule, remember that they had responsibilities for the welfare of their "inferiors". But inferior the rest of the people were and they ought never to forget it, and it was thought that the health of English society rested on the proper observance of this sense of "degree", that the "lower orders" should properly demean themselves before the "gentry" and that they should recognize their obligations to their "betters".

In England the "gentry" were often allied with commercial men and merchants, especially the wealthier ones engaged in trade with the East or West Indies or other places overseas. Many a noble family welcomed a profitable marriage alliance with such merchant princes, who in their turn were very pleased with the social distinction such a marriage might bring. To the merchant, buying an estate or marrying into an old landed family meant entry into the highest ranks of society—something which, of course, nearly all of them (and their wives) were very anxious for. Both parties thought they benefited, and it was said:

The mixture and confusion, as it were, which results from hence, between the nobility and the mercantile part of the nation, is an inexhaustible source of wealth to the state, the nobility having acquired an accession of wealth by marriage.

This meant, of course, that the nobility were not a closed caste, but that men who had made their fortunes by their industry could join the country's ruling classes. "My greatest pride is to be considered a private country gentleman," wrote one retired planter from the West Indies, "therefore I am resolved to content myself with a little [only about £100,000] and shall avoid even the name of a West Indian."

5. Australian Colonial Society

In the first half of the nineteenth century in New South Wales or Van Diemen's Land, the same sort of class structure existed for a time. At the head of society was the governor, who represented the English sovereign. Supporting him, in the upper strata, were his officials, the higher civil servants, lawyers, clergy, naval and military officers, wealthy settlers and a few merchants. Then, in turn, came the middle class, the smaller tradesmen, the labourers and the convicts.

Nearly all the officials and even a good number of the settlers looked forward to returning "home" to England and thought of the Colony as a place of temporary residence, but this did not stop them from trying to live as comfortably as they could in their place of "exile". As time went on more and more hoped to stay in the Colony and tried the more energetically to bring out or reproduce there the comforts and even luxuries of English life. Even as early as 1820 Commissioner Bigge had noticed that "of the older inhabitants, there are very few who do not regard the Colony as their future home". A generation later, a keen observer, the lawyer R. Therry, remarked in his reminiscences:

There are now in Sydney, as well as in Melbourne and other chief towns of Australia, all the materials of what may be termed good middle-class society that one can find in the principal towns of England, out of London.

Retired officers of the army and navy, with their families . . . form the principal class of settlers in the country. In Sydney, amongst the civil officers of government, are frequently found men of ability and superior intelligence. The majority of merchants have had the advantage of previous mercantile experiences in the United Kingdom; whilst the members of the bar . . . as well as of the medical and clerical professions, are quite on a par with their brethren . . . in the mother country.

At the balls and parties of Government House, and at private reunions, music and dancing and agreeable conversation supply the usual pleasant entertainment of similar evening associations at home. . . . Added to these materials of good and agreeable society we have a numerous magistracy, composed of the principal residents, with their families, in the interior, who come to Sydney in the season, in like manner as country gentlemen in England pay periodical visits to the capital. Naval officers and educated travellers now frequently visit the Colony. . . .

In the arts which polish life, and the accomplishments which adorn it, the towns and cities of these distant Colonies for a considerable time must of course rank secondary to those of the parent country. Of that class which constitute the high aristocratic circle of society in England there is as yet no representative circle in these Colonies; but the class which comes next to it, and that consists of the gentry in England, is creditably represented in New South Wales, and is quite on a par with . . . England.

6. The Treatment of Children

Where adults were divided into grades and classes, the education and training of children were bound to reflect the position of their parents. Even in the twentieth century there is a great deal of difference between the country children and city children. A country boy expects to help in his father's work, but a city boy cannot because his father has a special place to work apart from home.

Shipping wool across a creek in New South Wales.

Bullock team dragging sledges down an incline where no roads went.

Discovery of gold at the diggings.

(From the Newbold sketches, by courtesy of the Mitchell Library, Sydney)

A concert at the gold diggings. Note the predominance of males.

(From the Newbold sketches, by courtesy of the Mitchell Library, Sydney)

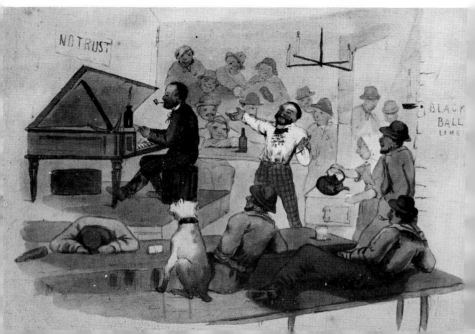

"Off to the Diggings—Flemington, near Melbourne." A contemporary picture showing gold-seekers travelling to a goldfield. Chinese miners travelling by foot in a long single line were a common feature of the gold-rushes.

Gold washing on Summer Hill Creek, near the site of Hargraves's gold discovery of 1851.

(From *Views of the Gold Regions of Australia*, 1851, by G. F. Angas)

Cricket in the Domain, Sydney. A match between England and New South Wales, Jan. 186?

(From *Illustrated London News*, May, 1862, by courtesy of the Mitchell Library, Sydney)

A game like hockey in Hyde Park, Sydney.

(From a sketch by John Rae in Views in Sydney, 1842, by courtesy of the Mitchell Library, Sydney)

In the eighteenth century, when most people lived in the country, boys were expected to help their fathers and girls their mothers. The rich had their sons tutored, and some were sent to boarding school or University. The children of the middle classes were generally sent to grammar school, and then at a comparatively early age they were attached to their calling. A banker's son might be made a messenger to a friend's home, or a younger boy sent to sea. Learning was simple and could be picked up at home, at some small local school or church, or from a private person who taught for a small fee in his or her home. The three Rs, reading, 'riting and 'rithmetic, were taught along with catechism and a few moral stories. Very few went to the grammar schools in England, but more went to the high schools of Scotland to receive training in Latin and Greek. A poor learned man could do little with learning except become a tutor, a minister, or a clerk. It was thought that men educated above their status become discontented.

The condition of children reflected that of their parents. The rich and the middle classes tended to treat children as little adults, dressing them in adult clothes and giving their small children adult's food. Some children were spoilt by their parents, others were over-regimented, and others again were neglected. As soon as children were able they were given work to do, and in most cases it must have been a relief from boredom and punishment.

However, though children had always been expected to toil in workshops or in the fields almost as soon as they could walk (they could earn their living when aged four, Daniel Defoe had boasted in 1707), new evils developed with the growth of towns and new industries towards the end of the eighteenth century. For example, some London orphans were sent to the cotton and woollen manufacturers of the Midlands. The parish guardians, who were supposed to look after them, paid the manufacturers a small premium to give them jobs. In 1802 an Act was passed limiting their work to twelve hours a day. Another Act in 1819 prohibited the employment of children under nine years of age in factories. In spite of these Acts, some witnesses giving evidence to a Select Committee in 1833 declared that sometimes children were kept working up to sixteen hours a day. Here is what a Nottingham mother said:

I have three children working in Wilson's mill: one eleven, one thirteen, and the other fourteen. They work regular hours there. We don't complain. If they go and drop the hours, I don't know what poor people will do. I suppose they'll take off the wages as well as the hours. I'd rather it continued as now. We have hard work to live as it is. It would make sad work with us. My husband is of the same mind about it. He works in the mill, and I am winding. My husband earns 12s. a week, I earn 2s., the eldest child 4s. 6d., the second child 3s. 6d., the third child 2s. 6d. Total, £1 4s. 6d. Out of this we have to pay house rent, hire and clothes, and food for six of us.

The reasons provided by this poor mother were not the only ones. When both parents were working, it was better for the children to be attached to some work. In new towns there were few amusements and much drunkenness and violence. Primary schools were not established for all children until after 1870, and there was very little suitable teaching material for children. If children were not cared for they often became thieves or vagabonds. Some youngsters who were caught were transported for life, and of these some suffered under the penal system of Van Diemen's Land.

It must not be thought that evil conditions were found everywhere. Certain areas in the large cities, certain mines, factories and ships were the worst offenders. A Factory Act of 1833 appointed inspectors to check on abuses under the law and to make reports. In 1842 a Mines Act forbade the employment of all women and all children under ten in mines and underground. In 1844, another Factory Act fixed twelve hours a day as a maximum for all women and all young people under eighteen, and six and a half hours for young children. Factory owners were compelled to guard machinery to prevent accidents. Shortly after, the working day was reduced to ten hours a day, instead of twelve. By 1850 conditions had improved greatly, and the public conscience in England was aroused.

Children were not quite so badly off in Australia. There was some cruelty and exploitation. In spite of government efforts, the children of the poor received very little schooling but they suffered more from neglect than overwork. The children of convicts tended to carry a grudge against authority. Many refused to work at "low" tasks in case they were treated like convicts. They seem to have grown up in the out-of-doors atmosphere that their parents had not known and to have developed a free and easy manner that contrasted strongly with the mannerisms of the well-to-do. Commissioner J. T. Bigge noted in 1820 that,

The class of inhabitants that have been born in the colony affords a remarkable exception to the moral and physical character of their parents: they are generally tall in person and slender in the limbs, of fair complexion, and small features. They are capable of undergoing more fatigue, and are less exhausted by labour than native Europeans; they are active in their habits but remarkably awkward in their movements. In their tempers they are quick and irascible, but not vindictive; and I only repeat the testimony of persons who had many opportunities of observing them, that they neither inherit the vices nor the feelings of their parents.

Abuses did develop in Australia, and though the British acts applied to Australia, there were no inspectors to enforce industrial laws. However, most of the industrial troubles in Australia did not develop until after 1850 because there was so little secondary industry. When secondary industry did develop, the primary school system was already established, and the liberal politicians and the trade unions were prepared to act on the questions of child labour. That they were alert and the public had a conscience about such matters was partly the result of the work of the humanitarians.

7. The Humanitarians

The humanitarian movement was a strong feature of English life. In the nineteenth-century hierarchical society, the gentry who were high on the scale believed they should show charity to their social inferiors. In the nineteenth century the rich were cut off from daily contact with the poor, and when they did come in contact, some were frightened, others thought that poverty was a punishment for sin, especially idleness, and others were indifferent. The humanitarians were those who could not accept and tried to abolish evils which some innocent humans suffered. On the whole these reformers did not give charity; they reformed the law and left the individual to look after himself once the obvious abuse was removed.

Perhaps the best-known humanitarian was William Wilberforce, who began the movement to abolish slavery all over the world. In and out of the House of Commons he battled for the rights of slaves. He was bitterly attacked by those who believed that charity should begin at home. The navy, which had to enforce the Act of 1807 forbidding slave trading from British possessions, suffered greatly during its patrols in equatorial waters, and the anti-slavery party was attacked for its meddlesomeness. Another humanitarian, John Howard, entered prisons and recorded a barely believable situation. His report shocked the House of Commons into action. Before his report, gaolers had been paid fees by the prisoners. Prisoners who were found "not guilty" by a jury were not released until the fees had been paid. After winning support in Great Britain, Howard toured Europe, visiting all places of detainment from France to Turkey and publishing his findings.

There were also some women humanitarians. Elizabeth Fry went into the women's prisons and demonstrated that changes could be made. She influenced the government to improve the conditions of transportation. Her example stimulated many others in Britain and on the Continent.

The humanitarians generally worked by forming committees, raising funds, founding institutions, and gathering evidence for the Press and Parliament. Most of the evidence had to be gathered by personal inspection because reports based on evidence were so unreliable. Lord Ashley, later Lord Shaftesbury, who was influential in passing the Factory Acts and the Mines Act, was attacked by John Bright for using false evidence and for seeking to cure the disease without dealing with the basic causes. There may have been some truth in what was said, but the results of the work were profound because their ideas were made into permanent practical laws which could be policed and publicly reviewed.

Besides the great individuals, the humanitarian movement was taken up by societies and newspapers and the general public. Permanent societies with regular paid secretaries and funds were able to stir up the government and help the unfortunate. Novelists took up the cause of the poor and distressed. Although the novel was meant to amuse, Charles Dickens found one of the great secrets of entertainment, that people enjoyed laughter after crying. He found too that his stories of the suffering of children won more sympathy than public lectures and preaching. In the mid-nineteenth century literacy was spreading, and publishers found a wide public for serialized novels which were sold for a small sum either weekly or monthly. Later in the century as newspapers became cheaper they found that reports of humanitarian topics were popular. By the 1850s the public was turning its gaze on nursing, insane asylums, the treatment of soldiers, native labourers, the care of waifs, and even the mistreatment of "dumb" animals.

Humanitarians, on the whole, wanted to relieve suffering, but they were not much concerned with political rights. Humanitarianism was strongest when poor people, of whatever colour or race, had the least chance of helping themselves to gain success. In New South Wales such an attitude was rare. Humanitarianism was never as strong as in England. Even the unskilled labourer could demand higher wages and better conditions than he could at "home", and the skilled tradesman was in a stronger position because his services were even more in demand.

8. The Utilitarians

The humanitarians were not typical of the well-to-do class from which they sprang. Most of the well-to-do in England were too concerned with their own affairs to take up causes. The gentry dominated political power and made up the bulk of the voters even after the Reform Act of 1832, which widened the franchise very little.

English cabinet ministers nearly always came from the families of the landed gentry and so did the most important civil servants, clergymen and lawyers. To give political power to men less well-off and less educated seemed dangerous to people of the time; if this were done, it was argued, men of this type would use their powers so foolishly as to destroy all the good things that social life provided.

Many politically minded Englishmen in the nineteenth century were called "utilitarians"; that is, they believed that the government should, as far as possible, follow a policy which should bring "the greatest good to the greatest number". In politics there should be no favours for any particular class or group, unless it could prove that if it were given privileges, they would in the long run benefit the whole community.

This doctrine might justify keeping political power in the hands of a small number of "men of property"; they would use their power for the good of all. But political reformers argued that utilitarian beliefs demanded a democratic form of government. Who could say what was "the greatest good of the greatest number"? Only the "greatest number" of the people themselves. So they all should have a vote to choose their member for Parliament. So we find that among utilitarians some were democrats and others were not, and the difference often depended on whether people thought the educated and wealthy upper classes could decide better than the large number of the poorer and slightly educated people what would be, in the long run, the "greatest good of the greatest number".

9. Self-Help

By and large, at this time most people believed that individual welfare depended on "self-help", and they rather distrusted the idea of State interference in their daily lives, and resented

it in practice, for where they had run against State officials in
the past, they had found them so often to be corrupt, inefficient
and oppressive. On the other hand, nearly all the miracles of
the new industries that were at this time sweeping across England during the industrial revolution, and setting up new life
in Australia, had been wrought by the hard work and inventive-
ness of individuals. If every individual were to try to look after
himself, he could do great things.

Australians tended to borrow their viewpoints from England,
but the views took on a new aspect in this country. Very few
people were sufficiently wealthy to devote themselves wholeheartedly to an humanitarian endeavour. Very few people were
able to advocate self-help without also asking for government
assistance. Most people held a mixture of opinions. The humanitarianism led them to set up asylums, schools and libraries as in
England. But the humanitarian sentiment was not strong enough
to protect the Aborigines or to provide a system of education.
The Governor's Councils were dominated by men of property
and officials who softened the laws against labourers only when
conditions suited them. It must not be thought that class difference alone prevented the growth of laws and institutions to
serve the "greatest number". Division among the churches played
a big part in preventing the development of a natural school
system. Other important factors were the natural wishes of the
settlers, their inherited political outlook and their previous
education.

10. The Upshot

By the middle of the nineteenth century Australian society
still reflected many features of British society, but the reflection
was largely illusory. Beliefs were not firmly entrenched and
class divisions were by no means stable. When William Wentworth suggested that Australian lords be created while the
organization of responsible government was being discussed, he
was laughed to scorn. Pity help the "new chum" who thought
he could do things in Australia just because he was "somebody"
in the "old country". In the next fifty years many of the "trap-
pings" of the old country were to be discarded and replaced
by Australian forms.

PART II
DEVELOPMENT OF ASPECTS OF AUSTRALIAN LIFE

CHAPTER 10

THE TRANSFORMATION
OF COMMERCE AND INDUSTRY

1. How Britain Led the Way

THE prosperity of Australia in the nineteenth century depended on certain changes that were taking place in Great Britain. These changes had not come suddenly, but their combined effect had transformed Great Britain. As these changes affected the whole outlook of the nineteenth century, it is impossible to see Australian history in perspective without reviewing them briefly.

The population of England grew from about 6,000,000 in 1688 to about 12,000,000 in 1811. This was partly due to the increased food supply which was made available by better farming methods and better distribution of products. Britain did not lose many men in the great continental wars. A peaceful war was won when the value of inoculation against smallpox was proved. Maternity hospitals and the diet of mothers and babies were improved. Most of the large population moved into the towns when there was not enough work. In Ireland they remained on the land with disastrous results. A potato famine caused many deaths through starvation and weakening the people's resistance to disease.

The British government's reply to the scarcity of food and its high price was to reduce the import charge on corn and other foodstuffs. After 1846 British farmers had to compete with overseas products. At first they responded to challenge, and, by applying scientific methods to their work they improved their crops and livestock, but about 1870 it proved impossible any longer to compete with the mass-produced wheat of the prairie farms and the chilled meat brought from the large ranches of the western United States. America's opportunity was Australia's chance also, as can be seen in Chapter 12.

By the second half of the nineteenth century, Britain's industry had grown to such an extent that she could afford to import much of her food supplies. Britain was by far the most important trading State, with a shipping trade and overseas investments to support her home industries. Australia, as a Colony of Great

Britain, was able to profit at each stage of Great Britain's advance.

Britain's experience in undergoing her agricultural revolution was of profit to Australians who borrowed ideas, good stock, and capital to establish grazing and farming in this difficult country. Britain's colonial achievement compares with the poor conditions in ex-Spanish and Portuguese colonies in South America, where primitive agricultural methods kept the ex-colonies poor.

The wool industry grew largely to supply the need of the Bradford-Leeds woollen mills. The mechanical processes of spinning and weaving were improved throughout the eighteenth century, and at the beginning of the nineteenth century the processes were made quicker and more regular by the application of steam power to the mills. Australian wool proved to be most reliable for the Manchester cotton mills.

The development of trade and commerce led to a demand for larger and more reliable cartage and shipping facilities. At the beginning of the century American ships were as good as the British. The Americans had a supply of good timber, while domestic British supplies were exhausted. But with the development of iron ships and applied steam power, Britain became so supreme that it could be truly said that "Britannia Rules the Waves". In the development of steam trains, British engineers played a leading part. Railways were faster and more useful than canals, and though canals continued to be used for cheap bulk cartage, the steam train became and remained until after World War I the most important means of land transport.

It is clear that steam power was the basis of many economic developments in the nineteenth century. The rest of this chapter will be devoted to the story of power in that century. Britain played a large part in this story, though in the later part of the century other nations play an increasingly larger part.

2. Steam Power

Steam has been known to be a possible source of power ever since the ancient Greeks. There had been several attempts to construct steam engines from the Renaissance onwards, but the engine that was to be the basis of modern development was made by Thomas Newcomen in 1710. His machine was the marvel of the age. A rhymester in the *Ladies' Diary* of 1725 described it thus:

> "On mighty arms, alternately I bear
> Prodigious weights of water and of air;
> And yet you'll stop my motion with a hair."

The people of those days were used to mechanical gadgets worked by wire springs, or wind-driven mills and ships, and even water mills, but Newcomen used fire to drive his machine. Denis Papin, a French scientist and refugee in London, had shown in 1690 how steam expanding in a cylinder could drive a piston upwards. Papin's model had been small, no larger than

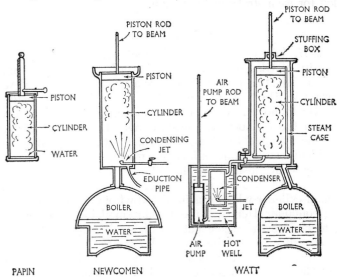

Developments in the use of steam power
(From *A Short History of the Steam Engine* by H. W. Dickinson)

an ordinary bottle. Newcomen had built a large cylinder (7 feet 10 inches high and 21 inches in diameter) over a boiler. The piston which moved up and down the cylinder was attached to a balanced beam to which was attached at the other end a chain and rod for hauling the water up from the mine. Making the large cylinder was not easy because iron casting had not developed at this early stage. So Newcomen made his cylinder of brass rubbed with sand to make it smooth. To make the piston tight he fitted the edges with leather and covered it over with water. To make the steam in the boiler contract quickly he invented a jet which poured cold water into the cylinder after the beam reached the top of its stroke (see diagram above). So successful was this engine that it was copied by other countries in Europe.

It was the pressure of air on the piston in Newcomen's engine that caused it to move down the cylinder when the steam contracted. This limited the force the machine could exert to atmospheric pressure, 14 lb to the square inch approximately, though in practice the greatest pressure achieved by an improved model in 1772 was only 6·72 lb to the square inch. In addition, by condensing the steam in the cylinder, Newcomen's machine wasted much heat because the cylinder had to be heated and cooled for each stroke of the piston.

3. James Watt

In 1757, James Watt, an instrument maker working at the University of Glasgow, was given the task of repairing a small model of an atmospheric engine. Watt was not satisfied with repairing it. He tried to find out the principles that made it work. He found that the amount of steam needed to move the piston in the cylinder was several times the amount required to fill the cylinder. In May 1765, while out for a Sunday walk, he suddenly worked out an idea about using a separate chamber to condense the steam from the cylinder. Within a few days he made a model of a separate condenser and connected it with the main cylinder which was insulated within another cylindrical steam container. Here was the working model of an engine that was to change the whole pattern of man's existence.

Much work had to be put in before the model became a satisfactory engine. He was assisted by Dr Black at the University of Glasgow. He was also helped by manufacturers. Matthew Boulton of Soho, Birmingham, saw that the machine would have to be "mass produced" to be economically worthwhile. Boulton wrote to Watt in February 1769:

I presumed that your engine would require money, very accurate workmanship and extensive correspondence to make it turn out to the best advantage, and that the best means of keeping up the reputation and doing the invention justice would be to keep the executive part out of the hands of the multitude of empirical engineers, who from ignorance, want of experience and want of necessary convenience, would be very liable to produce bad and inaccurate workmanship; all of which deficiencies would affect the reputation of the invention. To remedy which and produce the most profit, my idea was to settle a manufactory near to my own by the side of our canal where I would erect all the conveniences necessary for the completion of engines, and from which manufactory we would serve all the world with engines of all sizes. By these means and your assistance we could engage and instruct some excellent workmen (with more excellent tools than would be worth any man's while to procure for one single engine), could execute the invention

20 per cent cheaper than it would be otherwise executed, and with as great a difference of accuracy as there is between the blacksmith and the mathematical instrument maker. It would not be worth my while to make for three countries only, but I find it very well worth my while to make for all the world.

Boulton rightly saw that to manufacture large and expensive power engines needed a new approach to business. Mass production ruled out easy-going methods. Specialist workers had to be trained, precise measurements of dimensions and efficiency had to be worked out. James Watt undertook these tasks. In addition, good transport had to be provided and large markets found. Boulton himself undertook most of these arrangements.

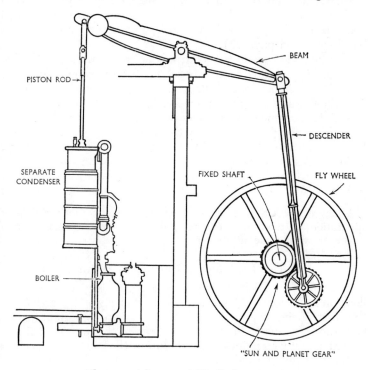

The essential parts of Watt's beam engine
(From the oldest steam engine of this type in the world, housed at the Museum of Applied Arts and Sciences, Sydney)

Another manufacturer who helped greatly was John Wilkinson. Five years after Watt applied for his patent and while he was still working on the engine, Wilkinson perfected a method of boring iron cylinders. Newcomen's brass cylinders would not have been strong enough for Watt's engine, and iron cylinders were badly centred. Besides, Wilkinson needed a steam engine for his blast furnace at New Willey, Shropshire, so that each inventor was able to supply the other's need.

Watt's first steam engine was only useful where "backward and forward" (reciprocating) motion was needed. But most machines need circular motion to turn wheels. Although a crank was already in use for changing reciprocating motion into rotary motion, it was covered by an expensive patent, and so Watt invented a gear called the "sun and planet". The "sun" and the "planet" were two cogged wheels. The planet was attached to the descender on the end of the beam and the sun was fixed to the hub of a large wheel. As the descender was driven down and up the large wheel was forced to move around (see the diagram on page 99).

This invention made the Watt engine much more useful. The first machine of this type was set up for John Wilkinson, the second was in a London flour mill, which was burnt down. The third was used in a brewery. This third machine, which is still in existence, is the oldest steam engine in the world. Strangely enough, it is not in the famous science museum in London, but in the Museum of Applied Arts and Sciences, Sydney. It is interesting to see this example of an engine which played such an important part in the story of the control of power. H. W. Dickinson, an historian of engineering, says of it:

A new era was thus ushered in, enlarging enormously the field of application of the steam engine; indeed, it now entered upon a career of world-wide utility.

4. The First Steam Engine in Australia

In 1813 John Dickson imported a steam engine to drive a flour mill in lower Goulburn Street, Sydney. The arrival of this first steam engine in Australia was an important event. Governor Macquarie himself went down to the mill in 1815 and started it. Other engines arrived during the next twenty years and slowly put the old windmills completely out of business.

5. The Steam Train

While the beam engine was being introduced into Australia, inventors were improving the steam engine and making it more useful. Every part of the beam engine was developed during the nineteenth century, the boiler, the pistons, the separate condenser, and the beam, until the engine was capable of many tasks. The first advance was to introduce high pressure engines. Watt did not approve of increasing pressure. He wrote in 1782, that "nothing much better than we have already done will be allowed by nature". Nevertheless, by 1798 Richard Trevethick of Cornwall had made a working model of a high pressure engine, which he perfected. He realized that his "puffer" was powerful enough to drive a carriage along a road. For his trial on Christmas Eve, 1801, he tried to drive it uphill but it would not move. On Boxing Day he tried again; it moved, but the road was so rough that the engine was damaged. His friends and he were satisfied, and so they dragged the engine into a shed and went off to a dinner "with roast goose and hot drinks". The fire in the engine was forgotten and both the engine and the shed were ruined completely. Trevethick ran another steam carriage in London in 1803. It made several trips and must have played havoc with roads, yet it aroused little interest. Late in 1803 he prepared a third one to run on rails. This first rail locomotive won a £500 bet for its sponsor, but did not make the locomotive popular. The locomotive was not accepted until 1829, when the directors of the Manchester to Liverpool railway offered a prize for a railway engine, and George Stephenson's "Rocket" won the prize by achieving a speed of 30 miles an hour and showing reliability. The following year regular passenger services were established, exactly 25 years before the Sydney-Parramatta service was opened.

6. The Steam Boat

Another advance was made by applying steam propulsion to ships. Some attempts were made to do this in the eighteenth century, but the first real success was achieved by William Symington, who was the first engineer to use a horizontal cylinder from which the piston shaft acted directly without a beam. Symington put a ten horse-power steam engine in a tug boat called the *Charlotte Dundas*, and though the paddle wheels damaged the embankments of canals, the pulling power of the steam boat was well demonstrated. Steamships were used more in the United States than in Great Britain. Old sea captains questioned the reliability of the steamer. One of the difficulties was to find engineers for each steamship to replace parts that were worn out and check pressures. Another difficulty was that coaling stations had to be set up. Steamships had to compete with magnificent sailing "clippers", which were comparatively cheap to run and reliable when they made use of trade winds. One of the great weaknesses of early steam-ships was the use of the paddle wheels. Whether placed in the middle of the stern or placed on both sides, paddle wheels were awkward. The first screw-driven vessel was designed in 1804, but screws were not accepted till they were proved. The British navy proved the issue in 1845 by arranging a tug-of-war between H.M.S. *Rattler*, newly built with screw propeller, and S.S. *Alecto* with paddle wheel.

7. Electricity

The most commonly used form of power today is electricity. Electricity had been known to exist for centuries, but it was not till the eighteenth century that electric current was dis-covered and only at the end of the century were batteries made. To secure a strong enough current for practical purposes it was necessary to find a mechanical means of producing electricity. The basic step in developing such a mechanism was made by Michael Faraday, a laboratory assistant at the Royal Institution in London. He found that when a magnet moved near a coil of copper wire a current was generated. The strength of current depends on the number of turns on the copper coil, the strength of the magnet, and the speed at which the magnet moves. Not till 1873 were dynamos* of sufficient power for industry created.

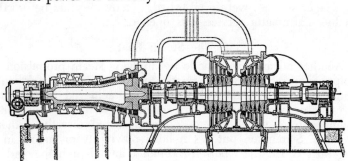

Parsons's steam turbine

To create the rapid movement necessary for generating electricity on a great scale two sources of power were tapped. One was the force of falling water. In mountainous districts it is generally easy to direct water through pipes from a suffi-cient height to turn a water turbine at the foot of the descent

---

* A dynamo is a machine for creating electrical current by setting a magnet in rapid motion.

Punt on the Lachlan River.
(By courtesy of the Mitchell Library, Sydney)

Collision between two paddle steamers, the *Emu* and the *Pelican*, on the
Parramatta River, 1855.
(By courtesy of the Mitchell Library, Sydney)

Bush travelling in New South Wales—Cobb's coach crossing a flooded river.
(From the *Illustrated Sydney News*, August 1875)

Glenelg, South Australia. The horse-drawn carriage and the steam train
formed a natural alliance, the steam train taking over the worst distances
and the heaviest hauls.
(From the *Illustrated Sydney News*, August 1875)

at great speed. This is hydro-electricity. Hydro-electric plants are generally expensive to install but inexpensive to run. Often they are expensive because they are too far from the cities where the electricity is used. Another source of power was the steam or gas engine, which would set the dynamo operating. Reliable electric current for industrial and domestic supply calls for generators with 1200 to 1400 revolutions per minute. Such speeds taxed the reciprocating motors of the nineteenth century.

8. The Turbine

That is why Charles Parsons's invention of an efficient steam turbine in 1884 is so important. There are many kinds of turbine, but the main principles of Parsons's machine are simple, because it is essentially nothing more than a series of windmills or fans mounted on a single shaft against which jets of steam are directed, so causing the shaft to turn. The use of this principle of reaction gives the turbine its name—the reaction turbine. Of course, the turbine is very carefully designed to make it as efficient and economical as possible. If it were nothing more than fans on a shaft it would be very wasteful of costly steam. The revolving shaft with its rows of fan blades is enclosed in a case so as to make use of the same steam again and again by making it travel along the direction of the shaft. To make sure that the steam does not lose its way, the case bears rows of blades which catch the steam as it leaves a fan blade and direct it on to one of the fan blades in the next set along the shaft. Because the steam would soon lose speed as it gave up its energy to the fans, the turbine is built so that each new row of fans is slightly larger than the one before it: the steam is thus allowed to expand, thereby recovers some of its lost speed, and is ready to do more work. When the steam enters the turbine it is at a temperature of almost 1000 degrees Fahrenheit and a pressure of perhaps 2000 lb per square inch. By the time it reaches the end of an efficient turbine, it has given up this energy of heat and pressure, and comes out at about atmospheric pressure and the temperature of boiling water.

The speed of rotation in Parsons's turbine was very high, ten times as fast as the reciprocating engine of the day. By 1896 Parsons had developed generation of 1000 Kilowatt capacity, a great advance on the 150 K.W. generators of a dozen years before.

Incidentally, we may note that Parsons used a turbine in a ship for the first time in 1897, when the 44½-ton *Turbinia* made a speed of 32 knots. Turbines were then tested in a naval

H

destroyer, the *Viper*, and in 1905 in the Cunard liner *Carmania*. At the present time turbines are used in all large ships. They have the advantage of taking up less space than reciprocating engines, and they run more smoothly, without jarring, delivering power as rotary motion which can be geared down to drive the propeller shaft.

9. The Use of Electricity in Australia

Australia watched the development of electric power carefully because so many problems could be solved with its aid. In the early nineteenth century the number of uses of electricity had been limited. Electricity was used for electroplating and other chemical processes.

Probably the most important discovery had been the telegraph. The first English public telegraph system had been set up in 1844. Nine years later the first telegraph in Australia was opened, and by 1872 Australia's leading cities were in contact by cable with London and most other great cities of the world. In the latter part of the nineteenth century electrical equipment was improved: the demand for electricity increased. The telephone and the electric arc light became effective in the 1870s, the incandescent electric light in the 1880s, and the silent movie film and wireless just at the end of the century.

The first electric arc lights in Australia were set up in 1879 to help the workers of the International Exhibition complete their building and exhibitions in time. In 1882 the Sydney City Council instructed the Town Clerk to write to Edison, the American inventor of the incandescent light, and to other authorities on the subject of electric lighting. Sydney was slow to act because gas lighting was well established and electrical equipment was expensive. The Legislative Assembly took from 1891 to 1896 to pass the Electric Lighting Bill authorizing the City Council to supply the public. Meanwhile several other towns, of which Tamworth was the first (in 1888), had installed electric street lighting. The Department of Railways had installed its first generator to provide lighting for Redfern railway station, then (1882) its terminus. The Department, after running trams on an electric traction system at Waverley and North Sydney, decided in 1898 to convert its existing steam lines to electric traction. Ultimo power station was built in 1899 and the first turbine used in Australia was installed there about six years later.

The first Sydney municipal power house for domestic supply was built near by at Pyrmont soon afterwards, though already

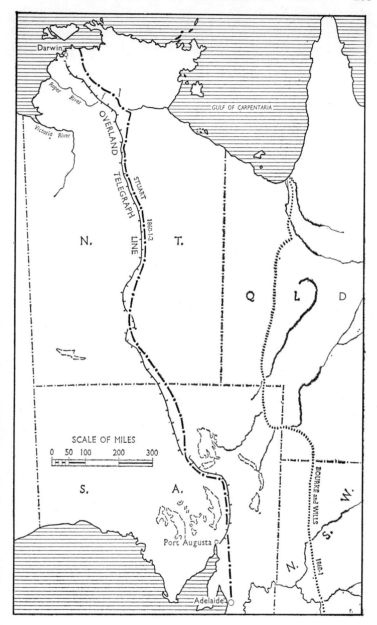

The Overland Telegraph Line, built in 1870-2, and the transcontinental journeys of Stuart and of Burke and Wills.

Redfern Municipal Council and five small private companies were in the field. In 1900 less than a hundred homes were lit by electricity, but before World War I domestic use of electricity was well established.

10. The Internal Combustion Engine

The generation of electricity in the nineteenth century was generally dependent upon a steam engine, either a reciprocating engine or a steam turbine, but the development of the internal combustion engine involved a different source of energy.

In the history of engineering, the internal combustion engine marks an advance on the principle of the steam engine because it burns fuel inside the cylinder and so it is more efficient. An engineer, Redtenbacker, wrote as long ago as 1850 that "the fundamental principle of the generation and use of steam is wrong. . . . It is to be hoped that steam engines will disappear in a not distant future, as soon as we really understand the nature and action of heat." The engineer saw the goal; it has not yet been attained. In trying to attain it several wonderful advances were made in the nineteenth century. In 1876 Nikolaus Otto of Germany perfected the method of exploding gas in a cylinder with a spark, and shortly after Daimler and Benz improved the method by using petroleum and an electric battery. In 1855 Daimler applied his petrol-driven engine to a bicycle. Within a year it was being applied to a three-wheeled car. In 1903 Orville and Wilbur Wright flew in a petrol-driven machine for over 800 feet. About the same time Rudolf Diesel perfected an internal combustion engine that used heavy oil as its fuel and relied on the heat of compressed air to burn the fuel. This method of burning rather than exploding the fuel puts a constant pressure on the piston and enables Diesel engines to work more efficiently than petrol engines. For this reason they are often used in ships, trains and electrical generators that require steady and continuous power.

CHAPTER 11

THE DEVELOPMENT OF STEAM
TRANSPORT IN AUSTRALIA

1. In The Days Before Steam

THE First Fleet took thirty-six weeks to come from Portsmouth
to Botany Bay. Better ships could have covered the distance in
just over three months, but most voyages to Australia took about
half a year. The ships were well laden, and some encountered
great storms which they survived with difficulty. In the new
Colony there were at first only a few weak horses and, of course,
no roads. In 1789 a small boat of ten tons was made out of the
unsuitable local timber to carry material to and from Parramatta.
The *Rose Hill Packet* was nicknamed the *"Lump"* because it
was so slow. Often it took over a week to do the round trip of
about thirty-two miles.

Australia, unlike the United States, has no great navigable
rivers apart from the Murray and Murrumbidgee system. Fortunately for the settlers the country was comparatively flat, so
that except for the Blue Mountains it was possible to clear earth
tracks which were useful in dry weather. From 1795 bullocks
provided most of the haulage. Horses were reserved for riding.
Until Macquarie's day there were no paved roads to make
coaches useful outside of Sydney. October 1, 1814, the *Sydney
Gazette* advertised a "Common Stage Cart to go from Sydney
every Monday at ten in the forenoon through Parramatta, Baulk-
ham Hills, etc., to Windsor and Richmond for passengers and
luggage at moderate charges". Both carts and carriages multiplied
after that, and in 1821 this advertisement appeared in the *Sydney
Gazette*:

Raffle—To be Raffled for, a handsome Stage-Coach, of the most recent
and fashionable construction, with Harness complete for four Horses.
Also, a COACH-WHIP—the whole perfectly new, and in sound repair—To
consist of seventy subscribers, at Five Pounds each. The Subscription
will be received at No. 8, Bligh Street, where further particulars may
be known.

If this suggests pleasure in travel, the picture should be
corrected by the reminder that travelling was dirty, hard and

dangerous. A solitary rider on horseback might travel fast, but had to be careful that nothing happened to his horse. Parties travelled very slowly because fording rivers like the Nepean was dangerous, and hill climbs over the Blue Mountains and the Great Dividing Range were very slow. A bullock team took two days to ascend the western wall of the Blue Mountains and had to be careful descending. From 1821 onwards coaching services developed, and after 1830 coaches were made locally. Regular two-day trips to Bathurst were made from Sydney. From Bathurst the parties went on by privately arranged transport. One of the common sights throughout the nineteenth century and well into the twentieth was the bullock team driven on by a dusty "bullocky" with fierce words and a large whip.

> "With eyes half-shut to the blinding dust,
> And necks to the yokes bent low,
> The beasts are pulling as bullocks must;
> And the shining tyres might almost rust
> While the spokes are turning slow."

After 1850, a number of coach drivers who had worked for American services, such as Wells Fargo, came to Australia in the gold rushes. Some noticed that American coaches would suit Australian conditions. Some enterprising Americans set up the firm of Cobb & Co. in Melbourne in 1853 using imported American coaches. The firm prospered and was sold and resold as it paid good dividends. The coaches were large and well sprung for the rough roads. A regular network of mail services was established from Bathurst, where the company set up its headquarters in 1861. The coming of the railways drove the mail coaches farther out, but their services were indispensable to supply the towns and stations off the railways. By 1870, Cobb & Co. serviced about 28,000 miles a week and employed 6000 horses a day. Motor transport displaced coach services, and the last coach was taken off its run in 1924.

While the sailing ship and horse and bullock played a notable part in the development of Australia in the nineteenth century, the steam engine was applied to shipping and railways, as you have seen in Chapter 10.

2. The Steamship on the Australian Run

The first steamship to come to Australia was a 256-ton paddle steamer, the *Sophia Jane*, which made the trip in five months in 1831. Two small steamers were built in Australia about the same time. The steamer was most valuable to the people along the New South Wales coast. The coastal rivers are mostly shallow and have difficult bars at the entrance. Sailing ships could not negotiate such hazards but steamships were quite capable of doing so. After 1836 regular steam services sprang up and encouraged coastal settlement and industries. A little later, regular steamship connection with England was established. The Peninsular and Oriental Company (P. & O.) started a well-equipped steamer, the *Chusan*, on the Australian run in 1852. Australia was linked with the world-wide network of shipping lines. Great Britain, with her world-wide possessions and industrial leadership, was supreme at sea until the end of World War I. Australia was more closely linked with Great Britain when the Suez Canal was opened in 1869 and the time of the trip to England was reduced to a few weeks by steamship.

3. Growth of Australian Railways

While steamships linked Australia with the outside world, steam trains were most important in developing communications within Australia. In the 1850s New South Wales, Victoria and South Australia opened their first railways. There were many difficulties in setting them up in a country as under-developed as Australia. The initial expenses of importing engines, work tools, iron rails and skilled workmen, as well as local expenditure on sleepers, railway stations and sheds proved too much for the Sydney Railway Company, when it was completing the Sydney-Parramatta line in 1855, and the New South Wales Government had to take over its assets two months before the line was opened. Private companies lasted a little longer in Victoria, but there too the government took over. The Colonies spent much money on railways to open up the country. If railways had been left in private hands few lines would have been built and many valuable areas would have been neglected. For the most part, railway construction in Australia involved no development of British ideas. The main challenges were distance and finance.

The development of the western districts of New South Wales was dependent on transport. The only link between Bathurst and Sydney until 1876 had been the Great Western Road, first built in Governor Macquarie's day. The Blue Mountains rose so steeply from the plains that they made any alternative route impracticable. Yet the road itself was inadequate. In 1857 the Chief Commissioner for Railways reported:

In winter the roads are impassable sloughs and in summer the rudest common earth roads. He esteems himself fortunate whose bullock drays accomplish, when the weather is bad, three or four miles a day and bears—as best he may—in addition to great inconvenience and severe loss, the inevitable heavy charges for the carriage of goods.

The solution to the problem was to build a railway alongside the old road and build elaborate ramps at the eastern and western approaches to the mountains. Great viaducts 120 feet high, a tunnel two miles long, and zig-zags running along a rock face from which 45,000 tons of rock were blasted, were constructed. The rewards were very great, for in the next twenty years the railway network spread over the middle west of New South Wales, the population expanded and primary industry was encouraged.

On the southern line Sydney was linked to Melbourne by 1883. The great drawback is well known. As New South Wales developed her railways, Victoria also developed hers. The gauges were different. The changing of goods and passengers from one railway system to another, especially at Albury on the main Sydney-Melbourne line, has been a great expense. The Commonwealth came too late as far as railways are concerned.

On the northern lines great development took place with Newcastle as the centre. The New South Wales railway joined the Queensland system at Wallangarra in 1888. The Newcastle-Sydney link was not completed until a year later because the railway had to cross the rough country north of Sydney and then span the Hawkesbury River. The piers of the Hawkesbury River bridge were sunk deep because the river bed was covered with a deep layer of sand which did not provide any firm base. When it was built the Hawkesbury bridge was the third largest in the world and a very expensive undertaking for a young country. When it was opened Sydney had gained a central position in the network of railway lines and it was possible to travel from Brisbane to Adelaide by rail, a distance of 1789 miles.

The last link in Australian railways was completed in 1917 by the Commonwealth government. This was the transcontinental line linking the Western Australian and South Australian railway systems. There were no engineering difficulties in building this line. The line runs dead straight for 330 miles with hardly any gradient. However, the country is so waterless and hot that a considerable organization had to be built up to look after the welfare of the construction parties.

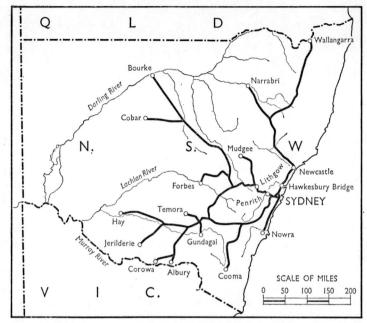

New South Wales government railways in the early 1890s, showing the central position of Sydney

Broken Hill was connected, by a privately owned line, with the South Australian system in 1888. Lismore and Mullumbimby, on the North Coast, were connected by an isolated line built in 1894.

Thus, in less than a century, all the Australian States were linked by railways.

CHAPTER 12

PRIMARY INDUSTRY

1. The First Farms

THE first cultivated farm in Australia was a failure in its first year. Governor Phillip was anxious for it to succeed, but he knew that success was not very likely. The amount of food that was brought out by the First Fleet was limited, and supply ships from England or the Cape of Good Hope or India could easily be delayed or lost in storms. If fresh food was not to be obtained in the Colony, the settlers might have starved, their health would certainly have suffered, and eventually they would have been forced to abandon the settlement.

There were many difficulties to be overcome. The grain brought out from England had not been tested under Australian conditions, and it had been badly stored in the ships during the eight-month voyage. The land around Port Jackson was hilly, covered with rocks, gum trees and scrub. To overcome these primitive conditions, the settlers had hand tools only: spades and mattocks, rope and axes, rakes and hoes. The men who had to do the work had no spirit for it: the convicts were careless and incompetent, and the soldiers did not encourage them.

The site selected for cultivation lay east of the main settlement beside a small stream that flowed into a harbour inlet which has been called Farm Cove ever since. The farm would have been at about the middle of the Sydney Royal Botanic Gardens. Governor Phillip wrote on 15th May 1788 to Lord Sydney:

The great labour of clearing the ground will not permit more than eight acres to be sown this year with wheat and barley. At the same time the immense numbers of ants and field mice will render our crop very uncertain.

The farm must have looked very unlike the English farms of that day. It was a rough clearing in the bush. The stumps of the trees were not thoroughly cleared away. The soil was light and sandy and there was no manure to improve it with; the only preparation was a light turning of the topsoil by spade and hoe, because no ploughs had been brought by the fleet. Although a seed drill had been invented in 1730 by Jethro Tull, it was considered an expensive device even in England and so the seed was sown by hand.

The first lesson was taught by the weather. There was much heavy rain in the first year and the grain rotted in the ground. A second planting from the grain reserved for the next year was tried and does not seem to have produced anything more than enough seed for the next year's planting. As Phillip could see that he could not put much reliance on the land near by, he himself set out to find better. Successful, he reported to Lord Sydney:

Near the head of the harbour there is a tract of country running to the westward for many miles which appears to be in general, rich good land; the breadth of this tract of country I have not yet been able to examine, but I believe it to be considerable.

In the month of this report two bulls and four cows escaped from their convict warders and the Colony was left with one cow, which later went wild and was shot. The only project that flourished was Governor Phillip's garden, where "the new settlers had the satisfaction of seeing the grape, the fig, the orange, the pear and apple—those delicious fruits of the *old* taking root and establishing themselves in their *new* world." There were some other significant developments. The rain cannot have been so bad for vegetables as it was for grain, and the development of this supply of fresh food cleared up the scurvy which had developed on the way out. The other livestock adapted itself to the country: pigs and poultry and goats survived the new foods and the attacks of hungry convicts, and the few indispensable horses could eat the native grasses. Whatever the results of the first year had been, the governor was not judging the new country by them. He thought that he had found "the finest harbour in the world", and he had faith in the new lands to the west. While rations were being reduced, and the spirits of all around were sinking, he wrote home for more supplies, urged the British government to send out good farmers, and gave orders for a settlement to be made at Rose Hill (Parramatta) in November 1788.

Thus, and not for the last time, a farming settlement followed up exploration and New South Wales began looking westward for future supplies. The government farm at Rose Hill looked like flourishing from the start, and the governor ordered a large barn to be built to store the grain. In 1789 he discovered more good land to the north-west along the Hawkesbury River. At the end of the year more than 200 bushels of wheat were gathered and stored ready for the next year's planting. About the same time (November, 1789) he decided that "in order to know in what time a man might be able to cultivate a sufficient quantity of ground to support himself, I ordered a hut to be built in a good situation, an acre of ground to be cleared, and, once turned up, it was put into the possession of a very industrious convict, who was told if he behaved well he should have thirty acres".

The very industrious convict was James Ruse. He earned his thirty acres by working hard, so improving on the methods used on the government farms that after fifteen months he had no further need to draw his provisions from the government stores. He described methods he used at "Experiment Farm" to Captain Tench:

Having burnt the fallen timber off the ground, I dug the ashes and hoed it up, never doing more than eight or perhaps nine roods in a day, by which means, it was not like the Government Farm just scratched over, but carefully done. Then I clod moulded it and dug in the grass and weeds: this I think about equal to ploughing. I then let it lie as long as I could exposed to air and sun and, just before I sowed my seed, I turned it all over afresh. My straw I mean to bury in pits and throw on everything I think will rot and turn to manure. I have no person to help me at present but my wife whom I married in this country; she is industrious. The Governor gave me for some time the help of a convict man, but he is taken away. My opinion of the soil on my farm is that it is middling—neither good nor bad. I will be bound to make it do with the aid of manure, but without cattle it will fail.

Ruse found the way to succeed, but he was not able to follow it up. In the days before fertilizers, cattle were a necessary adjunct to the grain grower. Besides, a farmer needed a kitchen garden and poultry to be self-subsistent. To keep all this going a farmer could hardly work without some assistants and money to tide him over hard times. Probably for these reasons, Ruse sold Experiment Farm in 1793 and moved to the richer lands of the Hawkesbury, where floods made him give up his land in 1809. But his example at Experiment Farm encouraged others to follow.

2. John Macarthur's Farm

The first balanced and financially successful farm was set up alongside Experiment Farm in 1793 by a well-to-do lieutenant of the New South Wales Corps, John Macarthur, who was supported by his able wife, Elizabeth, after whom he named his farm. He had spare cash, horses and cattle, a large property, the use of a fair number of convicts, and much energy. By 1795 the farm had expanded to about 400 acres, with a large well-stocked vegetable garden, an orchard, fifty head of cattle, a dozen horses, a thousand sheep of English breeds, in addition to fields of wheat, corn and maize. Even more important than the accumulation of farm wealth was the use of better techniques: the fields and paddocks were carefully set out and railed in, the first plough was used in cultivation, a dairy was set up, and good accounts were kept.

3. Farming on the Sydney Plain

In the development of the plains between Sydney and the mountains, Macarthur's farm proved the ideal, because the many activities tended to compensate and balance each other. The poorer farmers had a hard time of it, and many, like Ruse, who went to sea for the off season to make money, had to do odd jobs to raise enough money to keep themselves independent. Many gave up hope and did nothing. Governor Macquarie had little time for many of these farmers. Often in the journals of his tours he made comments such as these on the settlers on the east side of the Nepean:

On this side I was truly concerned to observe that the settlers have not made the smallest improvement on their farms since I first visited them in November 1810, *near five years ago*! No fences or enclosures or gardens made, and no new houses built or old ones repaired, and the settlers themselves living in the same poverty and sloth as they did then. This is a melancholy and mortifying reflection, but I fear there is no remedying these lazy habits during the existence of the present old generation.

Even now, it is easy to be deceived by the dilapidated appearance of some Australian properties. It is not easy to keep up appearances while living in the bush, and maybe some of these settlers were quite prosperous; but they had already begun to despise appearances. The "old generation" of settlers has been dead for over a hundred years and farmers in many parts of Australia still present a woebegone appearance to the world. (See the extract from the recent report on a mallee town in Victoria quoted on page 129.) Governor Macquarie, as you have seen from his interest in building, had very high standards and did not realize that Australia was not going to be nearly as trim as England.

By the end of Macquarie's rule as governor, the general pattern of coastal settlement was fixed. A few important colonists had vast estates with gardens, ploughed fields of grain and hundreds of sheep. Many hundreds of small farmers had small gardens, a few domesticated animals, and fields worked by hand. The grain did not do well: floods, fires and various forms of disease, especially rust, caterpillars and grubs, robbed the hard-working farmers of their profit. New South Wales had to rely on imported grain, much of which came from Tasmania. Although grain was cultivated at all times in New South Wales it was not till the end of the nineteenth century that she freed herself from imported supplies and then went ahead to become the leading producer. Farmers would have wrestled with the difficulties if they had gained an adequate reward, but good harvests brought prices down and bad harvests ruined the farmer completely.

4. John Macarthur and Wool

Thus for a century development in New South Wales was largely in the hands of the pastoralists, as you have seen in Chapters 6 and 7, and wheat followed slowly. Two great enterprises developed by John Macarthur set the pattern and the pace.

One of his first enterprises was the development of the techniques for improving stud sheep, though he soon had rivals in this field. During his long absence in England (1809-17) his wife kept watch on the security and general development of his merino flock. After 1820, the flock was kept at Camden Park, where one of his sons, William, had most of the management. Here is part of a letter written by Sir William Macarthur in 1865 in which he describes the way in which records were kept in this early period:

In 1825 each individual in the flock received a permanent distinctive number to correspond with a minute description in a large folio register. By dint of constant practice I had by this time acquired a keen perception of every shade of quality of fine wool fleeces, and each successive spring I made careful examination of every animal, recording the result opposite its number in the register for the year.

This document stated the parentage on both sides, weight of clean washed fleece quality, length, closeness and character of every portion, with the form, size and apparent constitution of the animal, adding such other remarks as the most minute examination might suggest, with reference to the fleeces, outside or inside, on the sheep.

Down to the present day breeders have worked along similar lines, using different stock or crossing various breeds and carefully recording their reactions to different climatic conditions and types of grass. The best merinos in 1820 gave a clip of about five pounds of wool: now clips of about 40 pounds are recorded. The average yield in 1820 was 2½ pounds; in 1901 it was 6½ pounds, and now is about 9½ pounds.

Macarthur's second enterprise was to interest English investors in putting their money into Australian pastoral development. He and the Reverend Samuel Marsden and many others had done as much as individuals could do to stimulate the industry here. English money was needed to pay for expansion, to buy good stock and provide transport and labour. While Macarthur had been in England he had interested many important people in Australia's possibilities. Largely as a result of his efforts, a great company was set up in 1824, the Australian Agricultural Company. It was given a royal charter, which set out its organization and rights, and a capital of £1 million. It opened up land around Port Stephens and developed the Liverpool Plains and Peel River areas. It also brought out good cattle and sheep and even started the coal industry in the Newcastle district as a commercial venture.

5. The Establishment of the Wheat Industry

The most notable new developments on the land in the middle of the last century were made by the free settlers of South Australia and Victoria. The agricultural implements and methods used in the older established Colonies of New South Wales and Tasmania were the same as those used in England. The farmers of South Australia began a series of inventions and adjustments that made it possible for Australians to make a profitable return out of the drier land of the interior, where wheat did not suffer so much from the damp weather and other troubles that had been noticeable on the coast.

The problem that faced South Australians in 1843 was the problem of harvesting a large wheat crop with a small labour force. Two inventors, Bell in Scotland and McCormick in the United States, had already invented reaping machines, but these were not needed in South Australia because the straw that was gathered with the sheaves was not wanted for fodder. Only the ears of grain were needed. The crop ripened so quickly in the heat of the South Australian summer that the operation had to be fairly fast. A group of farmers formed a special committee and offered a small prize of £40 for an improved harvesting machine. Sixteen designs were submitted to the judges, but they did not award the prize. Someone told the committee that a young miller, John Ridley, was at work making a machine.* Ridley knew something about engineering because he brought a James Watt engine to South Australia to drive his mill. When the threshing machine was successfully demonstrated two months after the competition, Bull, an entrant in the competition, claimed that the main principle in Ridley's machine had been demonstrated by his model. The idea may have been stolen, but the issue has never been cleared up. Many of the most important advances in science and engineering have been made by two persons at the same time. The general discussion of problems leads to several people covering the same ground at once.

Ridley's reaping and threshing machine solved one problem only. Farmers had to be persuaded that the machine was worth while. It was ten years before it was in widespread use. There was the cost of the machine in the first place, and then the farmer had to decide what to do with the long straw and trash it left behind in the field. As the harvesting took place in summer it was dangerous to burn it and if it was left till the wet season it was impossible to clear the field and the weeds took advantage of the spell to establish themselves. For some time men were not able to overcome these difficulties.

---

* The general working of Ridley's stripping machine is easily followed. "The body of the machine is about four feet six inches broad, covered in, built upon wheels like a cart, but much stronger, and driven forward through the standing iron by two horses or bullocks. Two sets of cogs are fixed in the inside of the wheels near the felloes, which drive two small pinions. At the ends of the rod on which the pinions are fixed, are two wheels about two feet in diameter; these drive the drum or beaters, which make 600 revolutions per minute. At the fore end of machine, in front of the beaters, is a metallic comb, the teeth of which are about eighteen inches long and one inch broad, and so placed that, as the machine is pushed forward, all the ears within the entire width of the wheel tracks are caught up by it—the straw only suffered to pass out, and the heads or wheat ears guided to the lower cylinder, where they are received by the beaters, and the grain threshed out, and thrown up a curve, whence it falls into the receiving box at the bottom of the cart, which in general will hold about nine bushels, and the chaff flies off through a kind of flue at the back end of the cart. With this machine it is usual to reap and thresh from eight to ten acres of wheat per day. The crop must be thoroughly ripe, and perfectly dry when the operation is performed, otherwise the beaters, instead of threshing out the grain, will drive the ears back whole to the end of the machine." (F. Lancelott: *Australia As It Is*, Vol. I.)

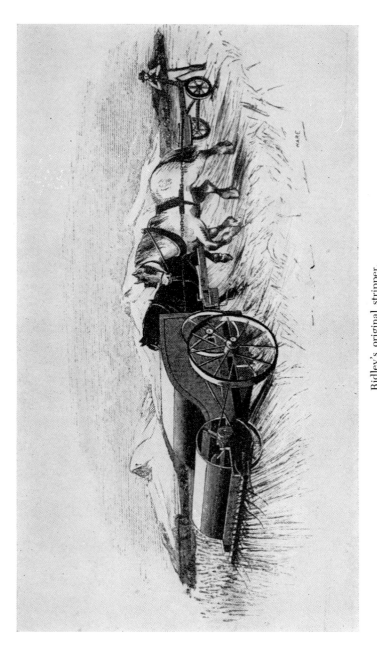

Ridley's original stripper.

(From *Romance of the Australian Land Industries*, by Robert D. Watt)

Running-in wild horses from the bush.

"Then fast the horsemen followed, where the gorges deep and black
  Resounded to the thunder of their tread,
And the stockwhips woke the echoes, and they fiercely answered back
  From cliffs and crags that beetled overhead."

(From "The Man from Snowy River", by A. B. Paterson)

Mustering day at a cattle station.

(By courtesy of the Mitchell Library, Sydney)

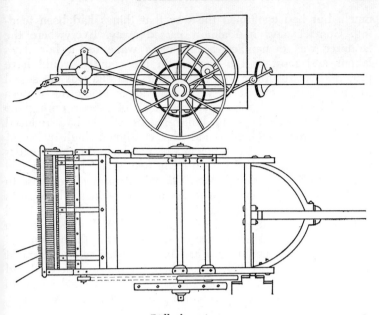

Ridley's stripper
(From *The Wheat Industry in Australia* by Callaghan and Millington)

The other problem was quite different. The price of wheat fell in 1843-4 to 3s. 6d. and even 2s. 6d. a bushel, while wages for labour were at least 3s. a day. South Australia had a surplus of 200,000 bushels which had to be sold at a loss. The Colony's income from exports was only £46,000. The settlers in the Port Phillip district gained £307,000 from the sale of wool, which required less labour than wheat. The wheat industry could not flourish until a market was available. Fortunately, New South Wales and Victoria found it best to import cheap South Australian wheat and their demand increased steadily until 1850. The gold rush brought a vast new population to feed and though labour for the farms was scarce when many men left to try their luck in the goldfields, there was an incentive to produce grain. The market was made. Moreover, with mechanical aids it was possible to make use of land with a low production per acre. South Australia remained the leading wheat-producing State until 1890.

6. Primary Industry by 1860

By about 1860 the main difficulties of setting up on the land were over. The gold rushes had not changed the pattern very

I

much, but had confirmed the way that things had been tend-
ing. Convict days had almost passed away. Everywhere the
labourer was demanding a fair day's wage for a fair day's
labour and most of the workers in the country would have
preferred "to run their own place". But Australia was not suited
to small farms except in very good areas along the eastern
coast. The pastoralists' response to lack of labour during the
gold rushes had been to build fences which had reduced
the need for shepherds, and the continued high price of
labour led to permanent fencing of paddocks in the decades
which followed. Barbed wire used in fences had been invented
in America a short time before. The wheat farmers' response to
the high price of labour was to use more machines. The various
governments' response to the demand for land was to pass Land
Acts which enabled men to select blocks of land, in New South
Wales between 40 and 320 acres, and to develop them. You will
read later that four Colonies had been granted self-government
in 1855 (see Chapter 17). Everywhere the man on the land, old
or new, faced the same problems of finding ways and means to
make the difficult country produce goods and then to sell them.

7. Science and Mechanics in Farming

Between 1860 and 1919 Australia underwent a series of
changes which linked her tightly with England and other
overseas countries. The great revolution in production, which
we call the Industrial Revolution, had earlier made England
the greatest manufacturing and trading nation in the world,
and now made a deep impact on Australia. As British manufactures had expanded and her towns and population had
grown, her food production had also increased. Many inventions, improved techniques and larger land-holdings had so
revolutionized agriculture and stock-raising in England that
she was almost a century ahead of developments in Australia,
and well ahead of the United States. Two men in particular
had raised the productivity of English fields, Sir John Bennet
Lawes and Sir Henry Gilbert.

Their work made practical use of the scientific studies of
the development of plant life made by Justus Liebig of Germany. For centuries men had improved the production of farms
by trial and error methods. Liebig was one of the first scientists
to use the new advances in chemistry to find out what chemicals
plants gain from the air, the earth and the rain. The results of
his researches were made known about 1840 in a work called
Organic Chemistry in Its Application to Agriculture and Physi-

ology. Lawes produced the first marketable chemical aid to growth in 1843. This was superphosphate, which he had extracted from rock salt. In 1843 he invited Gilbert to co-operate with him in running a research station at Rothamsted. These two men worked together for fifty years and gained much knowledge that helped agriculture.

English production was at its peak in 1855. Four million acres were under wheat and the yield per acre was high. But after 1855 production declined as cheaper grain became available from the United States. There grain was grown in bulk, as in Australia, and later on it could be transported cheaply by steamship. The United States had more suitable climate and soils for wheat than Australia, and was much closer to the home market. If Australia was to share in the market with America and to maintain wages, cheap methods of production had to be found. Slowly the limitations on Australian production and export were overcome. The first exports were made from South Australia in 1866, and despite some bad droughts and trade depressions, production mounted to 100 million bushels by the time of World War I.

As crops increased in the south of Australia, so cattle-raising in the far west of New South Wales and especially in Queensland became a major industry. Cattle could be run in country where the water supply was insufficient for sheep. Artesian water was first tapped in 1878 and was a great help to the stockmen. After 1860 salted and canned meats were sent to England but they were not very popular. For over ten years a French engineer, E. D. Nicolle, encouraged and subsidized by Thomas Mort, worked to perfect a method of refrigerating meat that would keep it in a satisfactory state until it reached England. A year after Mort's death, a cargo of 4000 sheep carcases was delivered to London on 2nd February 1880 by the *Strathleven*. By 1894 the process was considerably improved and Australia gained and maintained a fair share of the London market.

To increase production within Australia the men on the land followed their own devices. Their policy was almost a reversal of the careful and balanced English agricultural practice. They felt that there were no limits to Australia's possibilities, that they had land "to burn". While the number of different agricultural and pastoral activities was increasing the individual farmer generally devoted himself to one culture only. He was a dairyman, or a cattle man, or a grazier, or a wheat grower.

8. The Graziers, 1860-1919

The grazier remained the most important man on the land. Wool provided half the national revenue. The squatters bought their old leases and fenced them. The sheep improved in quality as they grazed naturally in the paddock without constant rounding up. The graziers were more concerned with the number of their sheep than with caring for the land. To increase the grass area, graziers ring-barked trees. As the trees died, erosion followed, for not only did sheep clear the grass off the earth, but rabbits began to ruin the pastures, so much so, that the first Rabbit Destruction Act was passed in 1883.

In 1885 a strange trial was held between an expert shearer, Dave Brown, and a mechanic using a sheep-shearing machine. The hand shearer did better time on his three sheep, but the onlookers noticed that his sheep were not as closely shorn as the mechanic's. Three-quarters of a pound of wool had been left on each of the three sheep clipped by the handclippers. Three years later the newfangled machines were tried at a station west of Bourke and showed themselves to be useful and reliable.

The graziers often had disputes with the rest of the community. To improve their properties with such things as rabbit-proof fences, dams, sheds and dips, they had to borrow money; banks and finance companies were accused of demanding excessive interest. In the days after the Land Acts which allowed farmers to select parts of their lease for farming were passed, graziers strenuously opposed the government in the faraway capital city, using every legal trick to retain possession of their leases, getting members of their family or their hands to select the best parts of their property along the creeks and near the waterholes. Where these tricks did not work, they sometimes tried something worse. They might burn off grass, but so carelessly that the fire set alight to the settler's wheat. One settler near Temora, Fisher, recovered £12,000 damages from a grazier named Wellman by proving that the fires were started maliciously. Not all cases were provable and tension was often very high. Another group with whom conflict went on all the time was the shearers, who had organized themselves into a strong union by the end of the century. All these problems were very serious. To solve them the graziers needed to understand human relations as well as business. They worked hard, took risks and were often extremely generous. They thought that as they had opened up the country they were entitled to some rewards and security. They were forced to work out compromises because in the last resort they and the people they dealt with had to eat to live.

Isolation in the early days was the cause of many of the troubles, but it also created a longing for better things. The station properties became little centres in the bush. Around the central homestead with its large verandas, gardens with trees were planted, large vegetable gardens were set up and a rough row of stables, outhouses and chicken coops straggled along in the home paddock. The large properties provided large woolsheds a few hundred yards from the homestead and quarters for the shearers. The homesteads and their surrounding buildings were Australian towns in miniature. The graziers kept themselves apart from the shearers in their huts, and apart from the hands on their own property, but they were very different from the gentlemen farmers of the older established properties. There was no job on the property that they could not turn their hand to, but they had little of the education or social polish that had marked the earlier settlers. When women went out to live on the stations, they gradually introduced the niceties of home life, such as furniture, flower gardens and varieties of food, gave a kindly welcome to strangers and started visiting neighbours whenever possible. Left to themselves, the men often lived roughly and thought that "anything would do" as long as it served the purpose. Growing wealth and the development of city boarding-schools changed this greatly by the end of the century.

9. The Wheat Farmers, 1860-1919

The wheat farmers were different in that most of them had a settled home from the beginning; but it was rarely of the size and importance of the squatters' stations. The main task of the wheat grower was to grow wheat, and when the more suitable lands were already taken up, the farmers moved out to the low rainfall areas. Some of the better-off settlers, like Fisher of "Mirrool" in New South Wales, obtained Chinese labour to clear their land. To sow his land Fisher "adopted the device of standing in the rear of a strong buggy, and in that way was able to hurl the seed over a much wider area, while a second person drove him steadily forward."

Rough and ready methods were the prelude to the use of mechanical aids. Ridley's stripper was the first Australian device, but it did one job only: it stripped grain. Others added to his machine. Finally, Hugh Victor McKay, at nineteen years of age and using bits of farm equipment, even kerosene tins, made a "combined machine" in 1884. In 1888 he set up a factory at Ballarat and in 1906 he founded a manufacturing town called Sunshine, now a suburb of Melbourne. His combine harvester not only stripped the wheat head from the plant but completed threshing, winnowing, and sieving the wheat, depositing it in a bag ready to be stacked and despatched.

The mallee country, which was opened up in this period, was the most difficult country to clear. The mallee bush is springy and tough. It sends long roots through the soil and these branch out and send up suckers even when the parent plant is cut. Clearing this ground cost about £7 an acre. The settlers could not afford this, and so one settler used a discarded steam boiler to roll down the scrub towards the end of winter. Then just as the shoots were growing in spring he fired the field. By attaching spikes to the roller it was possible to break up the ground enough for sowing at the same time as the bush was being levelled. The idea caught on because it saved so much money. It was found that if a field was rolled and fired for about five years in succession, the mallee died out. The fields were very difficult to plough because of the roots or stumps that were left in them and to meet this difficulty another settler invented a plough which would jump the stumps. The "Vixen" was the name given to the first "stump-jump" plough. It had three mould-boards each mounted on hinged beams. Each share could rise when the plough came to an obstruction and a 56-lb weight on the other end of the beam brought it back into the earth when the obstruction had been crossed. To increase the output of each man, many farmers used great teams of horses to drag multifurrow ploughs because horses were cheap and easy to feed.

Science was used to improve the crop production. In 1881 the South Australian government appointed a scientist as Director of Agriculture and later established an agricultural college. Here Professor Lowrie experimented with the fertilizers developed at Rothamsted in England to see the effect under Australian conditions. Superphosphates proved valuable because they raised production by seven bushels an acre, which added at least £1 profit per acre. Australian soils are deficient in phosphates and so nearly all Australian farms use superphosphate, though its cost has risen greatly.

10. Farrer

The other important development became public at the end of the century—the improvement of strains of wheat to produce

kinds that could resist rust and drought conditions. William
James Farrer undertook this work of his own accord. He was
a Cambridge graduate in mathematics who came to Australia
for the sake of his health. For some time he was a surveyor
and he saw the need for better types of wheat as he moved
about the country districts. Four years after he married he
settled down at Lambrigg, a property near Queanbeyan. Here
he planted the first plots of different types of grain, some local
varieties and some from overseas. The work was carefully
done. Each plot was laid out with a surveyor's exact measure-
ment. The rows were 15 yards long and there were 16 inches
between each row. In each row there were about one hundred
seeds five inches apart, sometimes more. When cross breeds
were made they were planted in a row beside the mother of
the crops so that comparisons could be made. The seed beds
were lined with manure and when the plants started to grow
the tops were dressed with manure. But this was only the
preliminary. Farrer described his testing work in the middle of
the season, November 1893, to Professor Lowrie.

I have been working like the very devil this year. . . . I have now
made 275 distinct crosses, and whereas last year I made 260 crosses,
I only operated on one side of an ear. This year I have mostly
operated on both sides. In order to do my work more effectively this
year, when I planted the seed I entered in my field book a description
of the grain—the size, colour, length, plumpness, depth of crease,
etc. I also sent to a milling expert samples of about 180 sorts that I
thought of using for parents, to be submitted to the chewing test.

This part of his work, crossing, recording his results and
checking with the miller reminds one of the work of the stud
breeder. The over-all results were the same. Many strains
were useless but some improved greatly. The government
appointed him Government Experimentalist on £350 a year
in 1894, and this gave him the opportunity to test his species
in different places and provided him with some assistants.
Farrer was one of the first experimenters in his field in the
world, and was at work at an important time. The farmers
needed his types badly. Not only had his varieties reduced
the menace of rust, but they gave better yields, were easier
to mill, and were easier for the farmer to handle at harvesting.
Some of them were capable of growing in the eight-inch
rainfall districts and made it possible to extend the area of
cultivation.

It was by using all these aids that Australia achieved the

greatest output per man of any country during World War I, when 18½ million acres went under cultivation as a result of a request from the British government for grain. So much grain was produced that the government could not store it and transportation was inadequate. After the war the government extended the railway lines further and built up a system of wheat storage, a network of wheat silos which were capable of holding 15 million bushels (55 million bushels in 1955).

11. Problems Faced by Primary Industry

The cost to Australia of this expansion was very great. The land itself suffered because no care was taken to put back into it what was taken out. The general well-being of the community suffered because over-production was followed by bad markets and loss of money and jobs for many people. This turning about of events is called boom and depression. But for the moment, the story will revert to the first problem of care for the land.

(a) Erosion

One-third of Australia is desert country. Nothing grows on the desert for long enough to hold moisture and sustain life. When the settlers cut down trees and allowed livestock to eat the natural grasses, and rabbits spread, the natural cover of the earth was removed and the sun dried out the soil, the winds blew the topsoil away and the rain created storm creeks which cut the land. Thus the area of desert was extended. A Royal Commission reported in 1901:

The evils wrought by the western sand-storms are various. The manager of Teryawynia Station, in the Wilcannia district, states that, out of the leasehold area of 460,000 acres, an area of 100,000 acres "is as bare as a floor, in spite of the great rain which they have had". . . . Witnesses also stated that large quantities of feed had been destroyed by being buried under the sand deposits. As to the ultimate effects of these sand-storms upon the western country, as far as its pasture-growing capacity is concerned, few persons profess to speak with positiveness; but there can be no doubt that if they are to recur frequently, they will add a new terror to the life of the western pastoralist by increasing enormously the cost of maintaining his improvements. . . . Another witness stated that upon his holding in the Mossgiel district he left one morning some weak sheep watering on a 400- or 500-yard tank. A dust storm occurred during the day, and by night time all traces of the tank, except the embankment, had disappeared, a number of sheep having been buried alive. . . . The destruction wrought by the sand-storms in addition to rendering useless valuable improvements, and involving the expenditure of large sums of money, has gone a long way towards taking the heart out of the western pastoralists by raising the question as to whether the experiences of the last few years are going to be of frequent occurrence.

Everyone knows the answer to the last question. The problem had come to stay and was world-wide. It was the problem of erosion. Land suffering in the same way in the United States was called "the dust-bowl". The problem was not just an economic problem for the pastoralists; it was the national problem of conservation of resources and so concerned the governments of Australia.

There were two other problems closely connected with erosion. The first was the exhaustion of the soil. The scientists had found many of the chemicals that the soil needed and, as was seen earlier, individual farmers and government stations had used phosphates to restore the fertility of the soil for crops. But the restoration of all pastures was a tremendous task, and here again it became obvious that the governments would have to step in.

(b) Pests

The other problem was the problem of pests such as weeds and cactuses, or rabbits and mice, that seemed to thrive on the weakened country. When the governments first intervened on these matters, they tried to make individuals responsible for cleaning their own ground. Regulations were important and have remained so, but the government's research has accomplished more than the farmers could achieve. The menace of prickly-pear was not investigated by the Queensland government until 1912. The wild cochineal insect was imported to deal with it, but the insect attacked only some forms of cactus. By 1926 it was shown that 60 million acres were covered by the pest. Investigators looked over many countries until a caterpillar was found in the Argentine. Carefully nurtured and distributed, the caterpillar made war on the cactus until the menace was laid low, and over 60 million acres of land became useful again. The recent victory over the rabbit brought about by the introduction of the disease myxomatosis, which spread rapidly in the summer of 1950-1, is fresh in many people's memory. However, rabbits are developing an immunity to the disease, and in the 1960s new methods were used to reduce their numbers.

(c) Marketing

The setbacks that the man on the land has to face on his property are not so difficult to meet as the setbacks that follow a collapse of prices on the market during a depression. In 1893 and 1929, following periods of increased production in Australia and throughout the world, the countryman has faced, along with the rest of the community, a problem which cannot be met by any form of direct action. Most expansion is carried out on borrowed money. When prices fall and products are sold at a low price, the money that is received has to be used to pay off debts. Crops still have to be planted, repairs kept up and children sent to school if the properties are to go on. Apart from economizing, and trying sidelines that will pay, the countryman is forced to apply to the government for aid and wait for better times. Many farmers had to leave their properties, but the level of production remained fairly high, except for two difficult years, because abandoned farms were often the ones that paid least and production was the only way to survive.

The governments made enquiries into the wheat industry in 1934. To tide over the market difficulties, the Commonwealth government fixed a high price for wheat, as it had done for sugar and butter in 1923 and 1926. This enabled the farmer to recoup himself for the lower world prices. In 1932, at Ottawa, countries within the Empire agreed to give preference to each other. Higher duties were placed on products from outside the Empire than on those produced within. This helped a little, but the other nations retaliated by putting up duties on Empire products.

Australia pulled out of the depression because world markets slowly recovered and because governments and people worked to make ends meet. During World War II many men were away on active service and the government created a volunteer land army. The Commonwealth took charge and directed the amounts to be produced and set the prices. Many controls are still maintained in order that prices may be stable, employment guaranteed and progress maintained.

12. Country Life Since World War II

The difficulties that the men on the land have faced must not hide the fact that life on the land has steadily become easier over the last fifty years. Isolation has been broken down by the wireless, the telephone, the aeroplane, the extension of roads and regular mail services. Except in the deep inland, schools, doctors and numerous shops and entertainments are fairly easy to get to. A modern country town may look like a "sleepy dying town" to a casual visitor. One wonders what Governor Macquarie would have thought of the modern country town with its long main street of shops and banks and untidy back paddocks and timber houses. To help see the difference between his day and ours, here is part of a description of the activity of a typical mallee town of about ten years ago:

No important section of the local population has time to spend about the town (even granted that there is little to attract them if they did). The children are busy at school, all working males are engaged in their tasks during the day, and very few are engaged in tasks which might bring them into the town; women are tied up with housekeeping during the mornings and only on occasional afternoons can they get away—when they can, such "breaks" tend to be taken on the Thursday market day when most organizations meet and when the Baby Health Clinic comes to town. Shopping, a major incentive for going to town, tends to be delegated to the children. Town mothers send their children on errands when they come home from school, while farm mothers phone in their orders to the stores and the children pick them up and bring them home on the school bus.

At harvest-time much more activity occurs in the town as the farmers and contract carters bring their wheat loads to the silo. At the same time small groups are to be seen making repair jobs at the garages and stopping briefly at the hotel to slake their thirsts and exchange news on the progress of harvests and incidents connected with harvest.

The work of the man on the land has become more complicated as time has gone on. By the end of the 1920s all the easily workable land had been taken up and ever since the 1930s advances have been made, not by expansion but by intensification of farming and care for the pasture. The land has been broken up into smaller properties. For instance, nearly 50 million sheep are grazed on properties each carrying under 2000 sheep. Only one-quarter of the sheep population is on stations each carrying over 5000 sheep. As properties are owned and not leased and the countryman wants to hand his property on to his son, greater care is taken to preserve the value of the land. This can only be done by giving up a single culture and returning to a balanced farm where different crops are planted in successive years and livestock are kept on wheat farms.* By varying the use of the land the soil is

---

* Look back to page 114 and notice the change; then look up the graph on page 131.

not exhausted. The pastoralist thinks twice before he removes trees now, and most often plants trees and grasses. Care for natural pasture and variation of crops have produced a revolution on the land, but have added to the cares of the farmer.

Here is a newspaper report of the way in which one farmer came to learn the new methods from a government adviser:

The Adviser called in again today and he had another look at my bare hill. You remember that I said it was too stony to cultivate. It is not stony all over, but has ridges of stone too close together for easy working. Well we decided that I would sow with grasses the country that I could get a combine over properly, which would be some time next year. We could run a series of contour furrows around the hill so as to stop the water running off. I wasn't quite sure what contour furrows were, but I didn't like to tell the Adviser that, so I waited till this evening when I rang Clarkson and he said that they were just single plough furrows ploughed around the hill on the level. Then the Adviser said that I ought to be prepared to top-dress the pasture every year, and that he thought he could get me an allotment of super for this. I started to tell him that I didn't hold with putting super on top of the ground—it should be put in the ground, but just as I was getting my argument going the Adviser said, "Yes, it was funny the ideas some of these old-fashioned farmers had." That rather knocked me, so I just gave in quietly. Then we started talking about what kind of pasture we ought to plant. He kept asking me what I thought, which was rather awkward because the only grass I know well is barley grass, because the seeds of that stick in my socks in the late spring. I said, after a bit of pressing, that I always thought that the lucerne would do well in the district. That wasn't quite true, because Clarkson has been trying to get me to sow lucerne for years, but I have always said that mine was a wheat farm.

But I couldn't very well say "What about sowing some barley grass?" to the Adviser, could I? He thought that we should try some lucerne, but it ought to be sown in the spring because of the lucerne flea, and it was too late to prepare the ground this year for lucerne. Anyhow, we decided to cultivate the arable portions to be ready to sow some grasses next autumn, and in the meantime he will do some more thinking. He's a terrible bloke for thinking. I don't hold with too much of it myself.

Then he went in and had some afternoon tea. He had remembered the names of the kids, so Mary fairly plied him with hot scones. Then he told Mary all about what we were going to do. Mary tried to look intelligent, and said that we ought to ask her cousin, young Fred, who is studying agricultural science at the University, to come up for his holidays, as he might be able to teach me a bit about grasses. That's the last straw. Young Freddie! He's only about 19, and now he's coming up to help me run the farm! At present I've got Mary Clarkson, the banker, my new book, Mr McLachlan, the Agricultural Adviser, and Grandpa helping me, and now I'm going to have young Freddie.

One can understand the difficulty faced by the farmer at times. The final result is that he takes each new task in his stride. At times he is a mechanic, at others a book-keeper, tractor hand, rough doctor, and odd-job man. Each new task he masters adds to the security of his property and generally to Australian production.

13. The Achievement

The first Australian farmers, the convicts at Farm Cove, used methods that had scarcely changed since the Middle Ages. Every bushel of wheat cost at least three hours of work. Now a worker produces a bushel for every eight minutes of work.

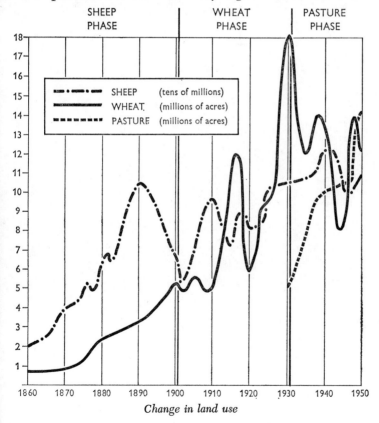

Change in land use

Here is an estimate of the number of acres harvested per farmer based upon average five-year periods.

Date	Acres	Date	Acres
1915	90	1930	300
1920	190	1935	290
1925	170	1940	380
		1945	380

The early increase is a result of opening up new land but the later increases are largely the result of mechanization. One of the most important developments was the introduction of tractors, which began to displace horses about 1924. This efficiency in production enables most people to live in the city and has released most of the working population for other industries.

Appendix A

Irrigation

The development of primary industry in Australia has been limited by rainfall. Only the eastern coastal region enjoys a heavy rainfall. Seventy per cent of the country receives less than 20 inches. Even in the favoured districts the rainfall tends to be unpredictable and seasons of floods and droughts make the work of the farmer extremely difficult. The large size of Australian farms and the low production per acre compared with other countries are the inevitable result of such conditions. Permanent use of the land can only be guaranteed by permanent supplies and intensive use of the land depends altogether upon the extension of irrigation.

The first farm irrigation project was begun in 1887 in Victoria. Two Canadians had visited the Mildura district and decided that an irrigation scheme was possible if the government would help with the land tenure problem. By pumping water from the Murray River into irrigation canals the Chaffey brothers transformed an unprofitable sheep station into a closely settled area, with a population of 3000 settlers who cultivated 4500 acres, including 900 planted with vines and fruit trees. Mildura still flourishes and is famous for its wines and dried fruits.

The success of this scheme encouraged many other projects. Irrigation by pumping river water can only be applied in comparatively flat country near large rivers. Larger schemes must depend on harnessing rivers near their source in the mountains and distributing the water by gravitational flow to the plains below. The first great scheme of this kind was begun in Victoria on the Goulburn River. When fully developed, this scheme supplied 375,000 acres and in the Goulburn River Valley irrigation area fruit canning became a major industry and fodder was grown to supply the fat lamb and dairying industries. New South Wales undertook a much bigger scheme when it built the Burrinjuck Dam on the Murrumbidgee, but it undertook the scheme too hastily. According to the 1913 plan, 200,000 acres were to be irrigated, and yet by 1938 only 100,000 acres were in use at a cost to the State of more than £9 million. The products from the irrigation area were expensive and there was no ready market for them. Nevertheless orchards and rice-fields were established and the area today is much greater because the markets are better, research has opened up new methods and canning industries have developed during World War II. Anyone who visits the Murrumbidgee irrigation area can see how much irrigation can contribute to the land. Outside the area the country is olive grey and brown and just across the first irrigation channel the country is green and the grass high. As Australia's population increases there must be need for more irrigated land.

The Commonwealth government saw the need and in 1946 took over from the New South Wales government one of the biggest projects in the world, the Snowy River scheme. The plan is simple: it is to divert the waters of a coastal river into two inland rivers and so prevent the loss of the water. Under the scheme the waters of the Snowy River will feed the Murray and Murrumbidgee Rivers and augment the water supplies of the Hume Weir and Burrinjuck Dam by over two million acre feet. This scheme involves the construction of seven major dams, fifteen power stations, 83½ miles of tunnels, 336 miles of race-lines and hundreds of miles of mountain roads. One whole township at Adaminaby is now submerged by the largest reservoir in Australia, which will eventually hold eight times the volume of water in Sydney Harbour. When the whole scheme is completed it is calculated that the value of additional foodstuffs produced will amount to £30 million per annum. The scheme adds to existing resources rather than changes the whole pattern, and, best of all, it provides power supplies to keep up with expansion and thus help maintain a balance in national development.

Basic plan of the east-west diversions of the Snowy Mountains Scheme

Sheep shearing in the 1860s. Note the women in the shearing shed,
the "spade" press, and the shepherd.

Cattle branding in the 1860s.

(From a sketch by S. T. Gill)

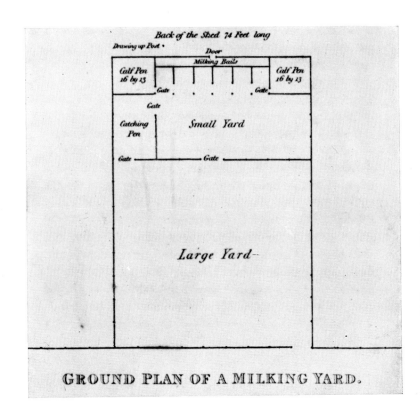

GROUND PLAN OF A MILKING YARD.

Plan of a model dairy, drawn to assist migrants to Australia in 1826.

(From *An account of the State of Agriculture and Grazing in New South Wales*, J. Atkinson, 1826)

O'Meara's homestead (a typical North Coast dairy).

(By courtesy of the Mitchell Library, Sydney)

Appendix B

The Dairy Industry

When the first settlers arrived at Port Jackson they were in urgent need of fresh food. Green vegetables were necessary to combat scurvy and fresh milk was necessary for the mothers and children. Yet as we have seen, the first cattle wandered off into the bush and were not discovered until seven years later in a region that was much better suited to dairy cattle than the bush around Sydney. The area was named the Cowpastures. John Macarthur gained a lease of 10,000 acres in this area and it has remained a dairying centre supplying milk to Sydney ever since. Most ships coming from England brought cattle, which were put up for auction. In addition, the government let settlers buy stock from the government herds. Gradually sufficient herds were built up around Parramatta, the Nepean and the Hawkesbury to supply Sydney's needs. The cattle were not well selected, the grass was often poor, many of the dairy hands would not have been very clean and there was no refrigeration. One wonders what the milk supply was really like.

The first record of an attempt to import pure-bred stock indicates that William Kent brought out some Shorthorns in 1800, and that other pure-bred stock arrived during the next ten years. The high prices that were paid for good breeders showed the value that the early farmers placed upon the animal and its products. When the land around Sydney was taken up, stockmen drove their herds southward beyond Liverpool to the richer lands of the South Coast. The new farmers were different from the gentlemen farmers about Sydney. They worked hard to clear the bush, making money at first by cutting cedar. When the bush was cleared, the dairy farm could start, generally with two sidelines, pigs and poultry. Dairy farmers were too far from Sydney to send their milk to market and so once a week, they made butter for the market from the cream, and used the skimmed milk to fatten the pigs. To get to or from their farms the settlers had to use narrow bush tracks which climbed up the steep rise of Bulli Pass. As the land was cleared and some fine herds were introduced conditions improved. By 1833 good quality butter in wooden kegs was despatched fairly regularly to Sydney by Alexander Berry, the leading settler of the Illawarra district.

As soon as the industry was well established, the price of good butter fell from about 3s. per pound in 1828 to 2s. in 1834. In time of glut, it fell as low as 3d. The farmers felt they had a grievance, for their work was hard. They compared their lot with that of the squatter who was given the convict labour generally denied them, and who often made a comfortable fortune without as much manual toil. The dairy farmer developed a different outlook and way of life from the squatter's. The smaller farmer, particularly, has had to employ his whole family to help him and works very

K

long hours. Nevertheless, dairy farming was a sturdy and independent life. Farms were small and could be bought fairly cheaply. The rainfall on the coastal districts was fairly reliable and so the pioneers found that their herds grew and it was possible to set up their sons on the land at a reasonable age. Dairying districts spread along the coast: Twofold Bay, the Hunter River and then the Moreton Bay districts were opened up.

In other Colonies dairying was started mainly to supply the capital towns with milk, butter and cheese. With small markets and poor transport, it is no wonder that farmers did not improve their methods much. Berry of Illawarra was a shining example, but he was ahead of most.

In the second half of the nineteenth century dairying was consolidated and methods of production and marketing were greatly improved. The gold rushes brought a large new population to the diggings and to Melbourne. Prices improved and the demand became more reliable. After the gold rushes many newcomers set up as dairy farmers and so prices fell again.

Better methods of management were demonstrated on the Wren-Tooth estate at Kameruka and Thomas Mort's property, Bodalla. Both of these estates were divided into farms placed under managers. All the milk was brought into the central factories, where good quality cheese and butter were manufactured. The products won them a reputation in Australia and Mort's cheeses won recognition in Europe. Both properties imported and bred good stock and Mort experimented with new grasses. These two South Coast farms set the standard which challenged other dairying districts.

The first regular transport services were established by the coastal shipping companies in the 1850s (see Chapter 11). The vessels of these companies were small enough to cross the bars at the entrance to the coastal rivers and sturdy enough to ride out storms that are so frequent along the coast. They provided cheap transport for butter and cheese. Later in the century the extension of railway services gave more dairying districts the opportunity to supply the cities with milk.

Machinery came to aid the dairy farmer. In 1873 refrigeration was introduced, though it took several more years to be fully established. Mort's experiments in refrigeration opened the English market to Australian butter. Cream separators, invented in Sweden, were introduced into Australia about 1881. They were more efficient than the old methods of letting the cream settle in open pans. Needless to say, they were cleaner. Pasteurization was introduced in 1889 and in 1901 the New South Wales government passed the Dairies Supervision Act, which forced dairies, milk vendors, creameries and butter factories to register and have their premises inspected by government officers.

The dairy farmers learnt that co-operation paid. On the South Coast and around Camden co-operative societies were established and they set up factories, arranged transport and market arrangements.

By the end of the nineteenth century dairy farmers possessed 1,200,000 head of cattle, supplied four million people with milk and butter, and exported dairy produce worth £2 million.

In the present century the dairying industry has continued to grow. The population of Australia has increased, so that there is a much larger internal market and there has been an increased market for by-products, such as condensed and powdered milk, casein and ice cream. The number of dairy cows is three times as great as at the beginning of the century. The value of exports has increased over ten times.

This is the result of a great number of improvements. Education of farmers has played a large part. Experts in farm management, cattle selection and manufacture travel through dairying districts and gather ideas from dairymen and pass on information. Agricultural colleges provide courses to train farmers. Journals, newspapers and radio broadcasts spread ideas widely and quickly.

Transport is much improved. Trucks and cars have speeded up deliveries and help dairymen to move about in their few hours off duty. Machinery has helped to speed up milking, haystacking and other activities and has lightened some of the drudgery. Improvements in breeding are constant. Artificial insemination has made breeding a much easier process. Diseases are better understood and there are many more easily applied remedies as well as good veterinary services at the farmers' call.

Management of properties and of the industry generally has improved. Co-operatives are established in every State. Health regulations and market organization have been worked out in great detail. The result has been a steady improvement in production figures. But Australian production has not improved as much as her overseas competition, and this has caused much concern. The reason seems to be that there is not enough incentive for individual farmers to increase their production. At the present time prices are stabilized by voluntary agreement between the Dairy Farmers' Associations in the States and the Commonwealth Dairy Produce Equalization Committee. As it costs a great deal to improve methods, farmers do not see much reason to change immediately. The industry is more dependent than any other on family labour. Cows have to be milked twice a day every day of the year. Very few labourers are willing to work in an industry that offers such hard work for no better reward than other industries offer. Every improvement costs the dairy farmer more of his own or his family's precious spare time. Whatever the reasons, the present situation is not healthy. The price of butter in Australia is very high and production per cow is low. On the other hand, there are plenty of remedies which can be applied: pasture improvement, irrigation, fodder conservation, and better breeding are just a few and if wise counsels do not lead to some of them being used more than they have been, economic necessity may force the industry to adopt them.

Appendix C

The Sugar Industry

The development of the sugar industry has been an interesting example of the way primary and secondary production have been linked, with both being influenced by the political and social background.

The first problem was to grow the cane. There were a number of early experiments in sugar growing in New South Wales, when the colonists were engaged in the search for a staple. At first these efforts were not a success, chiefly because New South Wales was too far south, and the climate therefore too cold for the grain. One Thomas A. Scott is often credited with successful sugar manufacture at Port Macquarie in the 1820s, but his claims are quite unjustified and he appears to have been rather an incompetent schemer, who managed to get considerable rewards from the government for doing very little.

With the opening-up of settlement in Queensland, the position changed. The climate on the coastal plains further north was excellent for the crop, and the area planted was 33,000 acres by 1895. During this period most growers widely employed coloured labour on the cane-fields. The Queensland Parliament passed an Act which allowed indentured Indian workmen to be brought in for the pastoral industry, but they were never employed in this way; white shepherds and cattlemen were better. But for tropical agriculture it was a different matter. At first they were used to grow cotton; but when cotton-growing turned out to be a failure, they were employed on the cane-fields, one of the first large-scale employers being Robert Towns, after whom Townsville was named, although actually the first important Queensland sugar-grower was Louis Hope, who opened the first sugar mill in 1865.

For a generation sugar was grown on fairly large plantations worked with black labour brought from the Pacific Islands. Many people claimed that these Kanakas were kidnapped from their homes, and in 1868 Parliament stepped in to regulate the way these workmen were recruited. The Polynesian Labourers Act succeeded in improving the treatment of Kanakas on the plantations in Queensland, but it could not control "blackbirding" in the islands. In 1872 the British government stepped in by keeping up naval patrols, but even so, the traffic remained a bad one. Even if the natives were not kidnapped by force or persuaded by fraudulent promises to "sign on", the "migration" still damaged island native societies whose men went away so often and came back to spread disease and drunkenness among the people. At this time most growers thought the industry depended absolutely on its cheap coloured labour; they argued that if this were prohibited it would collapse altogether. There seemed some reason for this, as the work in the cane-fields is very arduous and wages take up a large proportion of the costs. Sugar cane is really a giant grass, with stalks about nine feet high and more than an inch across. Cuttings are planted in furrows four or five feet apart. Nowadays planting is done by a machine which cuts the stalks, sprays the ground with weed-killer, drops them into the furrows, covers them and applies fertilizer, all in one operation; but before such machinery had been invented, this involved a lot of work.

After planting, the crop takes about 15 months to grow. Then it is harvested by cutting with large knives at ground level, after a fire has been pushed through the fields to get rid of snakes. Then the tops have to be cut off. After cutting, the cane is loaded on low trolley-cars on light two-foot gauge rail-lines and taken to the mill for crushing. The stubble left in the field soon produces a small ratoon crop; then the field is ploughed and a green manure crop grown before it is ready for another planting of cane.

All this was very strenuous work, which had to be done in intense tropical heat. Though now it is mechanically loaded and unloaded on and off the trolleys, no good harvesting machine had been invented until the 1960s, and much work is still done by hand. When planting was also a hand-labour job, one can see why the growers thought they could not manage without the help of cheap labour. But many Queenslanders, farmers, white labourers, miners and most townspeople in the south of the State were afraid that if many islanders stayed in Australia, they could create a colour problem like that in the southern States of the United States, and that the competition of their labour would lower the wages and living standards of the white settlers. Many years of very bitter political controversy on this question came to a climax when the Report of a Royal Commission of Enquiry in 1884 disclosed that a lot of brutality was still going on in the recruiting, hiring and employing of the islanders. The result was the passing of an Act in 1885 forbidding the indenture of coloured labour after five years, which meant that after all three-year indentures signed in 1890 had expired —in 1893—there would be no more black labour in the industry.

Before 1893, however, an economic crisis had persuaded the government to change its policy. Sir Samuel Griffith, author of the 1885 Act, had hoped to replace the large cane plantations with small farms, which would be owned and worked by whites. To replace the plantation mill, he hoped to open a number of central mills, which would crush the crop of a large number of the small growers, who would be saved the expense of building and running mills of their own. But the fall in prices made it seem that this plan would not work; white production seemed too expensive, and in 1892 it was decided to allow coloured labourers to continue working in the cane-fields.

But the issue was not allowed to rest. The establishment of the central crushing mills had reduced costs; so had the substitution of steam power for animal power in them. So they became larger and more efficient; in 1886, 166 mills had made 113,000 tons of sugar; in 1910, 49 mills made 210,000 tons of sugar. So Griffith's hopes of reducing costs were realized, and after federation, in 1901, the newly established Commonwealth government decided again to put an end to the employment of Kanakas. The Commonwealth government imposed high duties on imported sugar. This gave the industry a nation-wide protected market. By 1907 all coloured labourers had been sent home and Queensland sugar was grown by whites—the only example of such a thing in the world.

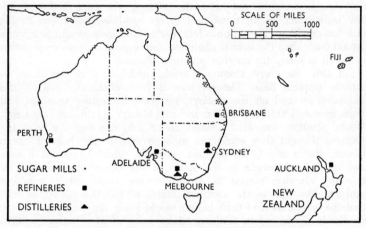

The sugar industry in Australia, 1959
Distribution of mills, refineries, and distilleries.
(From information supplied by the Colonial Sugar Refining Co. Ltd.)

Meanwhile, the refining side of the industry had been developing. Raw sugar is brownish in colour and contains some impurities; the refining process gets rid of these and produces the white crystals we see on the dinner table. The first refinery was built at Canterbury, now a suburb of Sydney, as early as 1841. At that time, naturally, it used imported sugar, but the market was small and it was cheaper for consumers to use imported refined sugar. But in 1855 the Colonial Sugar Refining Company was founded, a concern which has grown steadily until today it is one of the giants of Australian industrial enterprise. It gradually bought out the few other refining companies which were started in the second half of the nineteenth century, and concentrated its production in five refineries in or near the mainland capital cities, the last opened in 1930, being at Fremantle. Another refinery operating is operated by the Millaquin Sugar Company at Bundaberg. The C.S.R. Company has been unjustly criticized for its apparent control of the industry. It certainly has what appears to be almost a monopoly, but its profits have been due more to efficient production, research, the skilful use of by-products, and its trading activities in Fiji and New Zealand than to any "monopolistic exploitation". A succession of Royal Commissions of Enquiry has not found that the company has charged excessive prices for its refined sugar, and since 1923 it has acted as the agent for the Queensland Sugar Board in marketing and distributing sugar throughout Australia.

During World War I, the world price of sugar soared, and imported sugar was very expensive. The government wanted to make Australia self-sufficient, so it guaranteed to growers a price which would cover their costs. With this incentive, production increased and after about 1925 Australia began to export sugar overseas. Unfortunately, at this time world prices fell again, so that Queensland sugar was much dearer than imported sugar; but the government prohibited imports and allowed local growers to charge a high price at home to make up for the low price they received overseas. This caused much criticism during the 1930s, but after 1939 the position was reversed once more. "Foreign" sugar again became very expensive and the Australian consumer benefited greatly from his locally grown supplies, while the growers got good prices for exports. In 1951 a British Commonwealth Sugar Agreement imposed a limit on exports in order to keep up prices. The whole marketing and regulation of the crop is carried out by the Queensland Sugar Board, which buys all sugar grown in Queensland and New South Wales, contracts for its refining and local distribution, as well as setting its local price and supervising overseas sales.

T. S. Mort: Businessman

No man of his time worked harder to enlarge the industries of the country than he; no man had a wider grasp of its great possibilities and no man spent so much time and capital in developing its resources.

This was one verdict on the career of T. S. Mort, a Lancashire lad who arrived in New South Wales to seek a fortune in 1838 at the age of twenty-two. He had left home because the family cotton business had not flourished since his father had died a few years before. He did not want to be a humble commercial clerk; prospects seemed brighter in the colonies.

Mort was first employed as a clerk in Sydney too, in a mercantile firm, which sold to country storekeepers the manufactures it imported from England, and which exported wool. In 1843 he left it, and announced that he was "commencing business forthwith as an Auctioneer and Broker". Despite long hours at the office he preferred this life to the discomforts of pastoral pioneering, and in any case wool-growing was temporarily depressed; but he quickly succeeded as an auctioneer. He was helped by "knowing the right people", but more important was his ability to gain the trust of his customers. He decided to hold special, separate, auctions for wool, and so "to rescue the squatter from the claws of the exporter", and to ensure that he got a fair price for his clip; this was of particular help to the small-scale grower who could not afford to consign his clip to England for sale by auction there. Then he began to auction sheep stations, and to lend money to pastoralists to help them to buy properties they wanted. He also became a consigning agent as well. He attended the shipment of the graziers' wool, arranged for its sale in London, and lent money to the grower on its security. In 1850 he opened the large warehouse on Circular Quay, which was only demolished in 1957. Then he began to make long-term loans to the pastoralist, and to buy as well as to sell goods to his order. In this way he laid the foundations of Mort and Company, which later became, by amalgamation, Goldsbrough Mort and then Goldsbrough Mort-Elder Smith, selling wool, and sheep stations, providing credit, acting as banker, selling station supplies, and keeping the growers informed about their market.

But he was a man of many other interests too. He was a director of the Sydney Railway Company, and was interested in the Hunter River Railway Company. He tried to promote the production of sugar, silk, cotton and alpaca. He helped to plan the A.M.P. Society in 1849. In the 1850s he was active in gold-mining, and later in coal, and then in 1862 in copper-mining at Peak Downs, in Queensland. In 1854 he began the excavation of Mort's Dock at Balmain—the only dry dock south of the equator—where in due course he began to build ships, and after 1870 locomotive engines and metal bridges. In this year, worried by bad industrial relations, he suggested that the men buy half its shares, so both "should be bound together with the cords of common interest"—a plan for joint ownership with the leading workmen in the business. But the rank and file labourers could not afford to buy shares, and the better off who could cut themselves off from their fellows. The joint ownership was not a success, and in 1875 a normal type of company was formed, which closed down only in 1962. All this time Mort was extending his wool business, buying pastoral properties and lending money to graziers to enable them to buy and improve their land.

In 1860 he bought a 13,000 acre cattle station, Bodalla, near Moruya on the southern coast of New South Wales. It was partly a country retreat, but he also turned it into a model dairy farm. He hoped to make himself a landlord of the English type. He installed tenants and made share agreements with them. He drained the river flats and planted artificial grapes. Slowly the production of butter, cheese and, later, bacon improved. But though Mort virtually built the village of Bodalla, this share farming system was not a success, and by the 1870s Mort had taken the property back into his own hands, and was running it himself, with hired workers.

Meanwhile he had become interested in an invention, which, when it proved successful, was a great benefit—refrigeration suitable for ocean transport (see page 109). This achievement meant Australia could export fresh meat and butter to the old world. It would benefit both the industrial population of England, and the Australian primary producer. What he started as a commercial speculation, became for Mort almost an obsession.

I now feel that the time has arrived . . . when the various portions of the earth will each give forth their product for the use of each and for all; that the over-abundance of one country will make up for the deficiency of another, the superabundance of the year of plenty serving for the scant harvest of its successor; for cold arrests all change. . . . Climate, seasons, plenty, scarcity, distance will all shake hands, and out of the co-mingling will come enough for all.

Through years of disappointment he kept on with his experiments. "I am fascinated by it," he wrote, and this helped "to guard me against despairing thoughts". But success would also give "value to sheep which are now almost worthless . . . a vast amount of work for the Dock . . . and a profitable business for the Sydney and London farmer of Mort and Co." Enterprise, humanitarianism and profit might all go hand in hand, but the money Mort spent on it yielded no return in his own lifetime. The first refrigerated cargo in the *Northam* in 1877 was a failure, and Mort had died before a successful shipment of frozen meat left Australia in 1879.

Mort's life was a success story, and when he died his estate was worth £600,000—perhaps more than £2 million in today's money. He achieved his successes in ventures from which the community benefited too. He did not always manage them well and he often grossly underestimated the costs of the projects he was concerned with; but if they profited him less than he hoped, they benefited the community all the same.

In any case, he was not concerned only with making a fortune. He was a devout Anglican and he felt an obligation to serve his neighbours. He thought he could best do this by developing the material resources of the country; and he succeeded in doing so, carrying out many valuable enterprises. But he was also a generous supporter of the Church, of many public charities, and of organizations like the Philosophical Society, the Agricultural Society and the Society for the Promotion of Fine Arts. When his statue in Macquarie Place, Sydney was unveiled in July 1883, it was said that his was "a good, a great and a beautiful life", one "spent in work which meant the diffusion of public benefits"; this was not so far from the truth as speeches on such occasions often are.

CHAPTER 13

SECONDARY INDUSTRY

1. Manufacture and Secondary Industry

THE Aborigines of Australia and the first settlers were different from each other in many ways; but one of the greatest
differences lay in their ability to make things. The Aborigines
used tools and weapons of wood and stone. They could not
understand, let alone use, the metal tools of the British. They
had made little impression on the Australian bush or scenery,
because they could scarcely cut down a large tree with their
stone axes. The British settlers, as soon as they arrived, began
to alter the appearance of the country around Port Jackson.
Trees were felled, roots were dug out and burnt. A forge was
set up to shoe horses, to make nails and repair tools. Everything the British settlers used was manufactured; clothes, firearms, books, ships, tools, riding equipment and so on. Moreover, most of the things they used were complex. For example,
the clothes they wore had been cut and sewn by tailors who
used cloth that had been made from wool, which had itself
been in turn scoured, spun, dyed, and woven. These processes
themselves had used other manufactured articles: dyes, vats,
spinning wheels, and looms.

As manufactures play such an important part in man's life
the stages in the advance of man are often named after the
materials used in manufacture. Thus, the Australian Aboriginal
is said to have been living in the "stone age". Modern Europe
had passed through several stages and at the time the British
were settling in Australia, Great Britain was leading the world
into a new age called the "industrial revolution". Since 1800 the
means of manufacture have changed continuously, and have led
to the development of new patterns of life.

Before the industrial revolution of the eighteenth century,
most manufacturing was done in small workshops or in the
homes of the people. Shipyards and forges were the largest
establishments, though they were small compared with those
of today. Cloth, which is now manufactured in large factories,
was then manufactured in the homes of the people. In the
middle of the eighteenth century a series of great inventors made

machines which spun and wove materials mechanically. These machines were driven by water power, and early in the nineteenth century engineers applied steam power to the machines. The use of power-driven machines changed the self-employed craftsman into "a hand", a mere attendant on a machine. The old weaver had to use his judgment in developing patterns and setting his loom; the new hand merely set the machine operating and stopped it to tie loose threads and so on. If anything went wrong, a mechanic or engineer was called in. The worker did what he was told and understood very little of what he was doing.

When steam power was applied to machines, the wear and tear on wooden parts became very great and they were replaced by metal parts. During the nineteenth century iron and steel were used more and more. Bridge builders, shipbuilders and railway engineers, as well as factories, all made use of the product of the foundry. Thus "heavy industry" became central to all the other industries (see Chapters 11 and 16).

2. Advances of the British Iron Industry 1700-1850

Great Britain played the most notable part in the development of the iron industry. In 1747 Abraham Darby published an account of the way in which iron ore could be smelted with coke instead of charcoal. His father, the first Abraham Darby, had started this process, but the son perfected it in the 1730s. Coke is made from coal. Charcoal is made from wood. The new advance made the coal-field rather than the forest the best place for the forge. This was fortunate for England because her forests were dwindling. By 1750, Darby, making use of coal fuel, was able to turn out pig iron by mass production methods. The pig iron could be used for forging iron bars and by 1755 for casting. In 1767 the first iron rails were cast. In 1799 Abraham Darby finished a cast-iron bridge over the Severn River, with a span of 100 feet. In 1761, the draught for the blast furnace was made more powerful by Roebuck, who used water lifted by a steam pump to apply regular pressure to the bellows. By 1790 the blowers were being worked directly from the engine. In the 1780s Henry Cort introduced two new methods of production called "puddling" and "rolling". In puddling, iron bars stir up the molten iron in the furnace, thus enabling the air to contact the molten iron. The oxygen of the air combines with the carbon of the iron and this forms a gas which burns with a bluish flame. As the carbon was burnt off it left the iron stronger.

Then it used to be hammered into bars, but in Cort's process it passed between rollers to press it into bars or sheet iron, which was so much faster than hammering on a forge. Instead of 12 hours of hammering, one ton of iron could be rolled out in 45 minutes.

With these and many other improvements, British production of iron surpassed that of all other countries. In the hundred years between 1730 and 1830, British iron production grew from about 20,000 tons to 700,000 tons a year, as it was used for more and more articles, now that it could be made easily and cheaply. Britain's production was not overtaken by other countries until nearly 1900, when Germany and the United States caught up and passed her. In the early and middle parts of the nineteenth century only Belgium could rival England in the cheapness, quantity and quality of production. England was fortunate in having large supplies of coal and iron fairly close to each other in the Midlands and high grade ore could be imported from Spain and Sweden and used with coal from deposits near the coast. Mining had to expand to supply metal ores and coal for industry. Better pumps and lifting machinery made it possible for mines to be cut deeper than ever before. By 1700 some 2½ million tons of coal were extracted each year. In 1800 England used 10 million tons a year. Demand for the products of heavy industry increased enormously to supply England's own rapidly developing manufactures and her overseas trade markets. As England became the "workshop of the world", and sold more goods overseas, she expanded her mines, her furnaces and her factories more and more to keep them up to date in techniques and able to satisfy her customers. This period (1800-50) was England's "iron age".

But the iron age was not always a good one for the common people. The cheapness of England's goods was mostly the result of new methods of manufacture, but the wages that were paid to the men, women and children who worked in factories and mines remained as low as they had ever been. The increase of crime that created the penal problem, which led to the foundation of Australia, was also partly due to overcrowding in the English towns and other changes brought about by the change in manufacturing and agriculture towards the end of the eighteenth century.

3. First Steps to Secondary Industry in Australia

Since England produced goods so cheaply, there was not much need to develop secondary industry in Australia. Iron goods in particular were cheap to transport because after about 1830 they provided good ballast in the ships coming out from England to carry back Australia's wool. Until the middle of the nineteenth century the main secondary industries in Australia were such things as flour milling, tanning hides, manufacturing soap and candles from tallow, brewing beer, and making bricks. They were mostly concerned with treating the local primary produce. Perhaps Australia was fortunate in avoiding the first stages of the industrial revolution because the working conditions in the early factories were so bad.

The earliest mining and industrial work in Australia was carried on by convicts, and conditions were bad as one would expect. Sometimes heavy labour was used as a kind of punishment. The first permanent settlement at Newcastle in 1804 was established partly to give heavy labour to offenders. Seven miles south of Newcastle on the open beach the lime kilns were placed. The convicts had to keep fires going for long periods and had no protection from the fires. The lime had to be carried out to the boats through the surf on their bare backs. The coal-mining convicts in Newcastle were little better off. They had to descend a shaft 110 feet deep, cut the coal with hand tools, and draw it to the surface by hand windlass. Loading the boats by wheelbarrows was comparatively easy. Such were the labouring conditions of Newcastle in its first years.

Mining became more important about the 1830s because there was more demand for coal. The government could not supply enough coal with convict labour, for it had few skilled labourers among the convicts, and so, in 1826, the mines were leased and a monopoly in coal production was granted to the Australian Agricultural Company. The company took over in 1829. Private individuals opened mines at Bulli, Lake Macquarie and Maitland in the 1840s and the company unwillingly gave up its monopoly. Lithgow mines were opened about 1870 and by then coal was known to exist in all States except South Australia, where it was not discovered until 1889. New South Wales was found to have the best deposits, especially in the region northwest of Newcastle and around Port Kembla on the south coast.

Iron ore had been found in Australia as early as 1800, but no attempt was made to set up an iron works until 1848. The first works were set up near Mittagong, where small iron deposits were found near coal (even though of poor quality) and limestone, which is used in smelting. But the works were expensive to run against overseas competition. By 1870 Australia was still producing only about 500 tons of casting a year, and not long afterwards the Mittagong works were abandoned altogether.

4. From Iron to Steel

Meanwhile England was passing from the iron age to the steel age. In 1829 J. B. Neilson perfected the hot air blast which made production more efficient. In 1842 James Nasmyth patented a steam hammer which was capable of forging heavy steel bars and is still used for some steels. In 1854-6 England and France were at war with Russia in the Crimea and there was urgent need for superior metals for guns. Henry Bessemer patented a new furnace which converted pig iron into steel in 1856, and was producing better and cheaper cast steel than any of his competitors three years later. This meant that some firms began to suffer from what is called a "technical lag". Industrial equipment was so expensive that Bessemer's rivals did not change their methods till his competition forced them to do so. As the century went on, the capital expense to undertake any new method of manufacture grew greater. It was not just the cost of the new equipment; there were the problems of re-training workers, scrapping old materials, and then finding markets for the increased output. This was often achieved by driving rival firms out of business or by keeping down the workers' wages. Industrial competition was ruthless.

After about 1870 science became more important in the production of better steels. As chemistry and physics advanced the scientists were able to explain why irons and steels turned out hard or soft, brittle or malleable. Previously discoveries had been largely a matter of trial and error and the inventors needed to have some luck with their efforts. But in the 1870s Gilchrist and Thomas worked out a way to rid iron ore of the phosphorus which was often found in it. This discovery made it possible to use English ores in manufacturing steel. Even more important, this discovery made it possible to use extensive iron deposits in Germany and the United States and so created two important competitors for British industry. Alloys were developed in the same period. Galvanized iron, which is iron coated with zinc, was produced before 1840. The special metals which toughen steel were discovered by scientific research from 1880 onwards. The chief ores are manganese, tungsten and chromium. There are over 8000 alloys known today. To improve methods and test products, most iron and steel works set up laboratories.

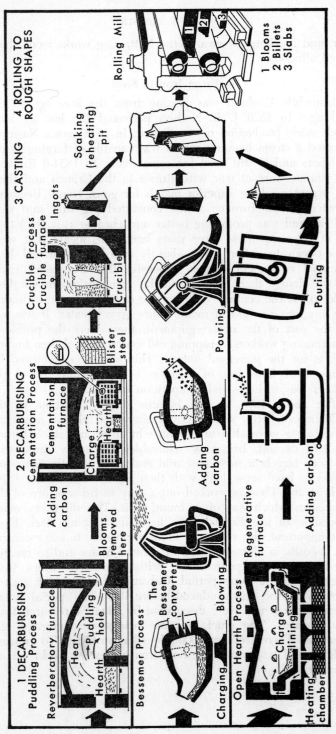

Stages in the development of Foundry Practice

1 DECARBURISING
Puddling Process

Reverberatory furnace
Heat
Puddling hole
Hearth
Blooms removed here

2 RECARBURISING
Cementation Process

Adding carbon
Cementation furnace
Charge
Hearth
Blister steel

The Bessemer Process
The Bessemer converter

Charging   Blowing
Adding carbon

Open Hearth Process

Charge
lining
Heating chamber

Regenerative furnace
Adding carbon

3 CASTING

Crucible Process
Crucible furnace
Crucible

Ingots

Pouring

Pouring

4 ROLLING TO ROUGH SHAPES

Soaking (reheating) pit

Rolling Mill

1 Blooms
2 Billets
3 Slabs

Jimbour Station, Queensland, in the early days.
(From *Strange New World*, by Alec Chisholm)

Victoria River Downs homestead. The homestead and station buildings alongside the Wickham River form a small township. This cattle property comprises more than 6000 square miles and is 300 air-miles south of Darwin.
(From *Northern Australia*, Australian Institute of Political Science)

Wheat-breeding and variety plots, Waite Agricultural Research Institute, South Australia.

(By courtesy of the Waite Agricultural Research Institute)

A photograph showing the depredations of rabbits, and the protection given by rabbit-proof fences.

(Australian News and Information Bureau)

5. Iron and Steel Industry in Australia

While England was advancing into the steel age of manufacture after 1855, Australia was catching up on the iron age. In 1875 the first large blast furnace for iron was set up at Eskbank near Lithgow. In 1886, the manager of the Sydney Wire Netting Factory, William Sandford, leased the works. He re-organized the plant for the production of rolled iron from scrap. In 1900 he set up Australia's first steel furnace. The New South Wales government placed many orders with the Eskbank works, but by 1907 the firm needed money for the building of a modern blast furnace. Sandford could not raise a loan and the Commonwealth government's promised bounty did not materialize. The very next year a well-established firm of iron manufacturers, G. and C. Hoskins of Sydney, purchased the works and made large additions. New quarries for ore and limestone were opened up. A blast furnace, three steel furnaces, coke-ovens and a rail-rolling mill were installed, and the works produced 30,000 tons of pig iron and 3000 tons of steel in the first year. This quick success was due to the firm's thirty years of experience, good management and equipment and government aid. The New South Wales government promised contracts for its railways. The Commonwealth government paid a bounty of 12 shillings a ton to encourage production in Australia. In return for the bounty, C. H. Hoskins had to promise to pay "fair and reasonable" wages to the workmen and to sell out to the State government if it ever decided to run the iron and steel industry itself. Without the aid of the government this first successful Australian iron and steel works would have had no chance of surviving. Lithgow was not the best place for a factory because transport costs by rail to Sydney were high.

It was clear that if any great expansion of the iron and steel industry was to take place, a very powerful company or one of the governments would have to undertake the task. In 1910 a Labour government came to office in New South Wales. As the Labour party had already clashed with Hoskins on political and industrial matters it called in an expert from England to report whether a government-owned steel works could be built on the coast. No sooner did the New South Wales government decide to build its works than a private company announced that it wished to build too.

6. Broken Hill Proprietary Company 1885-1915

The newcomer was the Broken Hill Proprietary Company (B.H.P.), which had been founded in 1885. This company

L

was extremely wealthy because of the huge profits it had earned from the silver and lead mines it had opened up at Broken Hill in the far west of New South Wales. In its first six years of operations, it mined silver and lead worth £7 million. Although the price of silver fell afterwards and there were serious struggles between the management and the miners' union, the company continued to expand. It set up a smelting works at Port Pirie on Spencer Gulf in South Australia. The company invented new processes which made it possible to treat zinc sulphide ore which had been dumped in the earlier stage of low-grade mining. Around Port Pirie the company developed subsidiary industries, which produced spelter, an alloy of zinc, superphosphates and coke. With an eye to the future, the company bought the mining rights to huge hills known to contain iron ore, Iron Knob and Iron Monarch, near Whyalla in South Australia. This was the position about 1908 when the company's main leases at Broken Hill were worked out and the price of silver had dropped so far that the company, after trying to cut the workers' wages (see Chapter 14) decided to close the Broken Hill mine and to establish a steel works, using the iron ore from Whyalla. In 1911 the company brought an American steel expert to Australia. He advised building the steel works at Newcastle, near the coal deposits. Iron ore was to be brought by sea from Whyalla and limestone by sea from Wardang Island in South Australia. The iron ore was brought to the coal deposits because three and a half tons of coal and only one and a half tons of iron ore were needed to make one ton of steel. Transport costs made Newcastle the most important centre of heavy industry in Australia.

Setting up the works was a lengthy business. The site selected was low-lying swamp land at Port Waratah. The New South Wales Labour government was anxious to have the industry set up in New South Wales, but there were no iron deposits in the State; lacking these, it gave up the idea of building its own works and agreed to help the company; it granted B.H.P. the land needed and agreed to dredge a channel 560 feet wide and 25 feet deep to the site. The swamp land was built up with silt from the channel. The company, for all its wealth, still had to borrow large sums of money. When neither private investors nor private banks would supply the capital, the Commonwealth Bank, which had just been founded (1912), made a special loan. Finally, the works were completed and the Governor-General opened the plant in 1915.

7. The Influence of World War I

World War I provided a great spur to Australian metal-manufacturing industries. England could not spare her products and sea transport from Europe was limited, being interfered with by German submarines. The Australian government wanted to make sure of essential supplies wherever possible from Australian materials. The Prime Minister, W. M. Hughes, appointed an adviser to work out a plan "to have, if possible, all ores and metals treated and refined within the Commonwealth". By the end of the war Australia was producing four hundred new kinds of manufactured goods; the production of pig iron increased from 47,000 tons in 1913 to 332,000 tons in 1919, while steel production exceeded 200,000 tons in 1919. Some of this production was begun only because overseas supplies were cut off or prices were high. When European supplies began to compete again after the war, even B.H.P. had to retrench and closed its Newcastle works between 1921 and 1923.

8. From World War I to World War II

From that period onwards, B.H.P. has done everything possible to keep down its prices by keeping its plant up to date and efficient, though it has always been helped by the high quality of its iron ore, situated so close to the coast. In the 1920s the company built its own electrical supply plant which enabled it to be independent of the local Council supplies, and at times to aid the local supply. The electricity supplied the rolling mills and other machinery as well as light for the factory and offices. Most savings were made by efficient use of fuel. The company mines and uses more than 750,000 tons of coal a year. The by-products of coal were very valuable. Engineers have made special ovens which preserve the residues from the coal. The company replaced the early ovens with Willpatte regenerative coke ovens in 1930. The main by-products saved are tar, benzol, naphtha, coal gas (enough to supply a city of a million people), coke and ammonium sulphate. The new ovens gave higher output for less fuel. The layout of the works was improved to bring furnaces and ovens and burners into the right position for continuous production. The three and a half tons of coal needed to produce one ton of steel in 1915 was reduced to one and a half by 1952. The company also set up bigger-than-average blast furnaces to keep up the level of mass production.

The battle for economy not only concerned production. If Australia was to produce steel to compete with overseas products and still maintain the high Australian wage, the shipping of supplies of ore and the selling of steel products had to be developed. The company built up a wharf frontage of 1800 feet on the Hunter River at Port Waratah, and a fleet of freighters to keep up contact with South Australia. Around the Newcastle steelworks a great ring of associated industries grew up. John Lysaght (Australia) Pty Ltd, which began production in 1921, specialized in the manufacture of steel sheet, both galvanized and uncoated. Many an Australian house is roofed with Lysaght's corrugated galvanized steel sheet and hundreds of sheds are covered with it. The Commonwealth Steel Company, founded in 1917, has grown since 1929 into Australia's chief manufacturer of special steels for machinery, motor cars, vacuum cleaners, trains and hundreds of other special uses. Stewarts and Lloyds began producing all kinds of tubular products from pipes to boilers. Ryland Brothers, established at Newcastle in 1921, make all kinds of wire products, and Australian Wire Ropes concentrates on cables and tension steel ropes. Many other industries in the region, some of which were established earlier than B.H.P., to be near the coal-fields and harbour of Newcastle, are now closely linked to the steel industry. One of the most important of these is the Walsh Island shipping yards now run by the State.

The industry has been greatly aided by Federal and State governments. The Federal government has protected it by paying bounties, for example, on fencing wire, galvanized iron and wire netting. State governments have built railways and cleared harbours for the company, besides placing large orders for steel and iron. Some of the biggest orders came with the construction of the Sydney Harbour Bridge, which was completed in 1932. Dorman, Long and Company, the English firm of engineers who contracted to build the bridge, undertook to use Australian steel and "the maximum of Australian labour, materials, machinery and stores". The State railway systems have continuously used iron and steel.

After 1928 B.H.P. faced a rival firm. The directors of the G. and C. Hoskins Ironworks at Lithgow decided to move their main works from Lithgow to the coast to reduce their transport costs. They chose the site of Port Kembla near Wollongong. They hoped to bring iron ore from the deposits in Yampi Sound on the north-west of Western Australia, and the government agreed to build a railway linking Moss Vale to Wollongong, to carry limestone from Mittagong to the coal area of Port Kembla. The firm of Hoskins could not build its new works to compete with B.H.P. without spending vast sums of money, so a merger of four large companies took place to help foot the bill. One of the other companies was Dorman, Long and Company. The new company was called Australian Iron and Steel. It built the largest furnace in the Empire, which produced 800 tons of pig iron a day. But the new company was always short of capital, and its first coke-ovens did not provide for the best production of by-products. Worst of all, it was set up just as the great depression, a world-wide decline in trade and employment, set in. The company just about made ends meet, and in 1935 B.H.P. bought all the main shares. Mr J. Darling became Chairman of B.H.P. and Australian Iron and Steel. B.H.P. became the sole mass-producer of iron and steel in Australia.

When Mr Essington Lewis, Managing Director of B.H.P., returned from a visit to some of the chief iron and steel manufacturing companies, it was determined, though the depression was just passing, to increase the capacity of the industry to keep pace with the rapid advances in such countries as Germany and Japan. The Port Kembla works were greatly enlarged. An even larger blast furnace producing 1000 tons a a day was set up. A modern coke-oven and by-product unit was installed. Three South Coast coal mines were mechanized to supply the works. The Newcastle works, too, were greatly developed just before World War II. Almost every year a new open hearth furnace was added to the great battery already in existence; the coke-ovens were improved; more machine shops and rolling mills were set up. All these mills were run electrically by the second year of the war.

In 1937 B.H.P. made a very important decision to build a blast furnace at Whyalla in South Australia. The efficiency of the coke-ovens now made it possible to take coal to iron, though transport costs were lowered by giving a return cargo of coal to the ships bringing iron ore from Whyalla to Newcastle. The South Australian government welcomed the new industry, as they had already aided B.H.P. by building railways and guaranteeing to extend its iron leases for fifty years. There was less industrial trouble in South Australia than in the older established State of New South Wales. In addition, the decision began a process called "decentralization of industry". In a war a country is safer if its industries are not concentrated in one target area. Decentralization helps to prevent cities from becoming too large for management and builds up the States that are smallest in population. But there are good reasons for industry being as centralized as it is in Australia. Heavy industry relies on markets, labour, transport and power supplies. Outside the main city areas it is difficult to find any of these resources. Decentralization of industry in Australia must wait on the growth of population and the extension of power supplies and other services.

9. World War II and After

Fortunately, Australian cities were not attacked seriously during World War II and centralization of industry did not prove to be a weakness. On the contrary, existing industry had to expand to meet the heavy wartime demand. Mr Essington Lewis, who had directed the expansions of his company before the war, was appointed Director-General of Munitions. Under his direction the iron and steel industry, the munitions factories, the army and the governments of Australia combined their efforts and Australia was able to equip an army of almost one million men mainly from local supplies. After Japan entered the war Australia had to rely on her own production. Some essential materials were still imported, but a great deal was done to improve local production of alloy steels for machine tools, weapons and armour plate. The experts of B.H.P. invented a new way of making armour plate by mass-production methods from Australian metals, and many armoured vehicles carried plates showing the marks of ballistic tests that were carried out on them.

After the war, the iron and steel industry continued to expand. During the war the iron and steel industry had concentrated on necessities and after the war there was a shortage of all kinds of manufactured articles, not only in Australia but throughout the world. Unfortunately, there were many industrial disputes and stoppages on the coal-fields, and coal supplies were quite unreliable. However, new developments were planned at Port Kembla and Newcastle. One of the most important developments was the erection of a plate and strip mill at Port Kembla, where one million tons of flat steel are now turned out each year to supply the manufacturers of motor cars, refrigerators, washing machines and other goods which have become so popular since the war. Western Australia has played a larger part in the production of iron and steel: the iron deposits of Yampi Sound have been developed, a blast furnace to produce high grade iron by using charcoal for smelting was opened at Wundowie in 1948, and a steel rolling mill set up at Kwinana near Fremantle in 1956.

The consequences of these and many other developments in the iron and steel industry are most important for Australia.

B.H.P., with its subsidiaries, has become Australia's largest manufacturing company, with about 100,000 shareholders and about £115 million capital. Australia has produced most of her own iron and steel to supply the needs of her growing manufacturing industry. Although Australia still imports some iron and steel, a small export trade has developed to counterbalance the imports and this export trade may grow in the future.

Most important of all, the iron and steel industry has stimulated the growth of other secondary industries. Mining, transport, electrical, motor manufacturing and many other industries have all been aided directly and many other industries indirectly. In 1934 there were approximately 27,000 factories in Australia, in 1964 approximately 60,000. This expansion corresponds with the period of expansion of the iron and steel industry, and there is no doubt that its development is one of the most important reasons for the general development in secondary industry.

Thus, in just over fifty years, the basis of the Australian economy has been fundamentally changed, for now secondary industry produces more of the national wealth than the primary land industries. The land industries still provide our largest income from overseas exports, but there has been a decline in prices for our primary products. When this has happened in the past Australia's general economy has been weakened because the country could not afford to import necessary manufactures. Should the tendency continue as at present Australia would be able to switch a large number of primary workers to industrial work. The future trend of production is largely dependent on two factors: the efficiency of our industries and changes in world markets.

G. D. Delprat: Industrialist

THE B.H.P. Company as we know it today is the product of many men of vision, enterprise and energy, even though sometimes they have not treated their employees as well as they would be compelled by law to do today; but perhaps the most outstanding figure in the history of the company is Guillaume Daniel Delprat. He was born at Delft in Holland in 1856, the son of a general and the Dutch minister for war. He left school at the age of thirteen, and one of his first jobs was that of powder-monkey on the first bridge over the Firth of Tay, which was soon to be destroyed by storm. In 1878 he went to Spain and worked as a metallurgist in one of the British owned mines in the Rio Tinto Valley. Four years later, he joined another mining company and travelled to most of the important mining centres of the world. In 1898 he was appointed Assistant General Manager to the Broken Hill Proprietary Company.

Here he soon made his mark by discovering a means of extracting more valuable metals, lead and zinc, from the mass of "failings", which had hitherto been discarded around the smelters. Then in 1902, helped by the company's metallurgist, he discovered the "flotation process" for extracting zinc (as well as lead) from other worthless matter brought up from the mine. Huge dumps of material had accumulated, containing zinc, but the zinc blende (sulphide of zinc) did not differ sufficiently in density from the worthless matter to allow it to be separated by ordinary mechanical methods. But Delprat managed to attack the zinc blende (sulphide of zinc) with a little acid, so that gas was given off; the gas bubbles then attached themselves to the minute particles of zinc blende and caused them to rise to the surface of a boiling mixture, so that the zinc could be skimmed off the top. As a result, while in 1903 about three-quarters of the material raised at Broken Hill had to be "dumped", thereafter all of it could be treated, as well as 6,000,000 tons of past dumps, which yielded minerals worth £30,000,000.

Between 1900 and 1908, B.H.P. extended its plant and improved its processes; output was high and profits were good. Then metal prices began to fall, silver from 2/9 to 2/- an ounce, lead from £16 to £12 per ton, so the Company decided to cut the wages it paid to its workmen from the beginning of 1909. The men appealed to the newly established Commonwealth Arbitration Court, but while the appeal was pending, the mine was closed. According to the Union, this was a lock-out.

During January there was unrest at the Barrier. The men were afraid the Company would attempt to work the mine with non-union labour and decided to picket it, though the Company denied that it wanted to do anything of the kind. For a time, Delprat and several of his senior officials were virtually besieged in the mine. Reinforcements of police were sent to Broken Hill. When some of the company officers left the mine they were assaulted and injured, though the union officials claimed that no member of the union was responsible. Certainly when Delprat, who was always popular with his men, left the mine to enter the city, he was not touched. He walked calmly through the picket lines, smoked his pipe, did his shopping and returned. Later he even attended a meeting of the strikers at the Trades Hall, announcing himself as "Daniel in the lions' den". He always showed as great a flair for dealing with his workers and negotiating with union officials as he had for his technical work.

In the Arbitration Court hearings, Mr Justice Higgins decided that the cost of living at Broken Hill was so high that the amount claimed by the men was the lowest wage that would allow "the healthy subsistence of the average family"; but Delprat told him that the company would lose about 1/4 on every ton of crude ore it mined, if it paid wages at that level; so the Judge felt that, although he could not allow employees to be underfed, or dividends to be paid "at the cost of the workman's breakfast table", he could not order the Company to re-open the mine either. So it remained idle until February 1911, by which time metal prices had risen again.

By then the Company was planning very different activities. It had always been on the lookout for chances of becoming more efficient and of reducing its costs; it had found that one way it could do this was by producing its own raw materials and using its by-products. For example, in 1904, it had decided to build a sulphuric acid plant and to manufacture superphosphates—thus using sulphur obtained from the "flotation process" in separating zinc from the sulphides, and also obtaining the acid it wanted more cheaply. As Delprat had pointed out,

Broken Hill has not really silver-lead mines, but rather silver zinc and sulphur mines. The Barrier ores contained large quantities of sulphur which in the old days was carried away in smoke from the chimneys. We could make sulphuric acid so cheaply as to supply it to all the mines which would go in for the acid process; and if we manufacture on a large scale we would use it in superphosphate.

As early as 1900, two other vital steps had been taken in widening the operations of the Company. The Port Pirie smelters always used large quantities of coke. Originally this was obtained from outside manufacturers, but the price was often high, and supplies sometimes unreliable and poor in quality. So the Company built its own coke works, at Bellambi, in New South Wales; and for fifteen years it obtained all its supplies from its own plant, at a much lower cost.

Iron too was needed, as a flux for lead smelting, especially after the building of the new smelting plant at Port Pirie in 1897. This is added to the ore in the blast furnace, so as to increase the yield of lead; otherwise some of the metal escapes into the air as smoke or fume, not only wasting the lead, but destroying all the vegetation in the neighbourhood. By the end of the century it was becoming difficult to obtain enough iron, so the Company took a lease of the mountains later known as Iron Knob and Iron Monarch, in the Middleback Ranges, some thirty-five miles to the west of Spencer Gulf in South Australia.

"I sent out prospectors to look for flux," said Delprat. "I went to a few places, but none of the places offered was big enough." Iron Knob and Iron Monarch were the only spots that were suitable. If he could not get flux from here, "it would pay better to sell the concentrates than to smelt", and "that would be a bad thing for Port Pirie", he told a Select Committee of the South Australian Parliament; but if regular supplies of flux were available, the situation would be different. So B.H.P. was given the leases and authority to build a railway line from their site to Hummock Hill on Spencer Gulf—that is where Whyalla is now. So the Company had obtained unrivalled supplies of ore, near the surface, so that they could be worked by open-cut, and near enough to the coast to be carried there cheaply. This was due, according to Mr Darling, one of the Directors, "to reports from the General Manager, who was looking ahead to the future".

Now that they possessed these deposits, the Company might think of setting up an iron and steel works, especially since, as we have seen, their silver-lead-zinc mines on the Barrier were becoming nearly exhausted. Delprat strongly supported the idea and in 1911 went overseas to collect all possible information about iron and steel works. In New York he engaged Mr David Blake, an American steel expert, to visit Australia and report on his plans, and in due course both men reported in favour of the scheme. "We have a solid basis for an iron and steel industry", wrote Delprat.

The fact of the Company holding an immense iron ore deposit in South Australia . . . made it incumbent on us to find out if this iron

ore could be turned to more profitable use than by merely using it as a
flux in the smelters at Port Pirie. This deposit is connected with the
coast by . . . a tramway, and a very long jetty facilitates the loading
of the ore. When the Company built this line and jetty, the market
for steel in Australia was very limited, and it would have been
unwise to erect Steel Works. However the demand for Steel has grown
steadily, and to-day the requirements are such that the urgent
necessity for having steel works in the Commonwealth is a well
recognized fact . . .

He pointed out that over 400,000 tons of iron and manufactured steel had been imported into Australia in 1910 and
argued that the demand would increase as Australia developed.
"The contemplated transcontinental railway will require enormous quantities of rails and other materials, and it is clear therefore
that there will be no difficulty in disposing of our product,
provided price and quality are satisfactory."

So much for the market. As to production, the ore supplies
were enough for "more than a generation", and its quality "the
very best that can be had for making steel". He said, "We
can lay out our works on the most up-to-date lines introducing
all the best-known labour-saving appliances existing and avail-
ing ourselves of the accumulated experience of Europe and
America." Coal for making coke for the blast furnaces could be
obtained both north and south of Sydney, near Newcastle and
Port Kembla; the works should be built close to the coal-fields,
and on both the sea-front and railway, so that raw materials
and finished products could easily be carried by train or steamship.

In fact he had already begun to negotiate with the New South
Wales government over the site. Baker, in his report, had recommended Newcastle:

As it takes more tons of coal than tons of your iron ore to make a ton
of finished steel, it follows that the works should be nearest the coal
. . . I have therefore considered two locations—Port Kembla and
Newcastle—and have decided in favour of the latter. It has the largest
supply of good coking coal suitable for iron blast furnaces. The coal
is cheapest and best adapted for your purpose. The harbour facilities
are best. The Company's land has good water frontage . . . and
provides ample space to take care of the growth of your works for
many years. It is the cheapest site offered. It is located on the main
line of a rail road and therefore offers ample shipping facilities for
the product.

Just at this time the New South Wales government was
thinking of establishing a State-owned steel works; but before

its Parliament had passed the bill to authorize it Delprat announced the plans of B.H.P. and asked the government to help it. He could set up the Company's works in South Australia, if the New South Wales government preferred, he said, "having regard to their own reported determination to erect similar works there". He therefore wanted to know if the government would give the Company "a fair deal", whether it would give an extended load of government land if it were necessary, and whether "we could count on the goodwill of the government to assist us in a friendly way—but this does not mean financial assistance or concessions".

During the winter negotiations went on, with Delprat continually pressing for "speedy replies", as "we have very little time to lose". The government declared that though it was their policy to establish a State-owned iron and steel industry, "any industry that may be established in New South Wales will receive encouragement and consideration from the government", and on September 27 an agreement was signed; the government promised to dredge and maintain a channel which would be 1700 yards long and 25 feet deep, up to the Company's wharves, so as "to give reasonable access from the Pacific Ocean to the Company's proposed works". They would also deposit the sand and silt removed from the channel on the Company's land so as to help to reclaim the swampy areas of the property, and would sell certain neighbouring land to the Company. The Company would pay for dredging the last 200 yards. Delprat also suggested that they should sign a ten years' preferential contract for the purchase of steel, but the government refused.

Delprat flatly denied he would want any other government help or tariff protection. "If I cannot carry on without Government assistance, I will not proceed at all," he said. He said he did not mind in the least the prospect of competition from a State steel works. It was not necessary to have a monopoly; on the contrary, "I would like to have people to compete against". If the government were to erect a steel works "they would not wipe us out", though they might "limit the extension of our works". But he did not think the government could carry on an iron works successfully. Why not?

To begin with the State has no iron deposits; and secondly I think that when the Government carry out such works the cost is more than if a private firm carries them out . . . The State could never get a contract if we competed against them, that is not on the same terms.

Still even if the State did get it (by preference) it would not

matter; "there would be plenty of scope for us even after that."
Delprat even asserted, "I believe we can compete with the
markets of the outside world," a belief which was proved true,
at any rate after 1933. However, for the moment he planned "to
make the works big enough to supply everything that is required
in Australia of iron and steel manufacture, and I intend to
expand them as the requirements of Australia increase." At first,
he would build only one blast furnace; but he would leave room
for eight. As he had said in his report to the Company,

I would propose to erect at once, one blast furnace of 350 tons daily
capacity and the corresponding number of open hearth steel furnaces
and rolling mills of sufficient capacity to deal with the steel made. I
would lay out the plant from the very start in such a way that it can
be extended indefinitely without having to tear down anything or
interfere with the operation of the existing plant. More furnaces could
then be erected as the demand for the products warranted and as the
staff of operators became more efficient. The erection of by-product
coke ovens should be taken in hand at once, so as to make sure that
the quality of the coke was all that we desired and the supply
assured. I would endeavour to supply the wants of the Federal and
State Government so that the works would gradually occupy in
Australia the same position that certain other firms occupy in Europe
and America.

While the negotiations with the New South Wales government
were going on, the Company's shareholders had agreed to the
scheme. Construction began at once, and on 9 March 1915 the
blast furnace was "blown in"; the production of pig iron began,
and of course the works were greatly expanded during the course
of World War I.

Not long afterwards, in February 1921, Delprat retired from
his position of General Manager of the Company. He took no
further active part in the affairs of B.H.P. He had never bought
shares in it; he had no wish to become a director. In 1918 he had
been made a C.B.E. He was the first man to be awarded the
medal of the Australasian Institute of Mining and Metallurgy,
instituted in 1935 for outstanding achievements in work of this
kind. In the same year he was elected an honorary member of
the American Institute of Mining and Metallurgical Engineers,
"in recognition of his distinguished achievements as metallurgist,
engineer and administrator in the production of ferrous and non-
ferrous metals." Two years later, at the age of eighty, he died.

Obviously it would be untrue to suggest that Delprat was
responsible for this entire growth. When he arrived in 1898,
B.H.P. was already a flourishing concern. Since he retired in

1921, it has trebled in size. While he was General Manager, he received able help and support. The Company's metallurgists, Carmichael and Bradford, contributed much to the flotation process. The chairman of directors, John Darling, backed him wholeheartedly in the steel venture, and supported his views by making a great contribution to the capital of the Company. The directors were ready to agree with his plans and to use the Company's reserves to help finance them. Even the government, that agent so often despised by private concerns, gave valuable support, in acquiring land, developing the port of Newcastle, dredging a channel to the Company's property and later giving tariff protection to the new industry, apart altogether from the underwriting of part of the £1,000,000 debenture issue in 1914 by the Commonwealth Bank, allegedly so ridden by red tape, and unwilling to take responsibility, in defiance of the advice of "orthodox" private banking opinion.

But the career of Delprat, in association with B.H.P., shows how much can be achieved by the initiative, foresight and efficiency of an entrepreneur, as well as giving a warning on the problems that beset the mining industry. At first he handled his mine in a most enterprising and efficient way, developing new processes cutting down his costs, but when the life of the mine seemed to be nearly at an end, he was not afraid to branch out in a new enterprise.

With the financial policy of the Company, Delprat had nothing to do. He was not a director; he was not even a shareholder. He was a salaried manager, working for his employers, serving them most efficiently and conscientiously, without the spur of personal gain, trying only to do his best, and gaining his reward by his fame and reputation. Such, paradoxically, was the man who did so much to build up this giant of Australian capitalism.

It is said so often that the *only* way to get work well done is to give men a personal interest, private profit, in their job. But Delprat was working on much the same conditions as the civil servant, for a salary, though responsible to his Board of Directors and not to a government.

Not least of Delprat's achievements was to win and keep the esteem and confidence of the men. He could not completely avoid strife; but he was always popular, and considering how difficult the problems of labour relations are in a dangerous and arduous industry like mining, and heavy industry, and the circumstances in which he was placed, his record speaks for itself.

It needs more than technical knowledge and organizing ability to be a successful industrial leader in Australia. One must be able to understand and appreciate the peculiar psychology of workers in a young, confident and strongly democratic country. Not every administrator from overseas, however great his reputation and skill could have succeeded at Broken Hill. But Delprat crowned a distinguished technical and executive career in other parts of the world with a brilliantly successful regime of twenty-two years as a general manager of the Broken Hill Proprietary Company. He was a captain of industry that Australia was extraordinarily fortunate to have, and even today, more than twenty-five years after he retired, the country still owes him a great deal for the work from which it is still reaping great benefit.

CHAPTER 14

WORKING CONDITIONS

1. Working Conditions in the Early Nineteenth Century

THERE are many records of working conditions in the early days of the Colony. One of the most interesting is the story of Alexander Harris, the "emigrant mechanic" who published the book on his adventures called *Settlers and Convicts.* After he landed in Sydney in 1825, he hung about for three weeks till a job turned up.

My engagement at last was more a matter of accident than the result of my own endeavours. The landlord of the public house, where I went every morning to look over the advertisements in hope of finding something that would suit me, had been brought up to the same trade as myself; knowing what kind of work I was seeking, he recommended me to a customer of his who had come up from Five Islands with a boat load of cedar, and wanted a snug little hut put up for his family; they had been there some time, but had been living, hitherto, under a few sheets of bark.

If the employer had been forced to live under such conditions, it was no wonder that the workman too was expected to rough it.

My agreement with Mr. ———— was soon made, for I knew so very little of the customs of the colony that I saw no objections to anything he proposed. It was stated in the agreement, which was a written one, that I was to proceed to Illa Warra and erect for Mr. ———— a house of such or such timber, of so many feet length, so many breadth and so many height, in consideration whereof, Mr. ———— was to pay me the sum of £75; supply me with rations at a rate specified for each article, lend me one of his convict servants to assist in cutting down and splitting the timber, and other work requiring two hands; and draw out of the bush the split stuff etc. as soon as it was ready. The bargain thus far concluded, he told me I could have if I chose an advance of £5 before leaving Sydney, to buy any extra tools I wanted. . . . I then found I should need to buy a cross-cut saw and some other articles which, however, I did with my own money, still having sufficient by me for that purpose; and having seen the tools, my own tool chest, and clothes, etc. aboard the boat, started along with one of Mr. ————'s men by land for the Five Islands.

This man was the convict who was to be my mate. In New South

The Ivel Agricultural Motor. Awarded a silver medal in 1904 by the Royal Agricultural Society of England, it was the first farm tractor considered worthy of mention by the society's implement judges.

(From *The Wheat Industry in Australia*, by Callaghan and Millington)

Irrigated lands in the Mildura District, on the Murray River.

(Australian News and Information Bureau)

"The Wayfarer." A typical family scene early in the nineteenth century.
Notice the clothing typical of that period.
(From the *Illustrated Sydney News*, November, 1878)

The Woolloomooloo fish market.
(From the *Illustrated Sydney News*, October 1875)

Wales it is not thought any derogation to travel with convict servants; in fact it is often unavoidable.

Harris went by bush tracks to Illawarra. Overnight he stopped in a hut made of bark and furnished with logs. He shared damper and tea with convicts and learnt how to fend for himself in the bush and even how to deal with some bushrangers who forced his mate to lead them to a settler's lonely hut and store. He noted:

The Australian settler undertakes, as a matter of course, to supply his labourers with rations; but he never thinks there is the slightest obligation on himself to make that supply a constant one.

At length the work was completed. After some days of what I considered very unnecessary delay, the chief of which Mr. ———— spent in walking round and round, and in and out of his new habitation, and looking at it from all mentionable distances and all possible angles, I got a cheque for the balance due to me, £43.

Harris had to find a new job, which meant another long trip and more negotiations. His next job was as a mate to a cedar sawyer. The work was heavy and the food cannot have been good; too much salt meat and poor bread. Harris comments, "A few months' residence and hard work in the bush leaves most men as pallid as corpses."

Later he was mistaken for an escaped convict and imprisoned. In the 1830s close watch was kept on the movement of all servants, free or convict. In some districts workers had to get a magistrate's warrant to prove that they were genuine travellers. Convicts were punished cruelly for attempted escape and even received 25 or 50 lashes for being impertinent to their masters. Harris thought they were often accused unjustly and he was revolted at the cruelty of the overseers.

The general attitude of employers was to be seen in government regulations and in the Masters and Servants Act passed in 1828. Any person who, it stated,

shall refuse or neglect to work in the trade, calling, or employment, for which he or she shall have been so hired or engaged . . . it shall be lawful for any one or more Justice or Justices of the Peace, to cause every person who shall be complained of as so offending, to be brought before him or them . . . and the Justice or Justices . . . shall hear and determine the matter of every such complaint, and if no reasonable and sufficient cause be shown to the contrary, such Justice or Justices shall commit every person convicted of so offending as aforesaid, to the common gaol, there to remain . . . for any time not exceeding six calendar months. . . .

M

On the other hand, employers who misused their employees were not punished. The magistrates simply cancelled the contract.

The worker's life was not completely unhappy. Many masters were fair and many had to work as hard as their labourers. Besides, there were joys of being with others in the new land. Harris recorded these new feelings:

It is during the three or four evening hours that elapse after his work that the sawyer enjoys himself. The success of the day, the prospect of a good cutting or an advantageously shaped log on the morrow, the pleasant perfume of the pipe, the cheering pot of tea again and again repeated, with each new yarn, or joke, or laugh, the busy and pompous excursions and barkings of the dog, the pattering shower, the clouds of fireflies that dance along in their countless angular courses . . .

Harris lived with rough and sometimes dishonest convicts and workers and in the worst of times and yet he recorded towards the end of his book:

There is among working men a strong and ineradicable and very correct sense of what is fair. Unless you act fairly to them, they will assuredly endeavour to right themselves.

The whole story of improvement of working conditions has been a struggle to achieve fair play. Conditions of work are constantly changing and there is constant need to review them and improve wherever possible. At the beginning of Australian history, the worker had little chance if things went wrong; the employers had the law too much on their side. In Australia, today, there is more of a balance and the worker is now free to organize to improve conditions.

2. British Conditions and the Beginning of Trade Unionism

Most of the problems about conditions of work can be traced back to England, where great changes in agriculture and industry were taking place about the time when the Australian Colonies were beginning to develop (see previous chapters). Machines, which should have made work easier, sometimes put men out of work. Factories were built for the profit of their owners, not for the benefit of people who worked in them. If there were more people wanting work than places for them to fill, employers preferred those who would take the cheapest wages. Children were employed on simple repetitive jobs from quite an early age; at eight or nine nearly all were at work. Women were employed because they were paid less than men. People brought up without education, with only one day a week to look after their homes, a 12-hour working day, and with poor food, were bound to be poor citizens. Thieving and drunkenness were common. Even where people remained decent, and many did, they were often filled with bitterness against the wealthy and the government. There were threats of violence; riots were not uncommon; at times there was even talk of revolution.

At this time government and employers believed that if wages were not kept low and hours long, factories would work at a loss and unemployment would result. "Better the bread of poverty than no bread at all," they said. Higher wages in England would only help Britain's industrial competitors and rivals. So they always tried to suppress the workers' attempts to unite to better their conditions. The Combination Acts which forbade the formation of trade unions were not repealed till 1824. Then, when the unions were made legal, the employers often refused to employ union members and "locked-out" the workers. The government was afraid, also, that working-class organizations, in trade unions and otherwise might lead to rebellions. Sometimes they prosecuted union members for stirring up violence or damaging property. The discontented were organized by leaders into a large-scale political party; they could not elect members to Parliament, for no poor men had a vote, but they drew up petitions setting out their grievances and sent them to Parliament. The Chartists gained few of their demands at the time, but their influence was felt, and a generation or so later the English political system was made more democratic.

These events in England had effects in Australia. The repeal of the Combination Acts prepared the way for the development of trade unions in Australia because English law applied in the Australian Colonies until self-government was granted. Many unionists and Chartists migrated to Australia and a few were transported as convicts. These men helped to build up a new outlook in Australia. By 1850 there were 25 unions in Sydney and 13 in Hobart. The country workers were too scattered to be organized, and since factory industry had scarcely grown even in the towns, the unions were mainly composed of skilled craftsmen such as carpenters and masons. The unions organized social meetings and tried to care for the widows of their members, as well as bargaining with employers on conditions of work.

One reason why the English government did not help the Labour movement in its early days was that the government represented well-to-do people and did not know or understand the workers' problems. However, it was concerned with the ill-effects of the industrial revolution and some of the injustices it caused. Through the Poor Laws, it made locally elected "guardians" responsible for administering "relief" to the unemployed. Through the Municipal Reform Act, it tried to improve local government, which administered markets, roads, building regulations and other similar matters. Most important of all, in 1833, it passed the first effective Factory Act. Four inspectors were provided to see that no children under nine years of age were employed in textile factories and that children under 14 did not work more than 48 hours a week. This Act was by no means satisfactory by modern standards, but it was a first step towards more general regulation. It took the rest of the century to obtain anything like present conditions of employment. The passing of the Act showed that the government recognized that it had to protect its people and to step in from time to time to see that all classes had a fair deal. Once such a principle was established, there was a chance that it would be followed to its conclusion.

After 1830 the English government helped to reduce prices of bread and other articles by removing high import duties and excise taxes. Yet England had such a lead in industry that she could increase her sales and pay higher wages. The machine was becoming a benefit to the worker.

The conditions of work for the skilled labourer in Australia after about 1830 were better than in England. The wealth from pastoral expansion encouraged the growth of towns and trades. Free immigrants were slow to try their luck in the new country, where work was so easy to find. The gold discoveries and the winning of self-government with a universal franchise in the 1850s stimulated a democratic movement in the eastern Colonies, as we shall see in Chapter 17, but the pastoralists remained in a dominant position for some time, because wool was important in the economy and manufactures were in their infancy. In spite of the Land Acts most Australians did not wish to work on the land.

3. The Eight-Hour Day

Meanwhile the average Australian from the very first wanted to get the best working conditions that he could. One of the first changes in working conditions demanded by Australian workmen was the introduction of an eight-hour day. Not many people noticed the first time that the slogan was raised, although a small procession was held in Melbourne to make it known. The leaders of this agitation came from the various building crafts. Skilled workmen could stand up for their rights more easily than the unskilled labourers, who could fairly easily be replaced on any job. At a time when many buildings were of stone, the stone-masons had very special needs of their own. Their work was extremely heavy and tiring and so they could not keep it up for very long hours without lowering their efficiency. Then they worked in the open, often in sun and heat or exposed to cold winds. Chipping at the stones also made a lot of dust. Then all the builders found that they were constantly changing the site of their work as they moved from job to job and this meant a long journey from their homes to their work when there were no trains or buses or cars to take them there.

The arguments used in the struggle for an eight-hour day are now familiar to everyone. Here are some of the main points from a report of the Victorian Operative Masons' Society made in 1884, twenty-eight years after the stone-masons had gained their eight-hour working day. First they said:

He [the Anglo-Saxon worker] might lead a more happy and enjoyable life. . . . We doubt whether as much work is not frequently done in eight hours as in ten. . . . In the morning a man is fresh and works with a will. . . . In the evening he is too often jaded and finds that every stroke he has to strike is a real effort and a bore.
The proposition is to divide the four and twenty hours into equal parts—eight hours for work, eight hours for repose, and eight for food and recreation.

The report denied that the worker would spend time lounging about:

He fills up his spare time by digging in his garden, feeding his poultry, milking his cow, teaching his children. . . .

Recent studies of the effects of fatigue have confirmed the argument that long hours tend to make people work badly, so that men are even able to produce more goods in a shorter time, say, an eight-hour day than if they had worked two hours longer. The argument that leisure would be used profitably has not always been justified by the event. Certainly, as the hours of leisure have increased the average life-span has

increased, but there may be other reasons for this as well; sport
has become almost universal and people go to theatres, or for
outings to the beaches or the countryside, but very few families
nowadays raise much of their own food or pay much attention
to education after the children have left school. But, they may
argue, they only want time to amuse and enjoy themselves and
this is a good reason for wanting shorter hours of work.

The struggle for the eight-hour day lasted well into this
century. It was first gained in building trades, then by women
and children and miners. Sometimes it was gained by strikes,
sometimes it was adopted because it was most economic, fitting
in best with meal times and transport arrangements, and finally
it was established by Acts of Parliament.

4. The Struggles of Trade Unions

During the 1870s and 1880s the trade unions were fully
legalized in Australia. The English Acts of 1824 and 1825, which
we saw above were in force here, merely said:

> Journeymen, workmen or other persons who shall enter into any
> combination to obtain an advance, or to fix the rate of wages, or to
> lessen or alter the hours or duration of the time of working . . . shall
> not be subject or liable to any indictment or prosecution for conspiracy.

Unions had more interests than "hours and wages", yet union
organizers were open to charges of conspiracy if they turned
their attention to anything but these. Union funds were not
protected and unions could not control their officials, who
sometimes ran off with union funds. As industry and communications grew in the last years of the century, the unions grew
larger. New unions were formed in one trade after another, and
they used the right to strike more frequently as they became
stronger and better organized. Often they did not gain the
improvements they sought, but their legal rights were conceded
by one Colony after another, because it was felt that if employers
could organize, the men should have a say in deciding what they
should be paid and what their working conditions should be.
The public came to realize that one man by himself was helpless
if he tried to bargain with his employer and that to give the
workers an equal say in such bargaining they must be able to
combine and to act together concerning the conditions of their
work.

In the 1890s there were several great strikes to establish
union principles. The Shearers' Union had been one of the most
difficult to organize because the men were scattered all over the

country. Pastoralists gave poor conditions and there was great need for a united front in the demand for improvements. After many setbacks the shearers had succeeded in forming a union and had won many concessions from the pastoralists. In their struggles they had been helped by the waterside workers, who had refused to load wool from a station which employed non-union shearers. Later, the seamen went on strike, when they thought that one of their men had been unjustly dismissed, and the shearers struck in sympathy. The pastoralists claimed that this was a "breach of contract"; they reasserted "freedom of contract", the right to employ any labour they liked, whether union or non-union. The waterside workers and coal miners joined in to support their fellows. But there were many unemployed in Melbourne and Sydney at the time. They were engaged to work on the wharves and pastoral stations and were protected from pickets by colonial government military forces. Some trade union leaders were charged with "conspiracy" and imprisoned for periods up to three years. The strikers ran out of money and one by one they had to go back to work. The Labour movement suffered a heavy defeat.

About the same time the B.H.P. Company (see Chapter 13) repudiated a wage agreement with the union: it claimed that a fall in the price of silver and lead had made mining unprofitable on the old conditions. The union called the men out on strike but it did not have enough funds. Its leaders were arrested, tried and imprisoned and the men had to accept the Company's terms.

These and other strikes failed in a period of economic depression in the early 1890s. The union at Broken Hill lost nine-tenths of its members in just over two years. The unions had to reconstruct themselves and re-organize. As industrial action had failed, they had to step up the political organization which they had already begun. They realized that very many Australians supported their desire to improve the lot of the poorer members of society. The Labour party quickly become a powerful agent of improvement.

5. Immigration Policies and Labour Standards

During the second half of the nineteenth century, unions and workers took a great deal of notice of immigration policies. The unions were not keen on too many migrants coming out with government assistance because they were often willing to accept working conditions that the union men were opposing.

When Chinese migrants came into Australia after the gold rushes, many people were afraid that Australia would be swamped by Asian peoples, who were willing to work for low wages and whose standard of living was thought to be "uncivilized", if not worse. There were several anti-Chinese demonstrations on the goldfields and the governments felt it necessary to restrict Chinese immigration. In 1878 the Australasian Steam Navigation Company employed Chinese seamen, but the white crews went on strike. They gained almost universal support. The Queensland government threatened to withdraw its mail subsidies. The shipping company decided to withdraw the Chinese seamen and so put an end to the question for the time being. The fear of Asian migrants was less justified at that time than the opposition to the Queensland sugar planters, who used Kanaka labourers from the Pacific Islands, "boys" who signed contracts to work in the sugar field. By 1885 it was proved beyond doubt that the "contracts" or "indentures" were a mockery for most of these native labourers, who were not able to understand what they were signing and who had been more or less kidnapped. The masters of six ships and their crews were tried on charges of murder, violence and fraud. A special Act of 1885 prohibited the use of Kanaka labour after 1890, but the Act was soon modified, as it was said that it would ruin the sugar industry. After federation, as we shall see, the Commonwealth government passed the Pacific Islands Labourers' Act, which stamped out the trade in 1904.

The Commonwealth Parliament could pass this Act because the majority of the Australian people did not want to see two labour systems in the one Commonwealth; a cheap native labour system in the north and a white labour system in the south. Most people could see that this would lead to bitter struggles in the future. The other implications were bad: that labour need not receive a fair wage, and that non-citizens could be worked for profit. These ideas are the fundamental ones that lie behind "White Australia". The first Federal government passed an Immigration Act which gave it the power to apply a dictation test in any language to any would-be immigrant, so that it could keep out cheap labour and preserve the living standards of Australian workmen.

6. Labour in Politics

Working conditions were regulated in the last two decades of the nineteenth century by a series of new measures passed by colonial legislatures. These measures were hastened generally by the formation of a political Labour party, though in Victoria they had been passed without this stimulus. The depression and the great strikes of the early 1890s encouraged the Trade Union Congress to organize politically. New South Wales and Victorian labour men co-operated with other liberal-minded men against the conservatives and introduced many social reforms.

7. The Introduction of Arbitration Courts

One of the most important was the trial of a new system of settling strikes. The original idea was quite simple. It was thought that a fair decision would be reached if cases that were causing industrial trouble were submitted to councils of conciliation made up of representatives of the Trades and Labour Council and of the Employers' Association, sometimes with an impartial chairman appointed by the government. But at first these commissions were not given power to compel either party to attend or to give evidence. So many people demanded compulsory arbitration in a court presided over by a judge. This system was introduced in several Colonies, but industrial unrest has continued and so have strikes. So often neither of the parties in a dispute accepts the basic views of the other about what is a fair profit or a fair wage and the arbitration courts have had to try to work out a policy for themselves, taking into account conditions existing at any particular time and what would be desirable from the point of view of the community, as well as the conflicting claims of employers and employees.

8. The Government's Social Legislation

Another way in which the colonial governments tried to introduce fair conditions was by Factory Acts. Victoria set up a Royal Commission which showed that women and children were employed under the worst possible conditions. A Factories and Shops Act was passed which limited the working hours of boys under 16 and women to a maximum of 52 hours a week, nine hours on five days and seven on the other. Similar Acts were passed by other Colonies, which also passed Acts to allow compensation to workers injured at work, and in 1900 New South Wales and Victoria adopted old age pension schemes. All these Acts were hotly opposed by conservatives, who argued that they would be too costly and were foolish concessions made by weak-kneed politicians trying to catch votes. But today, sixty-six years later, they are regarded as the beginning of a new policy of social welfare, for we now believe that everyone should share in the work of the community and everyone should expect fair treatment when too young or too old to work or when in distress.

"BEFORE THE LAW ALL MEN ARE EQUAL"

After the general strike of 1890, which led to the formation of the Australian Labour Party in New South Wales, Arthur Rae was charged and jailed for having incited 29 shearers to leave their work. The cartoon above, drawn by "Hop", was published in the *Bulletin* on 11th October 1890. Under the cartoon the following lines appeared:

Police Magistrate (at Hay, N.S.W.): "Defendant, you are clearly proved to have ordered or incited 29 men on one station to stop shearing and leave their contracts unfinished. I now fine you £5 5s. in each case—or, in default, 14 days' gaol in each case, the sentences to be cumulative."

Shearer Rae: "In other words, if I at one place, at one time and by using two words, called out a thousand shearers, you could sentence me to 14,000 days gaol!"

Query: Who made the Australian labour laws, the Workers or the Monopolists? And who are going to make them in future?

9. The Position in 1900

By 1900 the sense of justice and fair play which had grown up in the early days of the Colony had caused a wide-spread demand for much better standards of work and had led to the development of great new institutions, which were created to help to bring these standards about—political parties, trade unions, arbitration courts, and so on. In addition, the great wealth of Australia was being tapped by industries that provided new goods and materials as new industries and an expanding population increased the income of Australia. As industry became more efficient, it was possible for governments and industry to spend more on social welfare.

A Frenchman who visited Australia at the turn of the century reported:

> The Australian worker has become a "gentleman". He dresses himself after his work. He is housed and he behaves like a person of good society. If he has to attend a meeting, he will appear clean, freshly shaved, will be careful of his behaviour, will not speak out of turn, and will respect the authority of the chairman. More and more one can observe the external difference between the worker and the middle class diminishing except in working hours.

10. The Commonwealth Government and the Basic Wage

The Commonwealth government carried on the traditions that had been established. To protect Australian industries and so provide work for Australians, high tariffs were placed on certain goods coming into Australia. The Commonwealth government set up a Court of Conciliation and Arbitration to deal with industries which operated in more than one State. If industries were to be protected against the competition of underpaid labour in other countries while they were being asked to pay fair wages themselves, then it would be necessary to work out what a fair and reasonable wage was. So the newly established Commonwealth Arbitration Court was asked to do this. The judge, Mr Justice Higgins, after a long enquiry, decided that a fair wage should be based upon "the normal needs of the average employee regarded as a human being in a civilized community". He thought that this "basic" amount for an unskilled worker was £2 2s. at the prices ruling in 1907. From this decision arose the idea of a "basic wage", which the State sets up as the least that a man with a family should be paid. Most States have accomplished more than the farmers could achieve. They set up boards or commissions to lay down the basic wage.

There have been many disputes about the idea; some claim that a basic wage is nonsense and that industry can only afford to pay what is earned and that the basic wage should depend on productivity: workers claim that the ideal should be much higher than it is, and that they should share in the profits of industry, which they say are too high. But in fact, for a long time the basic wage has been prepared from a special list of prices of goods which are widely used in everyday consumption, called the "C Series Index" and issued by the Commonwealth Statistician every three months. This measured the changes in the price level and was based on Higgins's standard. But just before World War II a "prosperity loading" was added, and another £1 was granted in 1951. A shorter working week (40 hours) and holidays with pay have added to the real value of the wage, and in 1941 the Federal Government introduced a scheme of child welfare.

11. The Depression 1929-1933

From 1929 to 1933 Australia, like every other country in the world, suffered from a severe economic depression. The value of exports fell off by nearly half: 300,000 workers had no employment. People who could not afford to pay their rent had to move to tin shanties on the edges of the town. The State government paid out doles to relief workers, and there was a great deal of distress throughout the community. After 1934 business picked up slowly and employment became more normal. People did not understand why the great calamity had hit the community and many tended to distrust the politicians even after the depression. The coal-owners in northern New South Wales had locked the miners out in an illegal attempt to reduce wages. Suffering on the coal-fields was so great that the miners did not cease to oppose the government and the owners for a generation. Fifteen months of lock-out followed by depression wages led them to make a series of demands and strikes during World War II when the country needed coal and they were in a position to improve their conditions again.

12. World War II and After

The greatest changes of all came during World War II. The challenge of the war encouraged the national government to take up national schemes again. As we have seen, a system of child endowment was begun to help the family man in difficult

times. A National Welfare Fund was established to give relief
to any who should be out of work or sick. After the war,
ex-servicemen were helped to train themselves for work that
interested them. The government subsidized house-building and
encouraged immigration to improve transport, electricity and
water supplies; industry has been prosperous and there has
been very little unemployment; but people have complained
sometimes that there have not been enough homes, that prices
have risen too fast and that many services have been inadequate.
It is true that electricity and water supplies, for example, have
been short, and that roads, schools and hospitals need attention;
but the country is now being developed so rapidly that not
everything can be done as quickly as is desirable. The worker
certainly has a better share of the national wealth now than
he had before the depression, and the national wealth as a whole
is much greater too.

Today the Australian living standard is one of the highest
in the world. It was helped after the war by the high prices
obtained for primary products, particularly for wool and metals.
But war-time needs, the growing population and the profits
earned from the increased national income have all been used
to create new industries which are very efficient. Even if Australian primary products never bring such high prices again,
Australia is better equipped to face the future than she was
before the war.

If Alexander Harris came back as an immigrant now you
can see what kind of food he would have by looking at your
table at home and you can see the kind of work and house he
would get by looking at migrant camps. The huts may be built
of fibro, but they are lit by electricity and are very different
from the rough bark huts that he was often forced to live in.
The immigrant today is looked upon as a New Australian,
someone who will share the common citizen's rights as well
as the friendliness of his fellows. These changes show some
of the ways in which living and working conditions have
improved during the past hundred years.

CHAPTER 15

THE GROWTH OF SYDNEY

1. Sydney in the Eighteenth Century

IT IS difficult to find any remains of Governor Phillip's Sydney in the great city of today. Streets and buildings cover the Tank Stream beside which his little town grew. The cove where he landed has changed its shape as the quays have been built out. A small tablet on a stone in Bridge Street marks the place where he built the first Government House, but there have been disputes about the kind of house it was, since differing sketches of it remain. But it was Governor Phillip who made the original wise choice, that Sydney should be situated at Port Jackson. He also chose the site of Parramatta. The road from Sydney to Parramatta is the ribbon along which Sydney grew.

The first plan of Sydney was drawn up by Surveyor-General Alt, at the Governor's request. This plan was sent home with a despatch (9th July 1788), which stated:

As stores and other buildings will be begun in the course of a few months some regular plan for the town is necessary, and in laying of which I have endeavoured to place all public buildings in situations that will be eligible hereafter, and to give a sufficient share of ground for the stores, hospital etc., to be enlarged as may be necessary in the future. The principal streets are placed so as to admit a free circulation of air and are two hundred feet wide. The ground marked for Government House is intended to include the main guard, Civil and Criminal Courts; and as the ground that runs to the south-ward is nearly level, and a very good situation for buildings, streets will be laid out in such a manner as to afford free air; and when the houses are to be built, if it meets with your Lordship's approbation, the land will be granted with a clause that will ever prevent more than one house being built on the allotment, which will be sixty feet in front and one hundred and fifty feet in depth: this will preserve uniformity in the buildings, prevent narrow streets, and many inconveniences which the increase of inhabitants would otherwise occasion hereafter.

If Governor Phillip's plan had been followed, the centre of Sydney might have looked like some of the squares built in

London about 1800. These London squares were very dignified and orderly. A street of houses was planned as a single unit. Facing the main street each house had the best rooms and entrance halls. Facing the rear lane they had the stable quarters and service entrance, where supplies were unloaded and rubbish was thrown out. About 1800, English people's ideas about servicing houses were very simple. Only the well-to-do had water laid on. Such street lighting as existed was poor. By planning streets of houses, some of these difficulties could be pushed out of sight to the supply lanes at the back. As the main rooms of the houses overlooked the street, they were comparatively safe. A few oil lamps lit by a watchman could mark any movement along the orderly row, which provided no dark corners for footpads. In addition, the long row provided a magnificent vista for the eye. That is one reason why the best terraces in England and Australia have been preserved and cared for. Governor Phillip seems to have provided for vistas in his plan, because the main street led up to a site for Government House. There were nine blocks laid out symmetrically on both sides of the street, and at its other end it would have opened up to a view of Sydney Cove and the Harbour.

But the plan of Sydney was just a paper plan and it may not have been very suitable, as it ran contrary to the contours of land. As soon as Phillip left, the officers and officials took up estates wherever they wished, while the huts and other buildings straggled along roughly parallel to the Tank Stream and then along the roads that wandered into the bush. The buildings were put up hastily and were in constant need of repair. The first timber cut was not suitable and only the officers could afford imported house fittings such as door knobs and glass for windows.

2. Colonial Style

Although the plan of Sydney was irregular, the buildings were not. They matched each other better than buildings of later periods because they were built in a uniform manner or style. This style, which has been called "Australian colonial" by later Australians, held sway till the 1840s. It was a semi-classical style: Greek and Roman pillars and arches and balanced proportions were used in the design. As the builders worked in Australia, with Australian materials and simple fittings, the style was given a distinctly local twist, as you may see by

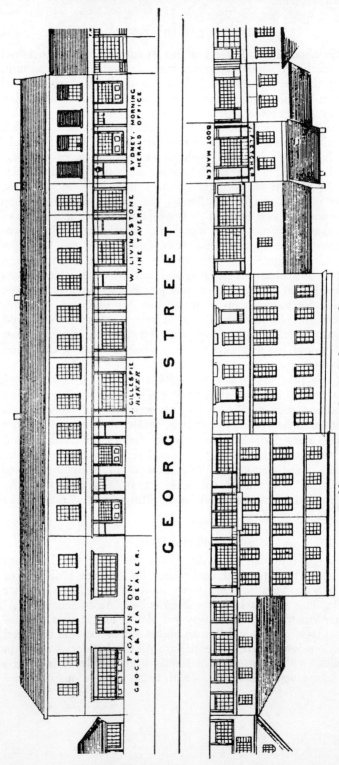

Buildings in George Street, Sydney, in the 1840s
(From *Sydney in 1848* by Joseph Fowles)

The swamps on which the Newcastle Steel Works were built.
(From *The Silver City*, by Ion L. Idriess)

The Newcastle Steel Works.
(From *The Silver City*, by Ion L. Idriess)

Sugar cane cutters. The cane has been burned before cutting. This is the outstanding example of the ability of Australians of European descent to carry out the arduous labour of agriculture in the tropics.

(From *Northern Australia*, Australian Institute of Political Science)

Stripping sugar cane by machine, 1960.

(By courtesy of Massey Ferguson Ltd, who developed the machine, a new Australian export)

comparing English and colonial buildings of the day. As you have already seen in Chapter 2, Sydney by 1820 had a distinct air. The handsome buildings built by Governor Macquarie's architect, Francis Greenway, dominated a town of two-story shops, stores and mansions, and of single-story cottages. The city thoroughfares had been laid out and built. It was a fine legacy that was left to the people of the second half of the century.

3. From Macquarie's Plan to Municipal Government

Sydney continued to be the chief centre in New South Wales after the initial period because it had offered several services to the growing agricultural and penal community. It was just as well that it ceased to be a farming community, because it was now able to concentrate on its main tasks. First of all it was the centre of government. The governor had his permanent residence in the town and the chief courts, barracks, gaols and other offices were set up there. After 1823 the governor's advisory council, the Legislative Council, naturally met in Sydney and this was the first step to the Parliament. It was also the chief port, where stores and wharves were set up. The stores, shops and markets were best situated near the port. It was also the centre of a network of roads, of which Governor Macquarie's road to Bathurst was the most important. Until the railway from Sydney to Bathurst was completed in 1876, this road was the only direct connection the western lands had with Sydney and the wider world.

Such activities as these led to secondary services being set up as well. For fifty years Sydney was the only lively social centre for thousands of miles. Its inns and shops and harbour-side roads provided for all sorts of entertainments, from horse racing and balls to gossip and heavy drinking. Many of the amenities of Sydney were invaluable to the wider community: the services of the Church, educational establishments, the light-house at South Head, the early newspapers, Simeon Lord's woollen mill run by water power at Cook's River, Botany, the windmills set up to grind corn, and many other enterprises tied Sydney to the country and the country to Sydney.

By 1828 the population of Sydney exceeded 10,000 and the city faced its first water supply problem. The Tank Stream proved to be an unsatisfactory supply of water. Between 1827 and 1830 a tunnel two miles long was cut by convicts to bring water from the Lachlan Swamps (in the flat area of the present Centennial Park) to Hyde Park. The convicts had only

N

hand tools and the work took a long time. Houses and horse troughs through the town were supplied by hand buckets and water carts. Even before it was finished this supply was seen to be inadequate and attempts were made to dam Cook's River at its outlet in Botany Bay. Water seeped from the Lachlan Swamps into East Lakes and then joined the Cook's River just near its outlet in Botany Bay. This area has been altered now to make the landing ground for Mascot aerodrome. So many difficulties were encountered with the Botany dams and the mains and pumps necessary to bring the water to Sydney, that the new scheme did not operate until 1859, when the population was nine times greater than in 1830 and the need for water was acute. When the water did come through, the reservoir in Paddington was not ready and the water over-flowed, threatening the security of the houses it was intended to supply. The reservation of the catchment area stretching from Paddington to Botany Bay preserved large areas for parks and playing fields in the eastern suburbs.

Here is one visitor's impression of the town of Sydney about this time.

Landing at the bottom of George Street, I strolled, stick in hand, my man following with my portmanteau in a cab, up to Petty's Hotel, a respectable quiet establishment. . . . I passed my first Australian evening in rambling slowly up George Street, the main artery of the city, and down Pitt Street, the second in rank, and should have been truly astonished at the immense extent of the former thorough-fare—the Broadway and Oxford Street of the Antipodes, 2½ miles long —and at the endless succession of well supplied and lighted shops in both, but that certain Sydneyites, my fellow passengers, had in so loud and high a key chanted the praises of their adopted city.

Sydney was so large and had so many problems that it needed special attention. The governor, with the advice of the Legislative Council, could not hope to deal with municipal as well as State problems. Governor Bourke himself suggested in 1832 that there was need for an elected body "for the repairing, cleansing and lighting the streets, the construction of flagged footways, and the introduction of water into public fountains and private houses. These useful objects may be obtained at no great cost by a rate levied on houses, according to their estimated value, and collected and appropriated by commissioners elected annually by ratepayers." Although the governor supported the idea, it was not until 1842 that the first City Council was set up. The people of Sydney had

become citizens of their own city. The free settlers of Adelaide
had been granted municipal rights in 1840, and those of
Melbourne gained them at the same time as Sydney. Both of
these cities had started with a regularly planned city, with wide
streets and small supply streets behind them, with proper provision for parks and public buildings.

The new Sydney Council found that the task of improving
Sydney with the small amount of money it received was too
difficult. The Council was attacked in the Legislative Council,
and the *Sydney Morning Herald* blamed it for neglect:

> Dead cats and dogs flung out on the footpaths and left to rot . . .
> plagues of broken bottles, the disgusting fragments of old shirts,
> old jackets, old hats, old shoes, these after six years of voting and
> taxing.

This wild attack the Council could deal with, but it could
not excuse itself from reports about its own meetings, where
it was said, "that offensive epithets and even oaths were used
in debate". New methods of electing the councillors were used
in 1850. In 1853, when the reform had not improved the
Council, it was abolished and three paid commissioners were
put in the councillors' place. But in 1857 the democratic system
of electing the city corporation was restored because the paid
commissioners had not been able to do the job. Until 1948 the
Sydney Municipal Council looked after the inner area of city,
that is, roughly, the area from Cleveland Street to the Quay
and from Blackwattle Bay to Rushcutters Bay. In 1948 it took in
eight surrounding councils with one-tenth of the population of
Sydney. Though the Council has undertaken many good works
in its history, it has never been responsible for controlling the
growth of the city, which has grown steadily to an area of about
670 square miles. Expensive projects such as railways and
tramways have always been in the hands of the State government, and many other major developments have been placed
under independent authorities such as the Metropolitan Water
Sewerage and Drainage Board. Independent authorities are
restricted to the specific activity for which they were constituted.
They are run by boards or committees and are responsible to
the government for carrying out their special tasks, but they
appoint their own staff and organize their own finances.

4. Social Changes in the Mid-nineteenth Century

During this period of the settling down of the Municipal
Council of Sydney other social changes had been taking place.

The gold discoveries of the 1850s had brought many new settlers, many of whom drifted back into the cities. The wealth of Australia increased rapidly and the cities were able to buy much more from overseas. While the established house-holders imported better furniture, such as pianos and pictures and fireplaces, and quarrelled about spending on footpaths and sewers and even Universities, the new immigrants were glad to get any sort of roof over their heads. Melbourne changed more than Sydney. There had always been a canvas town in Melbourne where people put themselves up till they gained accommodation in the town or the country. Canvas town rapidly spread and gave a most disorderly air to the orderly city. This "gave a Bohemian air to the whole place which the glitter of its American bars and the rowdyism of its lucky diggers tended still further to exaggerate. Money was quickly made and quickly spent in those days." Melbourne quickly became a much bigger city than Sydney, and it took Sydney fifty years to catch up with her rival of the south.

Another influence which encouraged spending was the Great Exhibition of London in 1851. In a vast "Palace" made of glass panes held in an iron framework, England displayed the innumerable manufactured goods which had displaced hand-made objects, and caught the eye of the householder with very elaborate but comparatively cheap articles. Who would put up with a simple fireplace when he could buy a "richly decorated" cast-iron one? Not only was there much to buy from England, but the time news took to reach Australia was reduced by the coming of the steamer. The first paddle wheel steamer, the *Sophia Jane*, reached Sydney in 1831 after a voyage of five months. All these things encouraged Sydney to shake off her old colonial dress and put on the latest fashion, if only to keep up with Melbourne.

In the 1840s George Street had been macadamized and gas lighting was introduced to private houses. Better sewers were laid down in the main streets and a new area for suburban settlement opened up when the first train line in the Colony, from Sydney to Parramatta, was declared open on 26th September 1855. Sydney's main station was Redfern, where passengers alighted and took a horse-drawn bus to town. The new suburban stations were Newtown, Ashfield and Burwood. Parramatta slowly became swallowed up in the Greater Sydney that was emerging. In the 1860s a tram service was tried in Pitt Street, but it was removed after a public outcry, because it was noisy and dangerous.

From the 1870s on, the population of Sydney has grown by at least 100,000 every ten years. This has been the result of the extension of communications and the growth of the industries of New South Wales. Sydney was linked with Bathurst by 1876 and with Albury on the Victorian border by 1881. By 1889, when the first Hawkesbury Bridge was built, Sydney was joined to Newcastle and the northern train routes and had rail links with every part of the State except the far west. The expanding industries and investments financed great new docks and warehouses.

5. Victorian Style

There was a demand that the simple old colonial buildings should be replaced by large and "well decorated" buildings that befitted the importance of Sydney as the capital of a growing State. St Andrew's Cathedral was completed and St Mary's Cathedral was rebuilt after the smaller earlier Cathedral had been burnt. The G.P.O. was begun in 1865 and finished in 1887. Most ornate of all was the great Town Hall built between 1863 and 1875. Mr Morton Herman says of this building that "there was scarcely a square foot of wall surface on the Town Hall that was not covered with elaborate decoration as the masons' chisels, under the architects' direction, tortured the stones into a multiplicity of fantastic forms. Where elaboration of stone moulding could not be applied, twisted and shaped metal was called into play to give further richness." The Town Hall of 1875 consisted of the vestibule and front office. The large main hall with its pipe organ was built between 1883 and 1888 to celebrate the centenary of the founding of Sydney.

In 1879 an International Exhibition was held. To house the exhibits a large "Palace" of concrete and steel, topped with a dome and lantern 210 feet high, was erected in the Royal Botanic Gardens near Macquarie Street. Fortunately for the beauty of the Gardens, it was burnt out in 1882. But the organization of the exhibition marked an important stage in the growth of the city. The first steam tram ran from Redfern to Hunter Street to cope with the traffic to the Exhibition. To enable construction to continue night and day, the first electrical plant in Sydney was installed and soon demonstrated the value of electric light to Sydney. The sponsors hoped that the Exhibition would encourage trade and industry. The editorial of the *Illustrated Sydney News* stated:

In some measure, the Sydney International Exhibition of 1879 bids fair to do for New South Wales what the London Exhibition of 1851 did for Great Britain. It will furnish a means of testing the industrial skill and excellence of colonial artisans, many of whom, it should be remembered, are natives of the colony or have been resident such a number of years as to practically become unacquainted with the advanced state of the industrial arts in the Mother Country.

Not all looked at the serious side of the exhibition. The *Illustrated News* also asked, "Will the International Exhibition exercise any marked influence on female dress fashions during the coming summer?"

The Exhibition remained open for 32 weeks and the total attendance was about one million. It had shown Sydney people many new machines and products and had aroused great interest in technical education. Many paintings and industrial exhibits were destroyed in the fire and the government was encouraged by the Press and citizens to erect, shortly afterwards, the buildings that now house the Art Gallery of New South Wales and the Museum of Applied Arts and Sciences.

Housing kept pace with the growth of the city. Near the centre of the city great rows of terraces sprang up. They were comparatively easy to build, as all the units were identical. The balconies were supplied with iron balustrades called "lace work" because of their complicated patterns, which showed up against the brown brick or painted cement walls. Those who did not have to live close to their work moved out into the western suburbs or along the new train line that extended north from St Leonards to Hornsby. The architects tried to give these houses and sometimes the terrace blocks as individual an appearance as possible, and so the streets lost their neat uniform appearance as every possible variety of style was tried out. (See Chapter 16, Section 4.)

6. Services and Amenities of the Larger City

The demands on the services of Sydney could not be satisfied. In 1885, for instance, there was only sufficient water in the Botany dams to last the city ten days. Drastic rationing was introduced and the engineering firm of Hudson Brothers rushed through a scheme for laying 1200 30-inch diameter cast-iron pipes from the nearly completed Prospect Reservoir to a wooden aqueduct, which led to the pumping station at Cook's River. The work was done in six months. The city suffered from many other growing pains. Great fires sometimes destroyed crowded city blocks. Minor epidemics were frequent. Industries were set up in residential districts near the city and added to the noise and dust. Redfern railway station proved to be too small for the traffic. This problem was solved later by building the enormous Central station, which was completed in 1904. About the same time the Railways Department pioneered the electric tram services in Sydney. At first they were feeder services to the railways, but by the end of World War I they had become the chief form of mass transportation.

In spite of these and many other problems Sydney was an enjoyable and even exciting city for the ordinary man. Surfing had established itself—though costumes were neck to knee. The esplanade at Manly and a pier at Coogee were only two of many harbour and beach attractions. Racecourses, theatres, sporting clubs and hotels were crowded on Saturdays. Sunday, a quieter day, found many people going to church in the morning and strolling or driving, if they could afford it, in the afternoon. The Domain orators, or the flower beds of Centennial Park and the Gardens, or the ferries, were some of the choices before the rambler. At Easter there was the Agricultural Society's Show. The Society had outgrown its first home near Cleveland Street School and had been granted 42 acres of its present site off Moore Park in 1882. Great halls were set up for animals and agricultural produce, and a crowd of side-shows followed the exhibition from its old site to the new.

7. The Twentieth Century

In the present century Sydney continued to grow, outstripping Melbourne because she was drawing on the resources of a larger State and because she had better supplies of coal near by. The reasons that led to the growth of Sydney in the first place still apply.

As the seat of the New South Wales government, Sydney is the centre for government departments that control railways, roads, law, education, agriculture, and numerous other matters. The pattern of State transport has changed, but Sydney has remained the centre. State coastal shipping has declined because of World War II, silting-up of the rivers, the development of road transport, and the high cost of labour. Many of the ships were requisitioned during the war and the fleets were never restored. Railways continue to carry a large volume of traffic, but for a number of reasons the more flexible systems of motor and air transport are robbing it of its profits. But these new services are just as much based on Sydney, with its port and commercial facilities, as ever the train service was. The market areas of Sydney have expanded, but not enough. The development of industries which took place after both the world wars led to great changes in outer Sydney. Between the wars a vast area stretching from Central railway station to Bunnerong on the shores of Botany Bay was slowly taken over by large factories. Since World War II developments have carried manufacturers to further outposts such as Port Kembla and St Mary's, but these satellites are tied to the city for supplies. As a social centre Sydney is more attractive than ever, having added modern theatres and television to her older entertainments. It is not that other places in New South Wales are without social attractions, but Sydney offers such a variety and in many matters of fashion sets the pace.

8. Planning Growth of the City

The result of all the developments is that the central part of the city, the two miles from Central station to the Quay, has become the nerve centre for the whole State and especially for the vast suburban area. But this vital area, which needed careful planning and control, was and still is under the control of 54 different government authorities. As early as 1906, one J. D. Fitzgerald had complained in a letter that people going to business might be held up "by sundry excavations in the streets caused by any one of the following authorities: the City Council, the Public Works Department, the Gas Light Company, the Hydraulic Company, the Water and Sewerage Board, the Federal Postal Department, or the Railway Commissioners".

In 1945 the government of New South Wales created a new body called the Cumberland County Council to draw up an over-all plan for Sydney. It is as different from the original plan of Governor Phillip's as could be imagined. It cannot be contained on a single map. It covers all land within a 35-mile radius of Sydney G.P.O. and deals not only with land allotments, roads, and buildings, but with a host of interlocking things, for example, power lines, pipe lines, railways and so on. The plan does not say how land shall be opened up, but rather how existing properties and services must be organized. The Professor of Town and Country Planning at the University of Sydney has explained that the plan means three things: co-ordination, consolidation and conservation. Co-ordination involves seeing that homes are placed near shops and schools and transport, or that factory areas are provided with power

lines and roads. Consolidation involves making the best use
of land left as waste in previous development. Conservation
involves preserving and protecting such things as "the fertile
soil, the water reserves, the best scenery and the finest buildings, aboriginal carvings and surfing beaches, native flowers
and useful forests".

The County of Cumberland Plan was drawn up in 1948 and
presented to the Minister for Local Government in the Sydney
Town Hall on 27th July 1948, and the necessary statutes were
enacted in 1951. It has started a large number of arguments
because it has set aside land for parks and roads that private
individuals had planned to use, and because it has suggested
some very costly public works, such as the building of a second
harbour bridge. Under the plan some areas have already been
bought for roads and parks, but the greater part of the plan
belongs to the future.

In the meantime Sydney had been changing its services and
its appearance and its shape.

The first great change of the century was the building of the
Sydney Harbour Bridge between 1924 and 1932. The great arch
makes a leap of almost one-third of a mile and has tied the
North Shore quite securely to the southern part of the city. Along
the train line and roads which it has linked to Sydney large
new suburbs spread quickly, so much so that the makers of the
Cumberland Plan were forced to work out arrangements for a
second bridge. The building of the bridge came almost at the
end of the extension of electric train services which had opened
up areas to the south, south-west and north of Sydney as
suburban areas. Since the war most new transport lines have
been opened up by bus services. Tram services are being
removed from the city because they hold up motor traffic. Not
seen in the city but just as important as the bridge has been
the development of Sydney's fifth great water supply scheme—
the Warragamba dam in the foothills of the Blue Mountains south
of Penrith. The Warragamba dam will store three times as
much water as all the other Sydney reservoirs. The dam should
also help to prevent any serious flooding of the Hawkesbury
River. When there is sufficient water it will be used to generate
hydro-electricity. The main supply of electricity for Sydney
comes from Bunnerong and Pyrmont power stations, and will
continue to do so, but the supply has been strengthened by
connection with the State network and soon will be reinforced
from the three new power stations near Port Kembla, Lithgow

and Newcastle. These new power supplies will help develop the outer Sydney metropolitan area and thus, perhaps unfortunately, make Sydney more than ever the centre of the State.

9. Modern Style

The large buildings of Sydney in the twentieth century are as plain as those of the last century were decorated. After World War I, ten- and twelve-story blocks of flats and offices were put up in the city and at King's Cross. At first the architects did not think that they could look as fine as the older buildings unless they were decorated with pillars on the walls or towers at the top. Gradually it was realized that these decorations were silly as well as useless. The huge size of the buildings, with their uniform rows of windows and their balanced proportions, made them fine enough. After World War II perfectly plain buildings appeared. The whole front was treated as a great window. This was made possible by the invention of the "curtain wall", a large metal frame enclosing many windows. The "curtain" frame fits neatly into the geometrical concrete frame of the whole building. The large new blocks built in this fashion make many of the older buildings look like tiny models. They are so large that although there are only a few of them, they dominate the city and have even made the Harbour Bridge assume its true proportions as a single link of the two parts of a great city rather than the dominant feature.

10. Present Day Expansion

If you look at Sydney from the air, you see how much the city has grown in the last half century. The old centre of the city from Circular Quay to Central Railway station is surrounded by two much wider rings. The first ring is made up of industrial areas and the terrace houses established in the Victorian period. Beyond this ring is an even larger ring of individual houses extending at places to about twenty miles along train and road routes which spread out from the centre like a disorderly spider's web. At places where roads meet, shopping centres are springing up, some of them forming the nucleus of new suburbs which may one day be as well-known as older centres like Parramatta, Redfern or Manly. There is a constant tug-of-war between the suburbs and the city. Shops, clubs, cinemas and other institutions in the suburbs compete with the city institutions. On the whole the city wins on the week days and the suburbs on Saturdays.

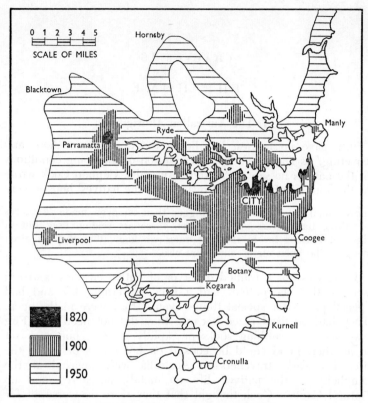

The expansion of Sydney, 1788-1950

The great spread of Sydney suburbs is a luxury, according to some planners, and they are calling on builders to build upwards instead of outwards and upon suppliers to centralize their stores and speed up deliveries. The general development of the 1950s has not followed this advice. It will be interesting to see what happens in the 1960s, especially when one can look back to the past and see what unexpected changes can be brought about by modifications of the available services, building techniques, engineering, and public taste.

CHAPTER 16

THE HOME

1. The Australian Aboriginal

"THEY have no houses, but lie in the open air, without any covering," is Dampier's brief description of the living conditions of the natives he saw in Western Australia. Captain Cook wrote in the Journal of his First Voyage that the natives' houses were

mean small hovels not much bigger than an oven made of pieces of sticks, bark, grass etc. and even these are seldom used but in the wet seasons for in the dry times we know that they as often sleep in the open air as anywhere else.

Cook was not a trained observer of native customs, and did not see that the natives had a fixed pattern of life and had special places for special things even if they were in the open. They had no fixed place because they did not need one. Fire was made by rubbing sticks or rapidly rotating one stick set in another. Food could be cooked on hot stones or under the fire. The early travellers to Australia were amazed at the simplicity of the natives' life—no metals, no stores, and no clothes! Captain Cook thought that they were no worse off for being without and as you have read in Chapter 1, he thought that "in reality they are far happier than we Europeans".

Some people may have agreed with Captain Cook, but no one brought up in England would have dreamt of living like a native and giving up "four walls and a roof" or "three meals and a bed" or any of the other conveniences and comforts of "home" as they knew it.

2. English Homes in the Eighteenth Century

Most of the first settlers in Sydney were not able to live in a home of their own, but the aim of every man who was not a convict was to set up a house as good as or better than the one he had left in England. The first house was built for Governor Phillip, and the officers soon followed his example. English houses provided the standards by which people judged, and so the early houses were as much like their English homes as it was possible to make them in the new country. In eighteenth-century England there were three distinct classes, the rich and the poor and the middle classes. The houses of the rich people were grand and elaborate, and those of the poor were simple and often untidy.

Although the rich had very few modern mechanical aids, they lived comfortable lives. Their houses were divided strictly into two sections, a living area and a service area. The service area was hidden from sight as much as possible. The rich did not want to see the kitchen, the pantry, the stables and the other work-rooms. All these services were placed at the back of the great houses, generally in separate wings. To step from the servants' wing of a great house into the main rooms was like coming into a new world. The main rooms were large and beautifully decorated. The walls carried large paintings, including portraits of their owners. The floors were of polished wood covered with carpets. Furniture was magnificently carved and often made to match the fittings of the house itself, so that the tables, chairs, sofas, picture frames, fireplaces and doors all fitted into the scheme. The principal rooms opened on large hallways, which were often two or three stories high, and had great staircases that were meant to impress the visitors with the importance of the owner. Many servants were needed to keep these great houses in order and to wait upon the master, his family and guests. There were fires to keep the big rooms warm, massive silver table services to keep food hot as it was brought from the distant kitchen, large vases to be filled with flowers. Beyond the house there were gardens and lawns, stables, coach-houses and kennels. Some of the greatest country homes in England needed 800 servants. These were exceptional, but all well-to-do people had servants and did not expect to do any housework at all. No wonder these people did not invent labour-saving household devices.

The ordinary worker lived in a small house or cottage. It generally had one large room in which the family spent most of their time. The central point was the fireplace, which served for cooking and general warmth. The furniture was useful and practical. Copper pots and saucepans hung around the fire, and tables and chairs were placed as near the fire as was convenient. The family slept in attics over the main room or in small rooms opening off the main room.

The middle class lived in small homes with several rooms. They "kept up appearances" like the rich by keeping the living area separate from the service area. They entered their houses from a small hallway, which opened on a parlour (now called a sitting-room) and a dining-room. The kitchen, pantry and scullery were generally hidden behind the staircase, which led from the hall to the bedrooms on the second floor. Even though the middle-class housewife had a servant or two to help, she generally supervised her own kitchen and was responsible for the tidiness of the house. Such homes were comfortable and homely even by modern standards, even though everything was done by hand, from stoking the oven in the kitchen to carrying water basins to the bedrooms. The daughters of the house, who rarely took positions before they married, helped the servants with the work.

As everything in the house was kept going by hard work, and housework was looked upon as drudgery, comfort was obtained by removing oneself as much as possible from work. So the rich made their houses as unlike the work-a-day world as possible. For instance, there were no food cupboards in the main rooms, though there would be a special side-board to hold food and drink before it was served at the dining table. Food brought to the table was "dressed", that is, arranged in beautiful patterns and decorated with jellies or icing. The portraits of the ladies and gentlemen show beautiful white hands that had never done any work, and clothes that were so fine it would be impossible to imagine them in the kitchen. The middle class found it impossible to keep up with the wealthy, but they, too, put on a fine show in the afternoon when work was done and on Sundays when attending church. The men were the first to break away from eighteenth-century fashions and most well-to-do men took to wearing trousers instead of knee breeches after about 1815. The ladies stood firmly by their full-length spreading skirts until World War I, when so many women took on men's work that skirts had to be shortened and petticoats made smaller.

The working classes had very little for show. They sometimes had a parlour with special furniture for special occasions and they generally had a good set of clothes for Sundays and holidays. Their good clothes had to last for twenty years and good furniture was expected to last many lifetimes.

The services which kept the everyday life of the house going were very simple in principle, though they were sometimes very elaborately worked out to meet the needs of the rich. The main services were provision of light and heat, storage, and disposal of waste matters.

Light was provided by oil lamps or candles. Candles were expensive, and the rich displayed their wealth by setting a large number of them together in chandeliers made of many glass lustres which reflected the light and sparkled, while the poor used candles sparingly and, as often as not, used the light of the fire while they sat about and talked or played at night.

Food supplies were difficult to keep, for refrigeration had not been invented. The country people lived off local produce and the city folk went to markets. The birds and animals were generally herded up to town and the arrangements for slaughtering them were primitive. In London you could select your goose alive and the vendor would wring its neck before your eyes. Fish were preserved in salt. In the homes of the rich large storerooms in cool basements held food. In the homes of the poor some food may have been kept in cupboards, but quite frequently flour and vegetables were left standing in bags or bins in the open room, while bacon and onions were tied to the rafters and preserved by the smoke of the fire.

Sanitary arrangements were very poor because people did not know that dirt caused disease. The rich had water-closets, more for avoiding discomfort and smell than for health reasons. It was not legal to empty waste into the drains of London by water flushing until 1815. Most sewers were open drains. Washing too was more for the sake of appearance than health. A hand basin and water jug provided most people with enough water to clean face and hands. Bathing was an upper-class custom and regarded as a luxury. Though some poor folk put out a weekly tub, others avoided it as a sure way of catching a cold.

These were the general housing and living arrangements of the men and women who settled in Australia in the late eighteenth and early nineteenth centuries.

3. Homes in Early Sydney

The homes in early Sydney and in the bush followed the English pattern. The contrast between the rich and the poor was very noticeable. Some of the large houses, such as Vaucluse House, most of which was built by William Charles Wentworth, can still be seen. Its front is made up of large rooms; the bedrooms are upstairs and the service quarters are grouped round courtyards at the rear of the house. On Miller's Point, near the southern approach to the Harbour Bridge, some of the small houses of the 1840s can still be seen, though the worst examples have been pulled down. This area was known as "The Rocks". Small houses were put up close to each other so that the workers would be close to the wharves and stores where they were employed. With so much bush about early Sydney, the builders did not see any reason to keep plenty of open spaces. People chose to live together for company as well as for convenience. Many of the houses built on The Rocks were very poor, scarcely more than four walls and a roof. The area had a bad reputation as a living quarter because there were many taverns in the area, and many birds of passage, sailors and ex-convicts, gathered in the lodging-houses and round the docks. To the north and south of the settlement another sort of house was being developed.

In 1825 one recorder described the new houses:

Generally speaking, the better sort of houses in Sydney are built in the detached cottage style, of white freestone, or of brick plastered and whitewashed, one or two storeys high, with verandahs in front and enclosed by a neat wooden paling, lined occasionally with trim-pruned geranium hedges; they have besides usually a commodius garden backwards, decked out with flowers, and teeming with culinary delicacies. Into the enclosures immediately around the house, the dogs are commonly turned out at nights, to ward off rogues. . . . The streets are wide and unpaved, but their durable composition, and the general dryness of our climate, render paving unnecessary; while an elegant set of lamps placed diagonally at fifty yards distance, by reason of the whiteness of our houses and clearness of our sky, effect an illumination equalling some of the best-lighted London streets.

These early Sydney suburbs set the standard for development. They were a compromise between the crowded tenement houses which had grown up close to the wharves in the heart of the city and large houses built further out by officials, successful graziers and business men. In this early description, the main features of the normal Australian house can be seen —the front fences, the back yard, the small shrubs and vegetable patches and the verandas.

The houses were quite simple inside. The simplest of all had two rooms opening off the front veranda and they had a back door opening on the back yard, with an outhouse for a wash-tub, wood, and odds and ends. Most houses had four rooms opening off a hallway that ran from the front door to the back door. In the country, this sort of house was surrounded with a veranda to give shelter from the heat of summer. The furniture of the houses was simple, too. Plain

The Sydney Post Office, built in the 1830s, predecessor of the present General Post Office.

(From *Sydney in 1848*, by John Fowles
by courtesy of the Mitchell Library)

In the market.

(From the *Illustrated Sydney News*, December 1853)

An early settlers' dwelling. Note the bark roof, and tall chimney to reduce the chance of fire. The design corresponds generally with plan 1 on page 208.

A typical nineteenth-century terrace house.

Brownlow Hill. A well-built colonial home, a development of the design shown in plan 2, page 208.

(From *Architecture* magazine)

A suburban house in Melbourne. This house corresponds generally to plan 4, page 208.

An open house. A modern house, of unconventional design, planned to fit its natural surroundings.

(From *Houses of Australia*, by George Beiers)

Government-built block of 309 flats, Milson's Point, Sydney.

(Australian News and Information Bureau)

Opening of the New South Wales Legislative Council, June 1854.
(From the *Illustrated Sydney News*, June 1854)

The Hustings. A Sydney election in the mid-nineteenth century.
(From the *Illustrated Sydney News*, May 1854)

big wooden beds, with down or horsehair mattresses, wooden tables scrubbed to whiteness, plain chairs and open fireplaces were the usual pieces. Many houses were not even equipped with ovens; the Sunday roast was taken to the baker, who charged a farthing or so to put roasts in the oven. Baking was a necessity in the country cottage, and yet since the kitchen with its fire was a menace to the safety of the house the kitchen was put up a few yards from the house and linked to the veranda by a short covered walk.

The growth of the number of four-roomed houses was very important in improving the outlook of the early colonists. In 1837 a document was sent to the British government pointing out that if a supply of good-hard-working emigrants could be sent to Australia instead of prisoners and fortune hunters, "the landed proprietor might multiply cottages upon his estates". The Colony was becoming economically sound. "Young men, when they had attained skill in their respective callings, might form the same ties which their fathers had formed before them, and seek the domestic comfort which every labouring man should be enabled to enjoy." The report also pointed out that

a family, crowded in single and often narrow apartment, which is to answer at once the ends of parlour, kitchen, bedroom, nursery and hospital must, without great energy and self-respect, want neatness, order and comfort. . . . The decencies of life can be with difficulty observed. The want of neat orderly homes is among the chief evils of the poor.

Every Australian government has been concerned with housing and has seen that ambition and decency are to a certain extent bound up with the right to have a home of one's own. If ideals have not changed much, prices have. A four-roomed house with veranda was built in the 1820s for £75 and the cost of the builder's food and provision for a free convict assistant.

Living in the 1820s was cheap compared with our present prices but in times of scarcity they rose sharply. Top prices in 1826 were:

2 lb loaf	7½d.	1 lb sugar	5d.
1 lb beef	6d.	1 lb tobacco	6s.
1 lb mutton	7d.	1 gal. rum	15s.
1 lb tea	3s.	1 lb soap	1s.

These prices were two or three times the English price. The skilled labourer could just afford to pay, but the unskilled labourer was poorly off. Luxuries, especially imported ones,

o

were expensive. Only the rich could afford to buy pianos and other costly articles of furniture. It took some time for city comforts to spread into the country.

The comfort and usefulness of a house is always limited by its surroundings. If a house is built in the bush, the owner may be able to have timber for his fires, a garden for fresh vegetables and cows to provide fresh milk, but it is difficult to send children to school, to fetch a doctor or even to buy provisions. In the early period of the Colony's growth the town of Sydney was the best place to build a house. It took a great deal of pluck to set up a home beyond the coastal plain around Sydney. Even in the area around the main settlement the provision of services were poor. Commissioner Bigge estimated than only 895 of 7568 children in the Colony were given any sort of education. There was no regular delivery of letters. The State-run hospital had no trained nurses. The story of the development of homes is linked with a steady improvement of these services and many others. Most services were established in the city first and gradually spread to the country.

4. Homes Built Late in the Nineteenth Century

After the gold rushes were over, Sydney and most other towns began to grow rapidly. The country areas were slowly brought into closer touch with the capital cities and the full effect of the great revolutions in industry began to be felt in the ordinary Australian home. The price of homes went up to over £500. £100 had to be spent on furniture and equipment. Every person who could afford it not only wanted "a home of his own", he also wanted a house different from everyone else's. The builder gained more clients by making his houses or terraces "just that little bit different" from every other builder's. This could be done by adding decorations, rich plaster ornaments, cast-iron work, or fretted timber which made the house look like houses of earlier romantic ages or of some European country like Italy. For example, some people wanted their houses to look like "medieval" cottages, with high gables and water spouts carrying carved heads; others wanted "Italian" villas with pillars and plaster statues and little fountains.

Slight variations were made in the ground plans. The most common change in the plan was to advance one of the front rooms and leave only half of the front of the building for the veranda. The veranda became so small in some houses that it was little more than a porch to protect one from the weather while looking for the key to open the front door.

The general appearance of the buildings in the mid-nineteenth century was changed by using brown and black paints instead of whitewash for the walls and ironwork. The new paints stood up to smoke and dust, but modern house-owners do not like the colour brown as much as the Victorian house-owners did; they thought that it was a rich colour and gave brick houses an appearance more like stone. Brick walls were generally covered with cement, which was marked with lines to represent stone blocks and then painted.

In the late nineteenth century most houses were built together as terraces. Near the railway stations in country towns, and for about four miles round the heart of Sydney row after row of terraces sprang up. It was the cheapest way to build because all the fittings were of uniform size. The houses were within easy distance of shops, trains and factories. It was easy to provide them with a common water supply and other services. But the terraces as they were built then had disadvantages. If the fronts were easy to keep tidy, the small garden allotments at the rear were too small for family needs. The central rooms did not have adequate light and air. They did not allow for much privacy. Most of the terraces were rented, and while most tenants kept their homes well, untidy and noisy tenants could easily upset their neighbours.

In the country and the outer suburbs of Sydney individual homes were the rule. North Shore and Western suburbs citizens could use ferry or train services to get to their work in the city, but until the development of trams in the 1880s it did not pay to build houses too far from the city. The extension of suburbs placed heavy demands on the roads and on water, postal, and food supply services. But all these services had to be paid for and only the well-to-do Sydneysider could afford a house with a garden at some distance from the city.

So the numbers of houses grew; the plans changed; the outside appearance changed. But more important were the changes taking place inside the houses. There was much more money about after the 1850s and there were more goods to spend money on. The age of mass production had arrived in England, and some of the importers took up the new styles, while colonial manufacturers adopted the new methods. Here are two advertisements that encouraged the home-lover to furnish or decorate his house in the 1860s: .

Oswald Allen of 360 George Street, Sydney, Artist Photographer, could supply large paper pictures, large vignette heads in monochrome, crayon portraits highly finished and photographic miniatures.

F. Lassetter and Company of 421 George Street, Sydney, were "wholesale, retail and export, ironmongers" and offered to sell, along with building materials and tools,

English, American and Scotch cooking stoves, superior Sheffield cutlery, spoons, forks, dish covers, cruets, tea and breakfast services, tea trays, urns, lamps, bedsteads, baths, toilet sets, etc., etc., and a really beautiful selection of statuettes, lustres, vases, Bohemian glass, and general ornamental ware.

Many articles that had cost a great deal to make by hand and had been possessed by the rich alone became available at a low price to everyone. It was possible to duplicate in cast iron the most elaborate bedsteads, fireplaces, table lamps and even statues. Electroplating made it possible to give a silver finish to metal objects such as coffee services, salt and pepper shakers and light brackets. Steel printing enabled copies of artistic masterpieces to be made in black and white, and photographers offered tinted or plain portraits at a moderate charge. The proud home builder of the period filled his house with the new articles. The plain practical furniture of the earlier colonial period was ignored. Rich dark wallpaper, heavy curtains and blinds and Indian carpet squares provided the background for big chairs and sofas, large sideboards and tables, numerous pictures and knick-knacks. The houses of the period before World War I were "cluttered and fussy", but the cheap and novel articles which manufacturers put into the hands of the home-maker were very welcome then. Most modern home builders prefer simpler articles and useful ones, and the people of today have become used to variety and have learned to choose carefully.

5. Hygiene

Another great advance of the period between 1850 and 1914 was made in hygiene. Before 1850 people avoided extreme dirtiness, smelly sewers and insects because of the discomfort and unpleasantness involved, not because they were un-hygienic. Advances in understanding the causes of disease led to great changes, because the people and governments of the day made war on the invisible enemies that caused disease. Louis Pasteur, a French scientist, discovered that germs caused disease, and Lord Lister, a Scottish doctor, discovered antiseptics, which killed certain types of germs and kept things clean. These discoveries and many others affected hospitals and nursing particularly, but they also had great significance for the home. Bathrooms ceased to be luxuries and became necessities. Greater care was taken to build closed sewers. Sinks were installed in kitchens and washing up with hot water and soap was insisted on.

It is interesting to see how advertisements changed after the introduction of antiseptics. As late as the 1860s advertisers offered to supply "soap and candles of the best quality at the lowest current rates". During the 1870s soap was made as a special and separate item and the word antiseptic became a common one in advertisements. Patent Californian borax was advertised as a "marvellous antiseptic, purifier, and arrester of decay, water softener, etc." Borax was a fairly mild antiseptic, carbolic was used in known infectious cases, and by 1900 other antiseptics were coming into general household use.

The public battle for cleanliness went on till the end of the century. The municipalities were in charge of local building standards. This made it very difficult to get uniformly high standards of sanitation. In the country it was easy to dig large cesspits clear of the house, though country towns were often careless of their provisions and paid the cost in sickness during the hot waterless summer months, when flies and other pests multiplied around unburnt rubbish or uncovered drains. In Sydney, the Press, encouraged by the Institute of Architects, took up the cause and published the facts about unsanitary practices. The Metropolitan Water Sewerage and Drainage Board was formed in Sydney in 1888 with the aim of providing every house in the metropolitan and then the suburban areas with direct water supply and drainage by mains. After many setbacks the inner city area was cleared up in the 1900s. As the suburbs have grown the network of water pipes has extended, but in 1958 more than a quarter of the houses in the Greater Sydney area still had no sewerage mains.

6. Services and Public Utilities

Science and technology were making other great changes by the end of the nineteenth century. New South Wales was fortunate in having good supplies of black coal handy to the coast. From coal, gas for domestic lighting supplies was made. The Australian Gas Light Company was established in 1836. Gas cooking stoves were developed in the 1860s, but were not widely used until the 1880s. The early stoves were made of sheet iron, painted black inside and out. The hot-plate was made of cast iron with large holes pierced through. The stove had no bottom—a drip dish was placed on the floor to gather anything that fell from the stove. About the same time, gas was also applied to fires. The first adjustments were simple and cost only 25 shillings. A single rod played a flame on the fire grate, which was filled with pieces of refractory material that glowed like hot coals. By 1900 gas coppers were being used to boil clothes in the laundry, and gas heaters were installed in bathrooms. Most of these new devices took twenty years to gain acceptance, and when they first appeared they were made to look like the objects they displaced. Not till 1930 did some builders stop building imitative fireplaces and chimneys for gas stoves.

Electricity followed gas. In 1872, nineteen years after the first electric telegraph service in Australia had linked Melbourne with Williamstown, Sydney was linked with London. This link was made possible by building the Overland Telegraph Line between Adelaide and Port Darwin, over 1973 miles of newly explored territory. The telegraph had already made family messages between the capital cities possible. The Overland Telegraph enabled householders to read the day's news from Europe in the newspaper at breakfast. The enthusiasm over this amazing achievement is forgotten in the age of television. Other household wonders soon followed. Public telephone systems were established in the 1880s and the electric light made its appearance. By 1900 fewer than 100 houses in Sydney were supplied, but the principle was well established in cities of Europe and America, and was bound to extend. Fires and flames could be avoided by using electricity. A force of great power could be conducted to any point in the house at the end of a strip of wire. Unlike gas, which had to be carried in cumbersome pipes, electricity could be conveyed cheaply even to houses in the country. No other form of energy has done so much to transform the arrangement of the home.

The Railways Department made use of electricity for lighting at Redfern railway station in 1882. The first electric tram was tried out between Bondi Junction and Waverley in 1889. A Rose Bay to Ocean Street tram line and the North Shore tram line were opened before the end of the century. The tram proved to be a cheap and efficient method of carrying great numbers of people to and from the city and opened up many new suburbs where detached single-story five-roomed houses became the standard dwelling in the twentieth century.

ization. Some were in the
hands of government and municipal authorities, others were run
by public corporations and others were left to private enterprise.
The house-owner had to co-operate by paying bills, caring for
household and public property, voting, and by joining committees
to plan for new hospitals, playgrounds and so on. Every new
convenience called for more planning and more responsibility.

8. The Early Twentieth Century

As the twentieth century advanced, all the new services
became solidly established. Builders and home buyers installed
the new services as the house was built. Electric light was
installed at first in the centre of the room, where the pipe
that supplied the gas jets had been placed. After the 1930s
lights were placed around the walls. In some modern houses
they are concealed in the walls or placed conveniently to
washing-up sinks and dressing tables. The cheaper and faster
methods of mass transportation led to a revolt against terrace
houses. After World War I hundreds of individual houses were
built, most of them as independent houses on small blocks of
about 50 feet by 120 feet. For those who did not want a
garden, blocks of flats were built. Flats were not as private as
houses, but they could share a common hot water service and
other conveniences. Most Australians prefer their own home.
Even in the cities three-quarters of the buildings are houses
standing on their own piece of land and the average number
of rooms for each house is five.

The five-roomed house is the typical Australian dwelling.
Despite the housing shortage, Australia still provides more
homes of this standard per head of population than any other
country. This is a record of which the country may be proud,

but it is a record that needs to be evaluated carefully. Many of the houses are very old and need constant repair. Many of the newer houses are built of flimsy materials, fibro and timber, which also need constant repair. The cost of houses has steadily risen as the price of materials and labour has gone up. By 1914 the average brick cottage cost £1000 and the price has steadily increased since, except in the depression years 1929-35. In 1960 it was about £4000.

The price of furniture and household equipment has also increased greatly. Most people today look on a refrigerator in the kitchen as a necessity. Refrigerators cost at least $200. The ice-chest or water-cooled cabinet of the last century cost about £3 or £4. To enable people to buy expensive articles, the stores provided lay-by systems during the depression and late in the 1930s hire-purchase systems, which provide immediate ownership in return for a guaranteed small weekly sum. The rise in the weekly wage of the worker (see Chapter 14) has enabled all these changes to take place.

9. Servicing Problems

Another problem has been to provide the three kinds of services that were mentioned before, to meet the needs of the new housing areas spreading ever further afield. It is not difficult to extend the system of electric wires, but the generation of sufficient power has called for the construction of costly power stations at Bunnerong and Pyrmont in Sydney as well as at numerous country centres. When coal, used as a fuel for generating electricity, was short because of World War II and industrial trouble, electricity was rationed and at odd times black-outs have reminded the householder that the old candle and kerosene lamp had better be kept handy, just in case they are needed. The development of the Snowy River scheme and the Warragamba dam and the three big new power stations being built will provide most of New South Wales with power for the next twenty years of household expansion. There are other plans to provide alternative lines of supply so that temporary blackouts will not be caused by the breakdown of some of the main supply lines.

Extending water, sewerage and road services to all the housing areas has been more difficult. The subsidiary services are also affected. Since World War II, hardly a day passes but the newspapers report on buildings encroaching on parks or reserved areas, the need for more school accommodation, lack of water for bush fire menaces and the need to decentralize the shopping centres. One typical article in the *Sydney Morning Herald*, 12th August 1958, stated:

Mrs Australia has often been referred to as a pack-horse—and will continue to be so until there are enough regional shopping centres with adequate parking facilities.

In the 1960s, about 75,000 houses are completed each year and many regional shopping centres have been built.

10. Development of Plan and Design

The plans of the houses of the twentieth century have changed even more rapidly than those of the nineteenth century. Most new houses have done away with the veranda and the hall. The nineteenth-century habit of sitting out on the veranda has largely died out. Young people prefer to be out of doors, and many families drive out in the car on the Sunday afternoon or in the evening. The verandas of older houses have been turned into rooms. The hall was rarely used and the valuable space it occupied is now often added to the main living-room.

The most revolutionary change has been in the conception of the relation between living and service areas. As work has been simplified in the house by use of such aids as electric cleaners and irons, and as the electric or gas stove has done away with messy wood or coal stoves, there has been less need to shut away the service area from the living quarters. In the 1920s the dining-room was left open to the kitchen and since 1940 the dining-room has often been made an extension of the living-room, with the kitchen placed in a recess or elbow bend off the main room. The design of kitchen material has made many of the articles attractive and simple, so that there is no need to put the work-a-day objects out of sight. The gleaming enamel stove, plastic containers and plain earthenware plates match the new wireless set and dining table. Broom, dusters and cleaning materials are stored out of sight in plain wall-set cupboards. The housewife can listen to the wireless or keep in touch with the family if the rooms are continuous or made into one. Not all homes are built on such an open plan, because most people still prefer to keep separate areas, but the necessity for division is decreasing. In the 1930s a famous French architect, Le Corbusier, described this new kind of house that was emerging as "a machine to live in". Though many people disagree with him, the services available in the modern house

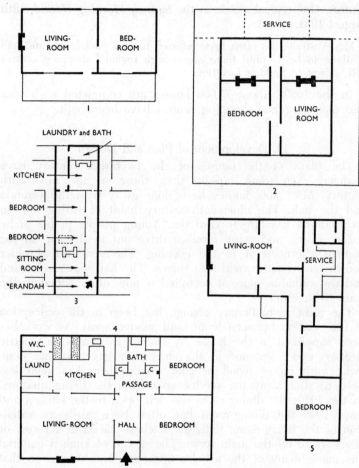

Ground plans of typical Australian houses

1. Simple form of an early home.
2. A four-roomed house—a common development of the type shown in plan 1.
3. Plan of terrace house.
4. Plan of a typical twentieth-century house.
5. The L-shaped house, a common variant of plan 4.

certainly make it a complicated arrangement of mechanical devices and the older plans with set rooms for definite purposes are giving way to plans which make special arrangements for the activities of the owners.

Work which was once a drudgery has become much simpler. Since World War II, washing machines have begun to displace hand washing; floor scrubbing is done by machine, or wall-to-

wall carpets are cleaned with a vacuum cleaner; cooking has
been slightly reduced by specially prepared foods, the tiling
of bathroom walls and the use of showers have cut down the
maintenance necessary in bathrooms. The housewife has been
freed from an unending task and has the wireless or television
set and telephone to keep her in touch with the outside world.

The outside appearance of the house has changed greatly.
After 1915 a new feature was often added to houses, the
garage. The family car was placed in a unit built beside the
house or in the basement, or under an open car port. But
now many homes make proper provision for a car and do not
add a garage as an afterthought. The house front is neater
now that eaves under the roofs are boxed in, pipes and wires
are concealed within the walls, wherever possible, and all
fittings are made flush with the walls. Ornaments on modern
houses are small and sometimes have a useful purpose. Garden
lights, house numbers or iron frames for fly-proof wire netted
doors are made fairly ornate to break the plain brick wall and
windows. The size of windows has increased as the century
has gone on. In the last century the idea was to shut the climate
and garden out of the house. More recent houses protect windows
from the direct glare of the summer sun, but make them almost
as large as the wall to take in as much of the view as possible.

Materials and designs for houses have changed so frequently
that in spite of the plainness of the fronts of the houses there
is no uniformity about the twentieth-century street. One house
will be built of yellow brick and the next of red, and the next
may be of white rough-cast stucco. The most noticeable differences are brought about by the use of coloured paint. The age
of almost uniform brown changed about the time of World
War I to brighter colours and then to two-tone painting, such
as cream and green. This preference gave way to pastel colours,
pale pinks and blues, and the present decade has added taste
for bright new shades with unusual trade names. All these differences add variety and interest to suburbs, and though some
houses are unpleasantly bright, grass lawns, shrubs and creepers
help to soften the lines and give a pleasant air to an otherwise
box-like series of dwellings.

The five-roomed house is the main form of the century. The
large house of twenty rooms or more is now rare. Most of the
large old homes are used as hospitals or schools; some are broken
up into separate flats; some have become boarding-houses. Large
houses cost too much to maintain without servants and very

few can afford, or want, servants these days. At the other end of the scale we have temporary huts and camps, especially migrant hostels and temporary housing camps. There has been much agitation to improve these living quarters. But even these camps are better than the humpies and canvas towns of the last century. Moreover, the State takes much of the responsibility for trying to improve the conditions in them. The story of housing is a story of rebuilding, extension and servicing, and there will always be a housing problem to be met.

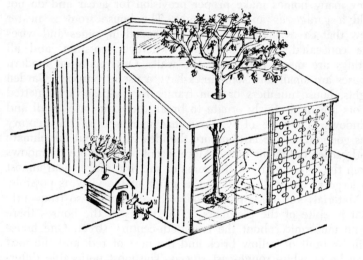

Bringing the garden into the home
(By courtesy of the *Bulletin*, 18th September, 1965)

1788-1855

SOCIAL

1796	Discovery of coal at Newcastle.
1797	Introduction of Merino sheep.
1803	First Australian wool sent to England.
1815	First road built across the Blue Mountains to Bathurst.
	First steam engine set up in Australia.
1828	Masters and Servants Act regulated conditions of employment.
1831	First steamship came to Australia.
1840	Transportation of convicts to N.S.W. ceased.
1843	Ridley's stripper used in S.A.
1851	Gold discovered in N.S.W. and Vic.
1855	Sydney to Parramatta railway.

GOVERNMENT

1788	Governor Phillip established the Colony.
1803	First settlement in Tasmania.
1809–1821	Lachlan Macquarie, Governor.
1823	First Legislative Council of N.S.W.
1829	First settlement at Swan River (W.A.).
1835	Foundation of Melbourne (Vic.).
1836	Foundation of Adelaide (S.A.).
1842	Act establishing representation in Legislative Council of N.S.W.
1852	Transportation of convicts to Tasmania ceased.
1855	Act establishing responsible government in four States.

Date lines, 1788-1855

1856-1900

GOVERNMENT

1856   First responsible legislatures met in N.S.W., Vic., Tas., and S.A.

1858   Manhood suffrage and secret ballot introduced into N.S.W.

1859   Queensland separated from N.S.W.

1889   Payment of members of Legislative Assembly of N.S.W. introduced.

1891   Federation Convention. Labour Electoral League in N.S.W. established basis of parliamentary Labour party.

1894   S.A. granted votes to women.

1897   Further Federal Convention met.

1900   Commonwealth of Australia Act.

SOCIAL

1856   Builders' Eight Hour Day in Melbourne established.

1858   Telegraph linked Sydney, Melbourne, and Adelaide.

1861   Two Land Acts passed in N.S.W. opened the way for selection of land lots.

1866   Public Schools Act set up universal education in N.S.W.

1872   Transcontinental telegraph completed.

1873   Victorian legislature passed first Factory Act.

1876   Sydney to Bathurst railway completed.

1879   Roseworthy Agricultural College established in S.A.

1880   First cargo of frozen meat sent to London.

1883   Sydney linked to Melbourne by railway.

1855   Formation of Broken Hill Proprietary Company Limited.

1900   Old Age Pensions Act (N.S.W.).

Date lines, 1856-1900

PART III

ACHIEVEMENTS IN GOVERNMENT
AND SOCIETY 1788-1900

Spring fashions in the 1870s.

(From the *Illustrated Sydney News*, October 1871)

A cooking class in Melbourne, 1875.
(From the *Illustrated Sydney News*, October 1875)

The Melbourne bicycle club's opening meet, 1878.
(From the *Illustrated Sydney News*, 1878)

A surgeon's hut in the bush.
(From the *Illustrated Sydney News*, June 1871)

Fishing in Port Jackson, 1878.
(From the *Illustrated Sydney News*, September 1878)

Holtermann's house, North Sydney. A typical ornate house built by a successful miner. Holtermann is most famous as a photographer.
(From the *Illustrated Sydney News*, December 1875)

The School of Industry Ball, 1875.
(From the *Illustrated Sydney News*, July 1875)

CHAPTER 17

THE ACHIEVEMENT
OF RESPONSIBLE GOVERNMENT

1. Autocratic Governors

ONE man was in charge of all matters when Australia was founded. His title was Governor of New South Wales. His commission from King George III stated:

> You are therefore carefully and diligently to discharge the duty of Governor in and over our said territory by doing and performing all and all manner of things thereunto belonging, and we do hereby strictly charge and command all our officers and soldiers who shall be employed within our said territory, and all others whom it may concern, to obey you as our Governor thereof.

Governor Phillip was responsible for everything in the Colony, for the food which everyone could eat, for the work to be done and for the conduct that all should observe. Such absolute power was necessary if the penal colony was to survive in the trying conditions of far-off Australia. The need for the government to provide help and direction for the settlers continued for a long time and made government in Australia rather different from the government of Great Britain.

The government of New South Wales was not a simple autocracy, the rule of one man. Behind the governor stood the government of Great Britain. Phillip's commission went on to state:

> You are to observe and follow such orders and directions from time to time as you shall receive from us, or any other of your superior officers according to the rules and discipline of war, and likewise such orders and directions as we shall send you under our signet or sign manual, or by our High Treasurer or Commissioners of our Treasury for the time being, or one of our Principal Secretaries of State, in pursuance of the trust we hereby repose in you.

So the early governors looked upon themselves as agents of the British government. As they received instructions from the home government, they had to send back clear and accurate reports so that their instructions would fit the situation. Each

P

report took many months to reach London and many months to return. The governors were not the only persons making requests or presenting points of view to the British government; the free settlers and even officials sent letters home or even made special trips to present their views.

2. Rights of Citizens in a Penal Colony

The form of government that was first set up in Australia was regarded as a special case and not as the normal government that British citizens should enjoy. If free citizens chose to live in a penal colony they did so at their own risk. Although colonists complained against the governors' actions, on the whole the settlers accepted the strong rule as a necessity. The well-to-do free settlers employed convicts as servants, and relied upon the government to keep order, build roads, supply stores and provide many other services. The free settlers did not want to meet ex-convicts, or "emancipists", socially and so they earned the title of "exclusives". They looked upon themselves as the "pure merinos" and upon the emancipists as the "black sheep" of the Colony. The political struggle between the two groups began under Macquarie and continued until the 1840s, when the leaders of the two groups gave up the struggle in the face of new and more important issues. As long as the division lasted, it was difficult for the colonists to work together to gain a more democratic form of government. Each party was frightened that if the governor's powers were reduced, power would fall into the other's hands.

3. Limiting the Governor's Power

However, the governors' powers had to be reduced and the ties with Great Britain had to be loosened. During Macquarie's rule, a Supreme Court was set up, and Judge Bent tried to prevent its sitting because he objected to emancipists appearing as attorneys. One man actually questioned the power of the governor to make laws that were binding on citizens and the lawyers were not able to speak definitely on the matter. Towards the end of Macquarie's term of office the British government sent out a special commissioner J. T. Bigge, to enquire into the government of New South Wales. One of the reasons for sending the commissioner was stated thus:

The Settlers feel a Repugnance to submit to the enforcement of regulations which, necessarily partaking much of the Nature of Rules applicable to a Penitentiary, interfere materially with the exercise of those rights which they enjoyed in this Country, and to which as

British Subjects they conceive themselves entitled in every part of His Majesty's Dominions.

The rights that were enjoyed in the other colonies were the right to trial by jury and the right to be consulted on laws of local interest. It is noticeable that the British government did not deny these rights in principle but took them for granted, merely inquiring to discover if it was advisable to apply them to New South Wales. The right of anyone to be tried by twelve of his equals had been established in England for centuries, but the question was whether the government could rely on the juries to give honest verdicts when so many of the prospective jurors were ex-convicts or related to them. As late as 1837 some well-to-do citizens claimed that "the sympathies of the numerical majority of the inhabitants are in favour of the criminals, whom they would rather screen from punishment, than deliver over to justice". Even if this statement was exaggerated it was difficult to set up a jury system or to have an elected body of citizens to advise the governor.

4. The First Legislative Council

But in 1823 the British government conceded some of these demands. Trial by jury was allowed for civil cases, though a military court still heard criminal charges; a Legislative Council was set up to advise the governor, but its members (seven in number) were to be appointed (nominated) by the government.

The council could make laws, but its powers were severely restricted. The governor laid the business before it, and if he thought that a law was essential for "peace and safety", he could enforce it against the wishes of the majority of the Council. On the other hand, councillors who dissented from bills could record the reasons. The laws which were passed by the Council were not effective until the Chief Justice certified that they were "consistent with the laws of England so far as the circumstances of the Colony will permit". Although the law could be enforced in Australia it still had to be sent to the British government for approval. A separate council was set up for Van Diemen's Land (Tasmania), which became in effect a separate Colony.

5. Representation Claimed

Almost immediately, the citizens of New South Wales demanded more rights. They claimed that the governor had too much power and that the Council did not represent them.

They appealed to the principle "taxation by Representation", which has been so important in English history. It had been one of the main claims of Parliament in its struggle against the Stuart kings in the seventeenth century, and it had been one of the main claims of the American colonists in the struggle that finally led to the setting up of the United States as a completely independent and republican State after 1783. The colonists did not wish for the complete independence that complete control of taxation implies, but they did want much more say in their own affairs. As the number of free citizens increased, the demands became stronger, so that within thirty years of the establishment of the advisory Legislative Council, self-government was established in New South Wales.

How did Britain regard the growth of this independence? The War of American Independence had taught her a lesson. Most people, including the members of the British government, thought that eventually all the Colonies would drift away from the mother country. No major war would ever be fought on that issue again. In the meantime the Colonies were part of the British Empire: Britain owed them sound administration and defence, and they in turn had to share in the expense of administration and render Britain what service they could. A special claim that Britain made was that the land in the Colonies that had not been taken up by settlement belonged to the Crown and was available to the British people. British ships had opened the way to the Colonies and the British navy had defended these lands from occupation by other powers. Therefore the revenue from land sales belonged to the Crown and should largely be used to help British settlers. In Australia, especially, the land had been developed by convict labour, and the settlers owed even more to the British government. Provided that the rights of the home government in matters of land, defence, foreign policy and costs of administration were respected, the government was willing to grant as much colonial self-government as the colonists were able to undertake for themselves.

Thus in 1828, only four years after the first Councils were opened, the Legislative Councils in New South Wales and Van Diemen's Land were enlarged to fifteen members, and the members were given the right to bring proposals forward themselves. The governor could refuse to present any proposal to the Council, but he had to record the proposal and his reasons for refusing to allow it. When Lieutenant-Governor

Stirling was appointed in 1828 to take charge of the new free settlement in Western Australia, he was given instructions which reveal the British government's attitude to a settlement that was not yet worried by the convict problem:

> You will endeavour to settle with the consent of the parties concerned a Court of Arbitration for the decision of such questions of Civil right as may arise between the early Settlers and until a more regular form of administering Justice can be organized.

Western Australia and South Australia were granted Legislative Councils soon after they were founded, and South Australia was promised more self-government as soon as the population reached 50,000.

6. Reform in Great Britain

This generosity of the British government was partly the result of great changes in England. You have seen in Chapters 10 and 13 how the pattern of industry in England had changed. As the industries had moved the population had moved too. Large new cities had grown up and old towns had practically ceased to exist and yet the electorates had not been changed. As ownership of property gave a man the right to vote, in some districts a small group of men dominated the voting and the rich and conservative land-owners dominated Parliament. In 1832, after many years of political struggle, a Reform Act changed the electoral districts in England. Many of the small electorates were abolished and some new towns were given representation. Some new voters were added to the electoral roll, but most people did not gain the right to vote, because the new Act retained property ownership as the essential qualification for that right. In the cities, the voter had to own a house or rent one that was worth £10 a year, and there were more complicated arrangements for the country. There were many reasons for not allowing more people to vote. The rich were frightened that the poor would use the vote against the existing order. They claimed that the poor were not educated to understand issues of government and that they paid too little in taxes to have a say in government expenditure. Nevertheless, the principle of the right to representation in Parliament was granted and the domination of Parliament by a small upper class was broken. Later in the century two further Acts extended the right to vote to most British male adults.

Closely linked to this reform movement was a new colonial reform movement which saw that the British Colonies were a necessary support to the growing power of Britain. The Colonies need not be a burden to the mother country, but friendly semi-independent States, sharing a common way of life with their founder. The surplus population of Great Britain could find a new home in these Colonies and, as they would mainly be agricultural societies, they would be able to supply Britain with raw materials such as wool and in return buy British manufactured products. By systematic colonization of new lands and friendly dealings with established Colonies, England would build a new Empire.

7. Canada

In 1837 there were armed disturbances in Canada, when the British governor threatened to dissolve the Legislative Assemblies which were elected by the Canadians in the two Provinces of Upper and Lower Canada (Ontario and Quebec), because they would not vote the money needed by the executive, the governor and his officials. Lord Durham was sent to Canada to quell the troubles and report on the situation. This Lord Durham did. His methods were prompt but high-handed, and when he was attacked in the British Parliament he resigned and returned to England scarcely six months after he had set out. With the aid of two colonial reformers who had accompanied him on his mission, he drew up a report in which he advocated uniting Upper and Lower Canada and, more important, giving to Canadian ministers responsibility for Canadian affairs. The two provinces were united, though Lower Canada was French-speaking and Upper Canada English-speaking, and neither wished to be united to the other. During the next ten years, with the assistance of a co-operative governor-general, the Canadian ministers took charge of the administration. It was not an easy process, particularly when the Liberal party, which was not too friendly to British interests, gained a majority in the elected Legislative Assembly, but it worked out in the end. Canada demonstrated that responsible government was possible and that Colonies did not have to break away from Britain forcibly, as the United States had done, in order to gain freedom of action. The idea that the ministers of the Crown should be selected from the party which holds the support of the majority of the elected representatives of the nation had only been established in Britain the previous century. The Canadian experiment showed that the British idea was sound and that the principles of parliamentary government could and should be applied in the Colonies when the elected representatives in the

Assemblies had strong and capable backing. Parties with capable leaders who do not control the administration make trouble for the administration and criticize unfairly. If they have to run the administration themselves and find the money for it, criticism becomes practical and constructive or the party loses power. More than that, the Canadian legislators found that they still needed help from Britain in financial, military and other matters and so co-operation and friendly negotiation replaced the older contentions.

8. Work of the Legislative Council

Meanwhile, in Australia, the Legislative Council of New South Wales was getting a grip upon local affairs. The Council was a very conservative body because all its members were officials and well-to-do citizens nominated by the Crown. It regulated working conditions in favour of employers (see Chapter 14), gave many grants to the churches of all denominations for church buildings and the salaries of the clergy, gave state aid to the schools run by the different denominations, and made regulations for land settlement; but it accepted trial by jury in criminal as well as civil cases, subsidized migration schemes, and discussed the working of the transportation system, though wanting it to continue. Many other issues were debated within the Council and outside it. Political groups became stronger and even though their demands were not met by the governor or the British government, party development prepared the way for self-government. Trade delegates began to put the views of the workers before public meetings. The "exclusives", who supported the established order while it provided them with cheap convict labour and guaranteed their land holdings, started petitioning for self-government when they saw that their interests in these matters were challenged. They were joined by the leaders of the "emancipists", who now wanted to protect landed interests too. Together they hoped to get control of government before the town merchants and workmen became strong politically.

Another important influence awakening people to political issues was the Press. In 1840 when the *Sydney Herald* (later the *Sydney Morning Herald*) became a daily, there were about ten newspapers in the Colony. The *Herald* proclaimed in its first editorial of 18th April 1831:

Whilst we are bound to respect Government, we are entitled to be independent in thought and speech. When these measures are evidently devised and executed for the general welfare, we shall promote and recommend them. When they are of questionable character, or work evil, we shall neither fear nor refuse to state our sentiments. . . .

The governments often found the newspapers troublesome and some of their articles unfair, but they did keep the small reading public in touch with British politics and discussed the activities of the Legislative Councils and governors vigorously. Their freedom to publish was defended by the courts on the ground that English law upheld freedom of the Press.

9. Representation Granted

In 1842, ten years after the famous English Reform Act, Australians were granted their first representative system. The Legislative Council was reconstituted. There were to be 24 elected members in the Council along with 12 other nominated members. As the English Act had stressed property qualifications for voters, so the Australian regulations stated that voters had to own a freehold property worth £200 or pay rent of at least £20. These were quite high qualifications for those days, and restricted the number of voters greatly. The electorates favoured the squatters, for Sydney was granted fewer representatives than its population warranted. The power of the squatters was so obvious and used so openly that their opponents, who agreed with them in demanding responsible government for New South Wales, became even more insistent that the vote should be extended to all citizens.

Another group of citizens who were disappointed with the Bill were the residents of the Port Phillip District, who claimed that it was difficult for their six representatives to attend council meetings in Sydney and that the revenue for their land was used to benefit the older Colony. Residents south of the Murray River protested without ceasing against the injustice until they were given a separate administration in 1850.

10. Responsible Government Demanded

It was obvious from the first that the Act of 1842 was not permanent. The elected representatives could not control the officials who carried out the laws they made. The governor was still the head of the executive and he was appointed by the British government. Moreover, the governor had wide powers; he could dissolve the Council and withhold consent from any Bill until it had been submitted to the British government. Such a system led to delays and lengthy correspondence between Britain and Australia. The colonists, therefore, made strong demands for responsible government.

The English government agreed to this in principle and called on the Legislative Councils in the Colonies to consider the broad issues of government involved. If New South Wales and the other Colonies were to be effectively governed, a wide plan should be prepared first to strengthen local government, second to create two houses in each Colony to discuss legislation, and third to establish some system of inter-colonial co-operation. The New South Wales Legislative Council replied that the setting up of district councils in the rural districts would be too expensive, as the districts were too large and the population scattered. It also thought that if an inter-colonial council was to be set up, New South Wales should be given a leading place in it because of her wealth and population. As the other Colonies feared this very predominance, no agreement was ever reached on the issue. What remained, according to the New South Wales Legislative Council, was the urgent need for responsible government in the Colony, and the right of the Colony to have some say in the conditions of self-government.

To meet some of the claims of the Colonies, the British government passed the British Colonies Government Act in 1850. Victoria was made a separate Colony from New South Wales. The four Colonies, New South Wales, Victoria, Tasmania and South Australia, were put on much the same basis. Two-thirds of the members of Legislative Councils were to be elected. The property qualifications for voters were lowered. The Councils were given a fair amount of control over finance and customs. They were encouraged to create a "House of Representatives" in addition to the Legislative Councils and to propose amendments to the Constitution Act. But they were not granted control of the executive or given the right to dispose of Crown lands, and these were the issues that concerned Councils most. In New South Wales the Legislative Council drew up an emphatic remonstrance and looked about for effective means of forcing the British government to grant their demands. In 1852 the Legislative Council of New South Wales decided not to grant supplies for the government in future. The British government did not allow the situation to get worse: the control of Crown lands was placed in the hands of the Legislative Councils and they were asked to draw up proposals for new constitutions.

11. Responsible Government Granted

The Legislative Council of New South Wales drew up its constitutional recommendations in 1853. The Council, whose tactics had won the concession of responsible government, was determined to maintain political supremacy for the squatters. The legislature was to consist of two Houses. The Lower House, the Legislative Assembly, was to be elected. The members of the Upper House, the Legislative Council, were to be appointed by the governor on the advice of the Executive Council. The Assembly was to be of 54 members, the Council of at least 21. The electoral boundaries were to be, as before, on the basis of population and interests, and this meant that the agricultural and pastoral districts were given more seats in proportion to the population than were the town districts. Property qualifications for voters were retained. "Balancing houses and lands, or sheep and cattle, against human beings," cried opponents of the proposals—in vain. Their only success was the rejection of a proposal to create an Australian peerage like the nobility of Great Britain to sit in the Legislative Council. The other States mainly followed this example and the various constitutional bills were forwarded to the British government.

Since the constitutional issue had been raised, Australia had changed rapidly. The gold discoveries (see Chapter 8) had increased the population and wealth of Victoria and New South Wales. The Colonies could well afford to administer their own territories. The growth of population had increased the number of problems facing the governors and there was no doubt that many of the problems were best handled by the colonists themselves. The English government made few alterations in the arrangements concerning the legislatures. However, the British government did indicate that there were a number of matters which should still be referred to the home government by the governors, such as laws affecting marriage and divorce, military discipline, and foreign policy. Very few Acts passed by the colonial Parliaments were overruled by the British government, and by 1900 the right of veto was hardly ever used. Queen Victoria signed the Constitution Act on 21st July 1855.

The four Australian Colonies then had to prepare themselves for self-government. The broad issues were understood but the details had to be worked out. The *Sydney Morning Herald* discussed the future of the governor-general:

The Governor-General has before him, if he retains office during the usual term, a long administrative career. The political changes anticipated will, however, give him Ministers. These Ministers will mould the policy and direct the measures of the Government. To enable them to do so, however, in harmony with the views of the constituency, or at least with the representatives, they, and not the Governor-General, will decide what work shall be undertaken,

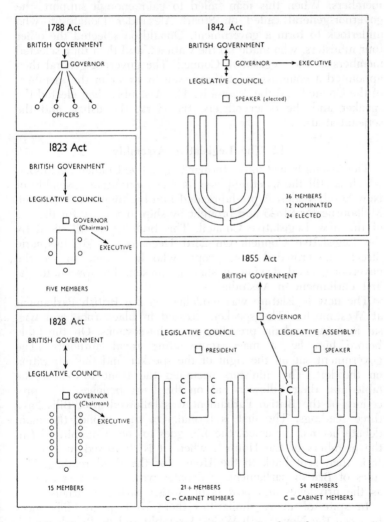

The evolution of government in New South Wales,
a diagrammatic representation

what offices retained, what taxes levied, and what public works accomplished.

The governor-general and the retiring Council prepared the way for the new responsible government. The elections were held and then the governor-general sent for the leader who he thought would have the support of the newly elected members. When this man failed to gain enough support, the governor-general called on Stuart Alexander Donaldson who undertook to form a government. Donaldson selected the other four ministers, who made up the Cabinet, and then they selected members of the Legislative Council. The governor-general then appointed a commission of three men to swear in the members of the Council and the Assembly. The Assembly then elected the speaker and the other officers, the clerk, the usher, and the serjeant-at-arms.

12. The Legislative Assembly

The Assembly met in the former Legislative Council's chamber, which is still the meeting-place for the Legislative Assembly of New South Wales. A pre-fabricated iron building was bought in Melbourne for £1835 and brought by ship to Sydney for the use of the new Legislative Council. This building is still used by the Legislative Council. On 23rd December 1856 Macquarie Street was crowded with people who had come to see the governor-general driving in state to present his speech to the first Parliament in Australia.

The new legislature was modelled on the British Parliament at Westminster. The speaker, dressed in black robe and wig, sat in a great chair, presiding over the sessions. On the table before him lay a mace representing royal authority. The government sat on the right of the speaker and the opposition on the left. The ministers occupied the front row near the table and their followers sat on the back benches. The procedure of the British Parliament was followed also. Bills have three readings. The first is formal. On the second, the main debate occurs. If passed, the Bill goes to the "Committee" (all the members of the House), where it is discussed by clauses. It is then sent back to the House for the third reading. The rules of British parliamentary debates were taken over as well as the privileges and powers of British parliamentarians.

In spite of many similarities there were many differences between the New South Wales Assembly and its British model. The Legislative Assembly was small and the standard of debate was poor. Members took a long time to master the difficulties of debate. Here is the *Sydney Morning Herald* report of part of a debate which shows the imitative nature and the weakness of the early Parliament:

Mr. Plunkett rose to a point of order. He put it to the honourable member if he felt justified in departing from the usual course, and reading a letter from the representative of the Queen. The name of the Queen or King is never named in the House.

Mr. Darvall said the Queen's name was frequently used in explanation in the House of Commons.

Mr. Donaldson said he had seen the Governor-General then.

Mr. Piddington said he felt convinced the hon. gentleman would not take the liberty to read such a letter unless he had the authority of the Governor-General. But I will again put it to the honourable gentleman in principle, whether it is right and constitutional to make use of the name of the representative of her Majesty to sway the opinions of the House.

Mr. Macarthur said he had been present in the House of Commons, when letters of a similar description to that alluded to by the honourable friend had been read. He also referred honourable members to *Hansard's* Debates.

Lack of experience in debate was matched by lack of experience of administration. Shortly after the new ministry took over its duties, the governor-general appealed to the former colonial secretary:

It is obvious that until some distinct and positive duties are allotted to each member of the Government, the term responsible government will be but a name. . . . I come now therefore to you with a request that you give me an outline of your views as to the distribution of the general business of the Government among the officers who will be responsible for it.

In reply it was pointed out:

It is assumed that the Ministers will direct those large measures of general policy for the promotion of which they have undertaken the labours and responsibilities of office, rather than the details, which will more appropriately devolve on the Heads of Department respectively placed under them. To prevent inconvenience, however, to the public service, there must be attached to each Minister a permanent Under Secretary and clerical staff; so that, on the assumption of office by any new Minister, the Department may continue to be conducted with due regularity. And this is how government business was conducted from then on.

The parties in the Legislative Assembly were ill-organized.

The first New South Wales government lost its supporters in a few months and several ministries succeeded each other rapidly. Gradually strong political leaders emerged, but for many years the parties had no fixed political programmes.

Personal leadership was far more important than party policy until the Labour party began to emerge at the end of the century. Labour demanded that its representatives in Parliament follow party decisions strictly. Labour made more radical demands than the two earlier parties because it stood for employee interests rather than for those of the employer, and this was a more fundamental division than had existed between the older parties.

13. Voting Rights

In the early party struggles several important constitutional reforms were made. Most Colonies removed the property qualifications for voters. These qualifications were difficult to prove and record. As prices changed, rents changed and the minimum qualification of six months' occupancy of a lodging worth £10 per annum was not so difficult to attain. About the same time as all men gained the right to vote, the Colonies introduced the secret ballot. It was seen that the vote of the employee was not genuine if he had to declare his vote publicly before his employer, who could take reprisals. On other occasions the mob could intimidate voters. One of the amusing and frequent faults of the open declaration system was that the candidates offered free drinks and food to their supporters and the elections turned into carnivals. Still, many conservatives supported the open voting system as "manly" and denounced the secret ballot as "furtive".

Australia was the first country in the Empire to use the secret ballot and other countries referred to it as the "Victorian" or "Australian ballot" until it was put into practice everywhere. One of the privileges accompanying the right to a free and equal vote for all was the right of any man to stand for Parliament. The conservatives found that they could grant this right because no working man could really afford to stand for Parliament unless his friends joined in to help him. Not till thirty years later, when the expense of serving in Parliament was a burden to all parties and no real hindrance to working-men's organizations which supported their representative, did the Parliament reimburse members for their expenses. By the end of the century all Colonies paid members for their attendance in the Assemblies and the last barrier restricting the working-man's entry to Parliament disappeared, in theory at least.

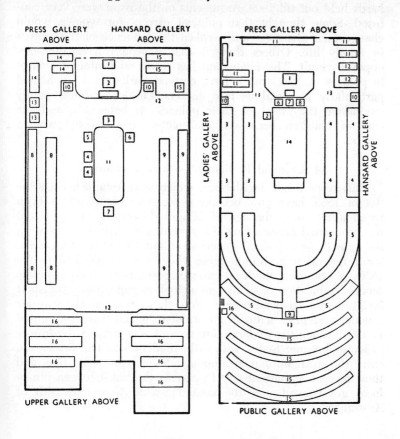

Houses of Parliament, New South Wales, 1960

Legislative Council Chamber: 1. Governor's Chair 2. Mr President 3. Chairman of Committees 4. Ministers 5. Clerk of the Parliaments 6. Clerk-Assistant 7. Usher of the Black Rod 8. Members usually supporting the Government 9. Members usually supporting the Opposition 10. Attendants 11. Table of the House 12. Bar of the House 13. Legal Officers 14. Private Secretaries and other Officials 15. President's Reserve 16. Lower Gallery
Legislative Assembly Chamber: 1. Mr Speaker 2. Minister in charge of the House 3. Government Benches 4. Opposition Benches 5. Cross Benches 6. Clerk of the Legislative Assembly 7. Clerk-Assistant 8. Second Clerk-Assistant 9. Serjeant-at-Arms 10. Attendants 11. Officials 12. Benches reserved for Members of the Legislative Council 13. Bar of the House 14. Table of the House 15. Speaker's Gallery 16. Speaker's Gallery Attendant

Just about 1900 most Colonies extended the franchise to women. South Australia led the way in 1894 and Victorian die-hards held out till 1909. Arguments on the issue were very confused. Some thought that political careers for women would change their character and weaken the influence of the mother in family life. Others thought that it would have the very opposite result. The innovation has made no profound change in politics. A few women have entered Parliament and helped particularly in social welfare matters. Politicians quite rightly emphasize the effect of their policies on home life and the care of children because these matters concern the women voters.

14. Colonial Parliaments—State Parliaments

Thus responsibile legislatures, which were established by the Act of 1855, have now become democratic organizations open to all adults over the age of 21 and do not merely represent the propertied classes. Colonial governments may have held up the growth of a federal government but there was little need for a federal organization when they were established in the 1850s. By building the local bases of government, such as public service, education systems, municipal organizations, transport facilities and financial organization, they prepared the way for a wider system of national government, which was inaugurated in 1901. When the Federal Government was created the former Colonies became States within the Federation. The States still carry the main burden of administration in the federation, and thus have an important role to play as the link between purely local government and the continent-wide Commonwealth of Australia.

Martin Place, Sydney, in 1910.

(From *Sydney Looks Back*, by Isadore Brodsky)

W. C. RENWICK,
GENERAL DRAPER, &c
86 KING STREET.

W C. R. has the pleasure to inform ladies in town, suburbs, surrounding districts, and the interior, he has issued an ILLUSTRATED CATALOGUE, for the purpose of assisting them in ordering goods they may require, and that great attention has been devoted to make it easy of reference, and will find that all the leading departments are included in it.

In presenting this catalogue for the perusal of my friends and customers, I beg to state that it ambition that my establishment shall present all the features of a FIRST-CLASS FAMILY TRADE, respect to Variety, Accommodation, Attention, and Economy, and by my persevering and conscientious exer to meet the desired requirements of my patrons. I have the honour to request their patronage and supp

Those who have not been supplied can have same sent free on application.

All Orders from the Country must be accompanied by remittance for goods required, but arrange can be made for quarterly accounts, upon satisfactory Town references.

W. C. RENWICK, 86 King Street, Sydney
PARCELS OF £5 AND UPWARDS CARRIAGE PAID.

ACCUMULATED PROFITS, £11,523 17s. 7d.

A newspaper advertisement showing a shop interior, 1878. This is a very fashionable shop with gas lighting, drapes, central aisle space, and cabinet shelving. It catered for "first-class family trade".

(From the *Illustrated Sydney News*, October 1878)

CHAPTER 18

THE INDIVIDUAL CITIZEN

1. Restrictions in the Foundation Years

BY 1900, partly as a result of the various activities of the governments we have been describing, the lot of the Australian citizen was very different from that of a century before. Of course, economic development and technical inventions had greatly altered his way of life, and had improved his standard of living; and apart from that, the attitude of government had altered too.

In the early nineteenth century, governments believed to a large extent in *laissez-faire*, i.e., they thought that they should not interfere with the activities of private individuals. They should not try, for example, to fix wages and working hours, to regulate factory conditions, or to improve rules about health or buildings or town planning and so on. The government should not even provide schools, if it could help it, but leave this, like everything else, to private people or institutions. All the government should do was to keep order.

Of course, since the first Australian colonies were penal settlements, the government had to do more than in England. As the employer of convict labour, and responsible for the prisoners' welfare, it had to determine the conditions of their work. In a community ill-supplied with public services, it had to provide more in the way of roads, docks, markets, churches and schools, for example, than was the case in England, where these had long been established, and were often provided by private individuals for profit. To keep order, it had to take on itself more drastic powers, because it had to deal with a possibly unruly population, and convicts who might attempt to escape. So it censored the Press, it made convict labourers carry passes, like the natives in South Africa today, and though free workers did not have to carry them, they were often arrested on suspicion of being escaping prisoners. The magistrates had unusual powers to try and punish offenders, and for a long time, as we have seen, the free citizen of New South Wales could not be assured of a trial by jury if he was accused of crime.

Q

2. The Rights of a Citizen

By 1900 the "rights" of an Australian were very similar to those of an Englishman. He had a vote. He had a right to trial by jury. He could not be held in prison without trial. If arrested and charged with a serious offence, he had the right to a speedy trial, or to be released on bail until his trial was held, if a magistrate thought this safe; if he was not satisfied that he was legally subject to confinement, he had the right to sue on what is called a writ of *habeas corpus*. This procedure compelled him to be brought before the courts, and they could at once order his release if he was being improperly held in custody.

In 1827 the local government wanted to impose on newspapers a heavy stamp duty, to make them expensive and so restrict their circulation, and to licence them, so that it would indirectly censor their contents by the threat of withdrawing the licence. The government in London refused to allow this, but permitted a very severe law of libel which often prevented the Press from criticizing public officials. Editors were fined and even sent to prison for their attacks on the governors; certainly these were sometimes rather scurrilous, but though there is no excuse for false attacks on officials or on private persons, and these must always be subject to the law of libel, in a democracy, everyone, including newspaper writers, must have the right to criticize government policies if he disagrees with them. Of course, the Australian colonies were not then democracies; but as we have seen, in due course they became so.

3. Government and Welfare

Meanwhile the government, while allowing greater freedom in this direction, was extending its authority in others. In New South Wales as early as 1862 an Act was passed to regulate working conditions in the coal-mines. This was amended in 1876, and by then Victoria had also passed an Act dealing with gold-mines. These were intended to try to reduce the number of accidents by improving their ventilation, their ladders and their lifts and enforcing other safety regulations. Acts were passed to regulate employment on ships, to see that the sailors were given decent accommodation, that the vessels were seaworthy and carried proper fire-fighting and life-saving equipment. In 1884 New South Wales established a State fire brigade system. In the 1890s it imposed a maximum nine-hour day in the coal-mines, and further tightened up their safety regulations. In

THE INDIVIDUAL CITIZEN 233

1896 a Public Health Act extended the supervision of infectious diseases and laid down regulations about the purity of food, and a Factory Act provided that dangerous machinery should be properly fenced. In 1899 a Shops Act compelled "early closing" so that shop assistants should not be kept at work night after night until nearly midnight. Next a series of "Truck Acts" forbade paying wages in goods, and insisted they be paid in money.

4. The Regulation of Labour

In much of this legislation, New South Wales, and the other Australian States whose progress was very similar, had merely followed, often rather slowly, English acts of the same type, concerning Public Health, Factories and Workshops, Ships, Mines and so forth, just as it had followed the English example in legalising trade unions (see Chapter 14); but on other subjects, the Australian Colonies were the pioneers—for example, on Industrial Arbitration, Immigration and Land.

Soon after the colonies were made responsible for their own affairs, they had passed acts "to unlock the land", or in other words to allow small farmers to buy blocks on fairly easy terms. But the terms were not easy enough. Few could afford to buy, clear, and equip their farms, and few had enough knowledge to cultivate them successfully. At the turn of the century governments made it even easier for settlers to buy land and established rural banks to make loans to enable them to stock their farms—all to help the "small man" prosper as a farmer.

Meanwhile the series of great strikes in 1890 and 1891 had brought home to the people the losses and inconvenience that industrial disputes could bring. "Citizens have the right to include strikes and lock-outs as one of the evils the State ought to protect them against," declared a radical leader in South Australia. At first both labour and employers were hostile to compulsory State interference, but the former changed its mind when employers refused to confer with union representatives, and when, after the labour defeats, the unions began to hope that they would gain more by peaceful arbitration than by striking. The first Act for compulsory arbitration was passed by the South Australian Parliament in 1894. In 1901 New South Wales set up a Court of Industrial Arbitration, with compulsory powers, "to hear and determine" industrial disputes. The new Commonwealth had been given in its constitution power to pass such legislation to deal with disputes which extended beyond a single State, and it established the Commonwealth Arbitration Court in 1904.

5. Immigration and the Standard of Living

As for immigration, before 1850, as we have seen (pp. 51-55), the government was anxious to encourage free migrants, both to offset the number of convicts then in Australia and to reduce the shortage of labour. In this period, nearly 200,000 free immigrants arrived, and more than 60 per cent of them were "assisted". The gold discoveries naturally attracted newcomers, but of the 600,000 arrivals between 1850 and 1860, one-third were still assisted, more than twice as many in the preceding *twenty* years. Away from the gold-fields the labour shortage persisted, and governments sought to lessen it but at the same time they began to impose restrictions on immigrants whom they looked on as undesirable. Previously the governors had passively opposed projects for Asian immigration; now that the governments were more subject to popular feeling, when Chinese were attracted to the diggings, first Victoria and then New South Wales, after race-riots at Lambing Flat, imposed poll taxes on their entry. However, these were not kept up for long, for when alluvial mining declined, fewer Chinese came, and in a few years the legislation was repealed.

But some hostility to migrants, whether European or Asian, remained. They appeared to many men as a threat to their employment, and there was constant agitation that they should no longer be helped to come out. "Assistance" was stopped in Victoria in 1873, though in New South Wales and Queensland it remained important longer. Then the opposition to the Chinese grew stronger again, especially after 1878 when one of the shipping companies began to employ them on its coastal steamers. Though withdrawn here, as they became more numerous they were represented, with some justice, as a threat to the standard of living of the Australian workman. During the 1880s one Colony after another passed acts restricting their entry to the country, and the 50,000 Chinese in Australia in 1888 fell to about 30,000 in 1901.

There were various reasons for objecting to them. Certainly the economic motive was an important one. But nationalist feelings were important too. Many Australians in the nineteenth century looked forward to what would be virtually a Utopia in this new country. They would cut themselves off from the international quarrels, the class struggles, outmoded superstitions and hereditary privileges of the old world—and this included both Asia and Europe. "The intellect of the people is freer, stronger and more original than in the age-old States of Europe," declared the *Bulletin*. Australia was the land of the future. Here the cult of mateship was growing up; but the "mates" were Australians; pommies and other foreigners had better keep away. When to these feelings race prejudice was added, the misnamed "White Australia" Policy was born, a policy which reflected a desire to restrict immigration and to keep Australia for the Australians. It was a product of nationalism, racial hostility, and economic fears, which are only slowly dying down today.

6. Political Activity

In all these developments much was accomplished by men of all political views. There were no rigid parties of the modern type before the 1890s; instead only a number of small groups, constantly coming together to achieve some objective and then drifting apart again. Changing political coalitions were frequent, and the political history of the period is extremely complex. But overall, one group pressed on by another and obviously with general support from the bulk of the community, we can see being enacted the achievements recorded here with others like the growth of tariff protection, except in New South Wales, the building of railways and of harbours to improve communications, and the development of education to foster the culture of the people.

7. Social Advance

When the colonists arrived at Port Jackson in 1788, as at the other settlements later on, their first thoughts were for food and shelter. Tents or wattle and bark huts were for a while their only protection against the weather, and later on, as we have already seen, the squatters' huts were little better. But even living in these conditions seemed better than in England—thanks to the climate. Except in Tasmania and southern Victoria, winters were very mild by English standards; the need for fuel was less (and what was wanted for cooking was, of course, very cheap when trees surrounded every settlement), and housing defects, ill-fitting windows and draughty doors did not cause the discomfort they would have brought in England.

Climate then made a big improvement to living conditions in Australia. In other respects the housing was very similar. As long as men had to walk to work, crowding was inevitable in and around the towns, for all the "wide open spaces" beyond. With crowding, dirt was almost inevitable, especially when people did not realize how much disease it was likely to cause.

Only in the mansions of the well-to-do was there much spacious-ness and elegance, and unfortunately the slums of Sydney or Melbourne compared all too closely with those of the cities, new or old, of Great Britain and Ireland.

But apart from this, the living standards of the poor rapidly improved, basically because wages were so much higher. For nearly a century there was a labour shortage. Unemployment was very rare, and appeared only for very brief periods in some economic crisis brought on by drought or flood or some upset in the English wool market. Opportunities for all again underlined the value for "self-help", as a democratic idea, and there was no need for the patronizing charity of the English upper classes.

This high wage-level was in fact one of the strong arguments used against the transportation of convicts from Britain. Trans-portation was certainly a severe punishment when New South Wales was first founded, and the convict seemed to be setting out for an unknown world, not knowing what might be in store for him. But as the settlement grew, many people in England began to feel, rightly or wrongly, that transportation was not a punishment at all. In 1820 Commissioner Bigge reported that to many "the prospect afforded by transportation to New South Wales is more one of emigration than of punishment. . . . The general opinion appeared to be that the period of seven years . . . was too short for the purposes of punishment to the labour-ing classes of convicts." Twenty years later Archbishop Whately was even more outspoken in his criticism of benefits he thought that the criminal gained by his "punishment".

To the great bulk of those who are sentenced to transportation, the *punishment* amounts to this, that they are carried to a country whose climate is delightful, producing in profusion all the neces-saries and most of the luxuries of life; that they have a certainty of maintenance instead of an uncertainty; are better fed, clothed and lodged, than (by *honest* means) they ever were before; have an opportunity of regaling themselves at a cheap rate with all the luxuries they are most addicted to; and if their conduct is not intolerably bad, are permitted . . . to become settlers on a fertile farm which with very moderate industry they may transmit . . . to their children.

Of course this was a prejudiced description, given by a man who had never been to Australia and who wanted only to convince his audience. Transportation had very unpleasant features which Whately did not mention; it involved exile from one's friends and a severe and sometimes barbarous discipline. But he was probably right to this extent—that wages were higher and employment more regular in the Australian Colonies than at "home". As a farmer the convict or free settler might not find things easy. As we have seen already, he would not know enough to be successful; he could not easily afford to buy land or implements for his farm—so that, as Bigge reported, "for the ordinary class of settlers the prospect afforded is . . . a forbidding one". But the unskilled labourer had neither the knowledge nor the money to buy and manage a farm successfully in England, so that in this his condition was no worse than before. But instead of being able to find only irregular work at low, even starvation wages, as was the case at "home", in New South Wales, his services even if unskilled, were always in demand, his wages were correspondingly higher, and his living conditions much better.

8. Manners and Culture

In the early nineteenth century, work was arduous wherever it was, in home, workshop or factory or on the farm, in Britain or Australia. With little labour-saving machinery to ease one's toil, nearly all operations depended on human muscles, whether to fetch and carry, to load and unload, to sweep, to dig or to manufacture. Hours were long, because without machinery it took a long time to do the work that was necessary for living, though some of the very wealthy might be able to employ other people to do it for them.

These were the people whose standards declined most by coming to Australia. There were fewer who were extremely rich; those who were had made their fortunes by their own hard work and had not enjoyed a life of luxury or relative idleness. The numbers of servants at their beck and call were few; complaints of their laziness, stupidity, drunkenness or other shortcomings were frequent from the very first. The new country lacked the opportunities for culture and gracious living that had existed in the old. There were very few libraries, books, picture galleries, theatres, private mansions, salons and literary or philosophical societies. All this did not mean that the upper classes were "barbarians" or philistines; but they were disturbed, as it was said, by "the fatal facility of making money", and this meant the growth of an uneducated wealthy class and a decreasing importance being placed on the intellectual and the artistic. "Money is so easily earned in this Colony," wrote one observer in 1851, "that parents, instead of educating their sons for the learned professions, or allowing them to remain at school until they have received a liberal education, send them to the bush with a few flocks of sheep, which is a surer and much shorter way of arriving at colonial eminence."

In any new country the opportunities for culture must be few. By 1850 there were beginning to appear on the scene mechanics' institutes, libraries both public and private, secondary schools, soon a University. This showed that intellectual interests were not dead; but the struggles of the early literary societies, schools and periodicals to survive showed the very narrow limits which such activities had. By migrating to Australia, men of substance were deprived of these interests; and this was perhaps the greatest difference between "polite" society in England and in the Colony. This was a loss for the upper classes, like the loss of their political privileges; the poor man, at this time not interested in such things, did not suffer by being deprived of them but rejoiced in finding that on the whole he was materially better off.

At the end of the nineteenth century primary education was provided freely by the governments, for all children and practically all adults could read and write. There were few homes which did not receive a daily paper or read a magazine of some kind. There was employment for writers, students, and artists of Australian background and training. The old sense of isolation was going. Some people thought that there was too much contact with Great Britain. The *Bulletin*, for example, not only encouraged Australian writers but also deliberately attacked English literature just because it was English. Despite this outlook, which was not taken very seriously, overseas artists found an Australian tour very profitable and, on the other hand, Australian artists found that a colonial background was no drawback to a career overseas. The most notable Australian artist to receive praise overseas was Dame Nellie Melba, whose singing was wildly acclaimed in Europe and America. She received an amazing welcome when she returned to Australia in 1902, after fifteen years' absence.

Popular taste was still simple. Horse-racing and boxing had larger audiences than Dame Nellie Melba. Mechanical mass entertainments were just about to begin. It is interesting to see how far-off Tasmania kept up at this time. Among reports of the usual entertainments of the day is one that is remarkably like the most popular entertainment of 1964, as this excerpt from the *Tasmanian Mail* of 6th July, 1901, shows:

Mr J. C. Williamson's exhibition of biograph pictures, just imported from England, and the entertainment throughout was instructive and interesting, whilst at times it was also very amusing. In addition to an entirely new series of moving war pictures of thrilling interest, and presented with astonishing realism, there were shown a complete set of films of unusual length, comprising the majestic pageant of the late Queen's funeral. . . . There were many other striking and historical scenes which were marvels of animated photography, such as His Majesty the King on his way to open the Imperial Parliament at Westminster, or the Duke and Duchess of Cornwall and York for Australia. . . .

Other scenes excited much laughter in the second half of the entertainment including the Reversed bathing, punting on the Thames, "a fisherman's luck", "marvels of science", "a restless night", and a motor car collision. The third part concluded with the pathetic historical narrative of Joan of Arc, in which animated and realistic panorama the whole story was depicted with wonderful realisms. The entertainment concluded with the pantomime of "Cinderella".

At the turn of the century people were amazed at the social development in which they had participated. Life in the country was still raw but the worst days of isolation were over. Most country dwellers lived within a reasonable ride's distance of a railway and received fairly regular mail. Homes had become more comfortable and food supplies were better so that the unhealthy diet of damper and fresh meat was only suffered on shearing trips or musterings. In the towns life was much easier because of the technical advances of the nineteenth century. We can read what view Australians took of their economic progress in 1901. Here is the *Sydney Morning Herald* account, which is typical, and though it glosses over some problems, is a fair description.

The conditions of life in Australia have changed much for the better during the last 20 years. People with good incomes in all the older settled provinces may now obtain domestic and municipal comforts and luxuries of as high a standard as are to be found in the finest European and American centres. To a proportionate extent, the salaried and wage-earning classes participate in these advantages. Communication is easy and cheap in all our capitals, and, generally speaking, food is not so expensive as in the English cities. Mr. Coglan, summarising the data supplied by various authorities, says "few countries approach Australia in the small proportion of income absorbed in providing food for the people". As to income earned by personal exertion, intellectually or manually, in the learned professions here, fees do not range so high nor so low as in Great Britain. The salaried classes are mostly better paid than they are in the home country. Working men, skilled or unskilled, drew astonishingly high wages during the period of the gold rushes from 1850 to 1858. For many years afterwards, their rates of pay were high and Australia received great access of population from all quarters of the world in consequence. Wages for tradesmen will still compare favourably with what is paid in Great Britain and America. Two-thirds of the trades at least in the federated colonies enjoy the benefit of the eight hour system. In Victoria, factories and shops legislation has improved the lot of the workers, and in New South Wales an Early Closing Act, recently passed, has emancipated the shop employees particularly, and other classes. This beneficial change has been brought about without reduction in the wages paid. There is, it is contended, still much to be done for the amelioration of employees generally. Australia, often referred to as the paradise of the working man, will probably never reach the ideal of socialist evolution, but as a first class all-round place to live in for people of all grades, admitting its present imperfections, it can certainly not be beaten. Minimum rates of wages are even paid for tradesmen and unskilled labourers alike in several of the colonies. In New South Wales the Government has fixed the minimum for navvies as high as 7s. per day. Figures showing the proportion of estate per one hundred deaths of the total population of the federated colonies, extending over 17 years, prove that there is a distribution of wealth over Australia not paralleled in any other part of the world. One out of every four adult males and females was found to be the possessor of property. Whereas in the United Kingdom, the richest country in Europe, only 9 out of every 100 possess £100. Few of our people are brought within reach of want. Our unemployed, persons supported by the State and by charitable effort, and criminal classes, do not aggregate more than 30,000 in a total Commonwealth population of 3,726,480. When it is noted there are nearly 9000 aborigines in New South Wales and Victoria, as well as many others elsewhere, most of whom receive State aid, the 30,000 seems indeed a small figure. There is certainly no hereditary pauper class in Australia. That life may always be as pleasant, as hopeful and as prosperous for the masses under federation in the years to come as it seems to be at the birth of our great promising nation, is a desire that every patriotic Australian must surely entertain.

CHAPTER 19

THE COMING OF FEDERATION

1. Six Colonies

TOWARDS the end of the nineteenth century, Australia was still almost only a name for six separate Colonies. True, "Australia" played test cricket matches against England. There had been inter-colonial conferences of trade unions dating from 1879—but not until 1891 was there reasonable representation from all parts of the continent. Employers in the shipping and stevedoring industries had inter-colonial connections; but manufacturers as a whole were still chiefly concerned with the local markets of their own States, as was to be expected when they were chiefly occupied in treating food and perishable products, and supplying the immediate needs of consumers.

A pan-Australasian Conference of Employers was held in Sydney in September 1890; it resolved that federal councils of all employers' organizations should be formed; but this was only a beginning. The premiers of the different Colonies had frequently held inter-colonial conferences, and some of them even joined in forming a Federal Council in 1885; but the colonial governments gave it little power. It could only deal with a few unimportant matters; it had no means of raising money or incurring expenditure—for its finance, and for enforcing its acts, it depended entirely on the goodwill and the action of each Colony; it remained "little more than a debating society". New South Wales and South Australia refused to join.

There had been talk of federation ever since Victoria and New South Wales had been separated in 1851; but no one was deeply interested. So long as poor communications prevented much inter-colonial travel, why should they be? Sydney and Melbourne were not linked by rail until 1883; Brisbane and Adelaide later still. The sea trip was slow and often stormy. The Colonies—particularly New South Wales and Victoria—were extremely jealous of one another; to bring them together would be no easy task. But by 1900 this task had been successfully carried out. Why and how was this done?

2. Foreign Policy and Defence

First, there was the question of foreign policy. Australians were becoming concerned about foreign countries in the Pacific —the French in New Hebrides, for example. New Caledonia in the nineteenth century was a French penal colony; might not criminals escape from there to Australia? And what about the Germans in New Guinea? To the Australian colonists these were important questions; but the British government did not seem to care about them. Might it not pay more attention to the voice of a federated Australian government? At any rate, many Australians thought so.

Then there was the question of defence. If it should ever be necessary to resist an invasion of Australia, would it not be much more effective to have the colonial military forces operating under a single control? In 1889 a British expert adviser, Major-General Edwards, reporting on the defences of the colonies, said:

> Before the completion of the railways which unite Adelaide, Melbourne, Sydney and Brisbane, it was impossible for the Colonies to co-operate for defence; and this is even now not possible, on account of their different organisation, and because the Colonies cannot employ their forces outside their own borders. Combined action for defence would be more economical and far more effective than the present system. . . . A common system of defence can only be carried out by a federation of the military forces of the Colonies. . . .

3. The Sentiment of Nationalism

Underlying this was the growing sentiment of Australian nationalism, a spirit of unity binding the people together. For some, this was partly a resentment against what they thought were the abuses of the "old world"; in Australia, they would build a new society, a Utopia. This is what William Lane, a Labour leader, wrote in 1887:

> Our principles are easily declared. They are Australian. Whatever will benefit Australia, that we are for; whatever will harm Australia, that we are against.
> We use Australian in its fullest, truest, broadest sense. To us it conveys an idea which we cannot adequately describe; a something far different from a vain and sectional clamour for the right to run amuck among the brawling nations of foreign lands, and to strike for conquests where we cannot rule. The Australian national movement is the setting in of one of those periodic tides which change and alter the whole life of the human race. . . .

We are for this Australia, for the nationality that is creeping to the verge of being, for the progressive people that is just plucking aside the curtain that veils its fate. Behind us lies the Past with its crashing empires, its falling thrones, its dotard races; before us lies the Future into which Australia is plunging, this Australia of ours that burns with the feverish energy of youth, and that is wise with the wisdom for which ten thousand generations have suffered and toiled.

4. Relations with Great Britain

Many even argued that loyalty to Australia should not be divided by loyalty to Great Britain, or any other European country.

. . . By the term Australian we mean not those who have been merely born in Australia. All white men who come to these shores —with a clean record—and who leave behind them the memory of the class-distinctions and the religious differences of the old world; all men who place the happiness, the prosperity; the advancement of their adopted country before the interests of Imperialism, are Australian. In this regard all men who leave the tyrant-ridden lands of Europe for freedom of speech and right of personal liberty are Australians before they set foot on the ship which brings them hither. Those who fly from an odious military conscription; those who leave their fatherland because they cannot swallow the worm-eaten lie of the divine right of kings to murder peasants, are Australians by instinct. . . .

Australia, wrote Joseph Furphy in *Such is Life*, is "committed to no usages of petrified injustice; she is clogged by no fealty to shadowy idols, enshrined by ignorance and upheld by misplaced homage alone"; her society should be free from the evils of the old world.

This criticism of the "foreign" was sometimes ridiculous, though since found, often enough, in the too common belief that nothing outside Australia is any good. The *Bulletin* wrote in 1887 of the University's "absurd reverence for the extrinsic and the foreign", which took it "outside the literature, the language, the life and the history of its own country to seek for specious inspiration in a museum of antiquities"—and this when Australia had barely begun to build an artistic or intellectual life of her own. Although this aggressive nationalism was self-conscious and exaggerated, it showed clearly that many people were beginning to cherish a feeling for independence. "My own particular vision of Australia," wrote Bernard O'Dowd, "is something like this. She is an entity with a new destiny—if she wills it. She is the fabled Astraea Redux, the Goddess of

Justice returning to earth as in the Golden Age . . . that is, if she wills it. If not, why simply Europe, with its aura of failure over again. . . ." The Australian believed in equality; he distrusted privileges and titles which he felt had rarely been properly earned.

When they pin the Stars and Garters, when they write the titles rare,
The men who earned the honours are the men who won't be there,

wrote Henry Lawson; this emphasized the hopes for a new country, which far from being "down under" would come to lead the world. To quote O'Dowd again:

> Antipodean? Whew! We are the head,
> The oceanic head, while you, slung low
> With lands that scrape the floor of heaven, gaze
> Far o'er the Bull your Europa wed
> Up to the Chambers of the South where glow
> Our pennant stars, our wider Milky Ways.

Many others had no wish to cut the ties with "the old country"; but they thought that government "under the British Crown" would be more efficient if the Australian Colonies federated. Most would have agreed with the veteran Sir Henry Parkes, when he asked in 1890, "Why should not the name of an Australian be equal to that of a Briton? . . . Why should not the name of an Australian citizen be equal to that of the citizen of the proudest country under the sun?" After federation, he thought, Australians would stop looking on Britain as "home", for they would create a "homeland" here. "Make yourselves a united people," he said, "and the dream of going 'home' would die away. . . . We should have 'home' within our own shores." The population of the Australian Colonies was more than three million—nearly equal to that of the American Colonies when they had become independent about a century before. Australians should form a federation in order "to enlarge their powers of self-government", as the resolution put it.

5. The Tariff Problem

One of the greatest obstacles was the tariff question. New South Wales had adopted the policy of free trade; for her there were no duties on imports. Consequently the prices of imported commodities were kept low (good for the consumer), but local manufactures were not "protected" against foreign competition. Victorian policy was the opposite. Quite heavy duties protected local manufactures; even though they might cost more than, or be not so good as, an imported article, at least they were made locally, and so provided work and encouraged local produce. The other Colonies' tariffs were protective too, but not as high as Victoria's. If the Colonies federated, there would be a single, uniform tariff throughout Australia; in fact getting rid of the "border duties", the customs barriers on the Colonies' borders on interstate trade and travel, seemed to many people one of the greatest advantages that federation would bring. But would the federal tariff be high or low? New South Welshmen did not want the former and her premier spoke of one teetotaller going into partnership with five drunkards; but the other Colonies did not want to give up their duties.

6. The Federal Conventions

In 1891 a convention was held to discuss federation. But its proposals were allowed to lapse. State jealousies seemed too strong. One Sydney politician referred to Victoria as a "cabbage garden"; New South Wales should certainly make no concessions to join *that* State. An economic depression, a series of strikes and a banking crisis all diverted men's attentions, and the Colonies had different opinions on the tariff question, as we have seen. So for a few years the question slumbered, while the colonial leaders wrestled with their other difficulties; but these very difficulties in time gave another spur to the federal movement. Was it not possible that joint action might have moderated the effects of the depression or shortened the strikes? Some people thought so, at any rate. "Federation is no panacea," wrote the *Pastoralists' Review* in 1893, "but it would be of considerable assistance in our present difficulties," while the *Journal of the Institute of Bankers* argued that a federal government would be able to raise loans in England more easily than the separate Colonies could, for they would be "among the best securities that could be offered in any part of the world".

In the Riverina, on the border of New South Wales and Victoria, federal sentiment was very strong; and after all, Riverina representatives had votes in the New South Wales Parliament. And even a national tariff would have its compensations; for there would be free trade between the Colonies. Both New South Wales and the Victorian Chambers of Commerce had pronounced in favour of an inter-colonial "customs union" as early as 1893, even if there should be no federation.

Propagandists were active; federal leagues were formed to "agitate for and advance the federation of the Colonies". Finally it was agreed that a convention should be held with ten representatives elected from each Colony who could draw up a draft constitution, and in 1897 this convention held its first session in Adelaide. Three years later, after long discussions and many changes in its proposals, the majority of voters in every Australian Colony agreed at referenda to the federation scheme, and the Commonwealth of Australia came into existence on the first day of the new century.

7. Reasons for Federation in the 1890s

Why did the Australian people agree to federate just then? Some of the reasons have already been mentioned—a growing sense of Australian nationalism, greatly strengthened by improvements in transport, which made it easier for people to travel about the continent and emphasized the "oneness" of the country as a whole. In addition, and partly arising from this, was the desire for a common foreign policy, common defence, a common policy to meet economic, financial and industrial difficulties, and a common customs barrier with interstate free trade. Of great importance in nourishing nationalist sentiment were the improvements in communications—by rail, ship, and telegraph. Formerly isolated and separate communities were now linked together; together they could face their common problems. On a smaller scale was the desire for a national postal service; on a much larger scale was the desire for a common immigration policy.

For a generation or more many Australian workmen had been afraid of the competition of cheap labour. For this reason they had often opposed assisted immigration; they often disliked the Irish; they were terrified of Chinese and Japanese, and the feelings of a meeting in Sydney in 1890, said the *Bulletin*, "were not the less commendable because the speakers and the audience were for the most part men who had personally felt or were afraid that they would soon feel the effects of the Chinese invasion—a dearth of work and a reduction in the rate of wages." By this time all the Colonies had laws in force which restricted immigration from Asia; but they varied in details and in Queensland there were Kanaka labourers from the Pacific Islands working on the sugar-cane fields. Would not the whole immigration question be better handled by one national government—especially if it was necessary to negotiate with foreign countries, or to stand up for Australian policy against British

"Let There Be Light." A cartoon illustrating the view taken by the Victorian
Press of its own activities.

(From the *Illustrated Sydney News*, December 1875)

A Royal Commission's plan for Circular Quay, Sydney, 1909. It is just as well that not all plans are successful and this one would soon have been outmoded, though the basic idea of an overhead railway is retained in the present plan.

(By courtesy of the Mitchell Library, Sydney)

statesmen? So the federal leader, Barton, soon to be the first prime minister of the Commonwealth, could argue that federation "would enlarge the powers of self-government of the people . . . (because) it is an enlargement of the powers of self-government to include within the scope of action the dealing with national affairs which previously we could not touch."

8. The Various Viewpoints

Strong support for the federal movement came from the outback, especially in New South Wales, Queensland and Western Australia, where many in the capital cities opposed it. In the West, the miners on the recently discovered goldfields around Kalgoorlie even petitioned to the British government to separate them from their State if its government refused to join the federation, so that they might then join it themselves. The government in Perth had never cared for the miners' interests, they said, but only heeded the wishes of the old settlers near the coast, who used their power "harshly, arbitrarily, and unjustly. . . . They have passed laws and applied public moneys for their own special benefit and to our detriment and have otherwise . . . oppressed the inhabitants of the Eastern Goldfields" by imposing special taxes on gold mining and "heavy Customs taxation on food and other commodities, so devised as to . . . oppress us for the advantage of their monopolies", by refusing to build a railway from the goldfields to the south coast and ignoring their needs for public works. Most of these complaints were in fact unjustified, but they show the hostility so often felt towards the cities by the man in the bush. In Queensland many farmers and manufacturers in the south were afraid of competition from New South Wales if there should be no tariff "protection" along the border; the majority in Brisbane and on the Darling Downs voted "No" in the federation referendum. But the majority in the north, disliking the Brisbane government and looking for an Australian-wide protected market for their sugar, were able, though rather narrowly, to carry the day. Though the Brisbane *Worker* was hostile, many Labour men must have voted "Yes", perhaps looking for any stick to beat the then rather conservative Queensland Parliament with; after all, even the *Worker* agreed that in the federal convention "upon every point of conflict between Conservatism and Democracy, Conservatism has gone down heavily. . . . Our Democratic readers, groaning under the rule of the most unprogressive, reactionary of governments may take this to heart that the

R

government as provided for . . . is more liberal than the provincial Government existing in Queensland at this moment."

On the whole, Labour supporters did not take this view. Many were indifferent to federation; it did not seem to them likely to bring any social reforms which would immediately benefit the working man. Some, even, were hostile, especially in New South Wales, fearing that the working-class strength there might be outvoted by what were thought to be the more conservative feelings of the people in the smaller States. Hence New South Wales Labour men wanted to try to strengthen the position of their State in the federation, and to make sure that the federal government, even if it should be dominated by the representatives of the smaller States, could not endanger the social reforms of the mother Colony.

There were, of course, many others who were afraid that federation might hurt their particular colonial interests. We have already noticed, for example, how some economic groups were nervous of the effects of interstate free trade. In New South Wales many people thought that their State was being imposed upon by the others—the whole federation idea seemed to them to be a conspiracy directed against her. The federal capital, it was argued, would be in Victoria, and federal laws would therefore be passed to favour it (why this should be the result was not explained—but then political campaigners often do not explain their deductions). New South Wales, they said again, would not be represented strongly enough in the federal Parliament; not only would she have to sacrifice her free-trade policy, but her people would be heavily taxed to support a costly federal government which would only harm her; the States would be "pauperized" and New South Wales would lose her prosperity. The New South Wales premier, George Reid, though he supported federation, criticized very frankly what he thought was wrong in the proposed constitution, and pointed out all the "blots" in it. He said he would vote for it, but because of his lukewarmness he was called "Yes-No" Reid.

At first there were not enough supporters in New South Wales, and a few concessions had to be made to her. This, for example, explains why a new federal capital came into existence. Although New South Wales was a free-trade Colony and some free-traders strongly opposed any change, even the tariff question, which a keen federationist had once called "the lion in our path", helped in the end. The customs houses on the borders were being felt to be more and more intolerable. Railway passengers coming to

New South Wales had to have their luggage looked at at Albury or Wallangarra or Echuca or wherever they might cross a border. At least federation would put an end to this. From the very beginning it had been said again and again that "trade and intercourse between the federated Colonies, whether by land or sea, shall become and remain absolutely free"; there would be no more interstate customs; they at least, would go for ever; and free-traders were able to console themselves by reflecting that even if Australia did impose tariff duties on imports from overseas, at least there would be free trade throughout the length and breadth of the continent, while protectionists were glad to see a tariff on imports from overseas.

9. Federation Achieved

In the end, as we have seen, the draft constitution was approved in referenda in every Colony, although without compulsory voting less than sixty per cent of the electors bothered to vote at all; there were plenty who remained quite indifferent, and only in Victoria did more than half the electorate actually vote "Yes". Still the majority of those who voted were in favour, and that was enough. A delegation took the draft to Great Britain and the British Parliament passed the Commonwealth of Australia Act in good time for the new Commonwealth to come into existence on 1st January 1901.

BIBLIOGRAPHY

Books for General Reference

Books marked with an asterisk are recommended for teachers only.
Australian Encyclopaedia, second edition, 10 vols. (Sydney, 1958)
* Atlas of Australian Resources (Department of National Development, Canberra, 1953 ff.)
Clark, C. M. H., Sources of Australian History (London, 1957)
Clark, C. M. H., Select Documents in Australian History, Vol. 1, 1788-1850 (Sydney, 1950); Vol. 2, 1851-1900 (Sydney, 1955)
Crawford, R. M., Australia (London, 1952)
Evans, L., Australia and the Modern World (Melbourne, 1955)
* Grattan, C. Hartley, The Southwest Pacific to 1900—a Modern History (Michigan, 1963)
* Greenwood, G. (ed), Australia, A Social and Political History (Sydney, 1955)
Palmer, H. G. and Macleod, J., The First Hundred Years (Longmans, Melbourne, 1954)
Palmer, H. G. and Macleod, J., Makers of the First Hundred Years (Longmans, Melbourne, 1956)
Palmer, Vance, National Portraits (paperback, M.U.P., 1960)
Pike, Douglas, The Quiet Continent (Cambridge, 1962)
Shaw, A. G. L., The Economic Development of Australia (fourth edition, Melbourne, 1960)
Shaw, A. G. L., The Story of Australia (Faber paperback, London, 1962)
Ward, Russell, Australia (Spectrum paperback, New Jersey, 1965)

Books for Further Reading

CHAPTER 1

Dark, Eleanor, The Timeless Land (Sydney, 1941)
Erdos, Renée, John Hunter (Great Australians series, O.U.P. paperback, Melbourne, 1964)
* O'Brien, Eris, The Foundation of Australia (Sydney, 1950)
Roe, Michael, Philip Gidley King (paperback, Melbourne, 1963)
Tench, W. (ed. Fitzhardinge), Sydney's First Four Years (Sydney, 1961)

CHAPTER 2

Barnard, Marjorie, Macquarie's World (M.U.P. paperback, 1949)
Barnard, Marjorie, Lachlan Macquarie (Great Australians, O.U.P. paperback, Melbourne, 1964)
Dark, Eleanor, Storm of Time (Sydney, 1948)
Dark, Eleanor, No Barrier (Sydney, 1953)
* Ellis, M. H., John Macarthur (Sydney, 1955)

* Ellis, M. H., *Lachlan Macquarie* (Sydney, 1952)
Fitzpatrick, Brian and B. J. Munday, *Readings in Australian History*, Vol. 1 (Cheshire, 1965)
MacMillan, D. S., *Enter the Merchant* (Australian Landmarks series, Longmans paperback, 1961)

CHAPTERS 3 AND 4

Cumpston, J. H. L., *Charles Sturt* (London, 1951)
Fitzpatrick, Kathleen (ed.), *Australian Explorers, a selection from their Writings* (London, 1958)
Gardiner, Lyndsay, *Thomas Mitchell* (Australian Explorers, O.U.P. paperback, Melbourne, 1962)
Kennedy, Donald, *Charles Sturt* (Australian explorers, O.U.P. paperback, Melbourne, 1958)

CHAPTER 5

* Bassett, M., *The Hentys—a Colonial Tapestry* (London, 1954)
Cunningham, P., *Two Years in New South Wales* (Sydney, 1966)
Curr, E. M., *Recollections of Squatting in Victoria* (M.U.P., 1965)
Fitzpatrick, Brian and B. J. Munday, *Readings in Australian History*, (Cheshire, 1965)
Harris, Alexander, *Settlers and Convicts* (Melbourne, 1953)
Joyce, Alfred, *A Homestead History* (Melbourne, 1942)
* Roberts, S. H., *The Squatting Age in Australia* (Melbourne, 1964)

CHAPTER 6

Kiddle, Margaret, *Caroline Chisholm* (M.U.P., 1950)
MacMillan, D. S., *John Dunmore Lang* (Great Australians series, O.U.P. paperback, Melbourne, 1962)

CHAPTER 7

Dutton, G., *Founder of a City—the Life of Colonel William Light* (Melbourne, 1960)
Hasluck, Alexandra, *James Stirling* (Great Australians, O.U.P. paperback, Melbourne, 1963)
Hasluck, Alexandra, *Portrait with Background* (Melbourne, 1960)
* Pike, Douglas, *Paradise of Dissent* (Adelaide, 1957)

CHAPTER 8

Blainey, G., *The Rush that never Ended* (Melbourne, 1963)
Fauchery, A., *Letters from a Miner in Australia* (Georgian House, Melbourne, 1965)
Historical Studies, Eureka Supplement (paperback, Melbourne, 1965)
* Serle, G., *The Golden Age* (Melbourne, 1963)

CHAPTER 9

Boyd, Martin, *The Montforts* (London, 1928)
Eldershaw, M. Barnard, *A House is Built* (London, 1929)

Lindsay, D., and Washington, E. S., *Portrait of Britain, 1688-1851* (O.U.P., 1956)

Nadel, G., *Australia's Colonial Culture* (Melbourne, 1957)

Roe, M., *The Quest for Authority in Eastern Australia* (Melbourne, 1965)

Thomson, D., *England in the Nineteenth Century* (Pelican, 1950)

Ward, Russel, *The Australian Legend* (London, 1958)

CHAPTER 10

Court, W. H. B., *Concise Economic History of Britain*—from 1760 to recent times (C.U.P., 1958)

CHAPTER 11

Department of Railways, New South Wales, *The Railways of New South Wales* 1855-1955 (Sydney, 1955)

MacMillan, D. S., *Tall Ships and Steamboats* (Australian Landmarks, paperback, Longmans, 1961)

Mudie, Ian, *River Boats* (Sun paperback, 1965)

CHAPTER 12

Allen, Noel D., *Concerning Australian Sheep* (Rigby, Adelaide, n.d.)

Barnard, A., *Thomas Sutcliffe Mort* (Great Australians, O.U.P. paperback, Melbourne, 1962)

* Barnard, A., *Visions and Profits* (Melbourne, 1961)

Donath, E. J., *William Farrer* (Great Australians, O.U.P. paperback, Melbourne, 1962)

Forster, H. W., *Squatter and Selector at Tongala* (Australian Landmarks, Longmans, Melbourne, 1964)

Palmer, Helen, *Fencing Australia* (Australian Landmarks, Longmans, Melbourne, 1961)

Penton, Brian, *The Landtakers* (Sydney, 1935)

Russell, A., *William James Farrer* (Cheshire, 1949)

Wadham, S. and Wood, *Land Utilisation in Australia* (M.U.P., fourth edition, 1965)

Watt, R. D., *Romance of the Australian Land Industries* (Sydney, 1955)

Wright, Judith, *Generations of Men* (M.U.P. paperback, 1965)

CHAPTER 13

* Hughes, Helen, *Australian Iron & Steel Industry*, 1848-1962 (Melbourne, 1964)

MacMillan, D. S., *Iron and Steel* (Australian Landmarks, Longmans, Melbourne, 1964)

Morris, W. A., *The Rise and Progress of Australian Industries*

CHAPTER 14

Ebbels, N., *The Australian Labor Movement, 1850-1907* (Sydney, 1960)

Gollan, R., *Radical and Working Class Politics* (Melbourne, 1960)

Harris, A., *Settlers and Convicts* (M.U.P., 1953)
Palmer, H. G. and Macleod, J., *W. G. Spence and the Rose of the Trade Unions* (Australian Landmarks, Longmans, Melbourne, 1964)

CHAPTER 15

Barnard, Marjorie, *Sydney, the Story of a City* (Sydney, 1958)
Grant, J. and Serle, A. G., *The Melbourne Scene, 1803-1956* (Melbourne, 1957)
MacMillan, D. and Birch, A., (eds.), *The Sydney Scene* (M.U.P., 1962)

CHAPTER 16

Boyd, R., *Australia's Home* (M.U.P., 1952)

CHAPTER 17

Martin, A. W., *Henry Parkes* (Great Australians, O.U.P. paperback, Melbourne, 1964)
Persse, M., *William Charles Wentworth* (Great Australians, O.U.P. paperback, Melbourne, 1964)

CHAPTER 18

Palmer, V., *The Legend of the Nineties* (Melbourne, 1957)

CHAPTER 19

Deakin, Alfred, *The Federal Story* (second edition, paperback, Melbourne, 1963)
* La Nauze, J. A., *Alfred Deakin*, 2 vols. (Melbourne, 1965)
La Nauze, J. A., *Alfred Deakin* (Great Australians, O.U.P. paperback, Melbourne, 1962)

INDEX

INDEX

Aborigines, 17, 27, 43-6, 83, 145, 194
Adelaide, 30, 70 (diagram), 72, 185
Agriculture, 4-5, 112-131
Alt, Augustus, 180
Angas, G. F., 69
Antiseptics, 203
Arbitration Courts, Act for, 233; introduction of, 175-8
Australasian Steam Navigation Company, 174
Australia Day, 3
"Australia Felix", 31
Australian Agricultural Company, 117
Australian Gas Light Company, 203
Australian Iron and Steel Ltd, 155

Ballarat, 75; Reform League, 80
Banks, Joseph, 3
Barton, Sir Edmund, 247
Basic wage, 177-8
Bathurst, Lord, 18
Benelong's Point, 11
Bendigo, 75
Bent, Ellis, 216
Bentley, J. F., 80
Bessemer, Henry, 149
Bigge, J. T., 19, 86, 88, 216
"Blackbirding", 138
Bligh, William, 9, 10
Blue Mountains, 13, 14, 21, 34, 107-8
Bogan River, 23-4
Botany Bay, 3, 15
Boulton, Matthew, 98-9
Bourke, Governor, 34
Bright, John, 90
British Colonies Government Act (1850), 223

Broken Hill Proprietary Company (B.H.P.), 151-165; Union, 173
Burrinjuck Dam, 133-4
Bushrangers, 43, 48-50; Act, 49

C Series Index, 178
Caley, George, 4
California, gold rushes, 74
Canada, 220-1
Campbell, Robert, 10
Castlereagh River, 23, 24
Cattle, 10, 121, 135-7
Child labour, 86-9, 168-70; in Australia, 88-9, 175
Chinese immigration, 174, 234
Chisholm, Caroline, 61-4
Church, in England, 84; division in Australia, 92, 183
Classes, English social, 195-6
Climate, 14, 50, 113, 235
Coal-mining, 146-8, 153, 161, 178
Cobb and Co., 108
Colonial Society, 83-92
Colonial Sugar Refining Company, 140-1
Colonies, new, 59-73
Colonization, systematic, 65-73
Coloured labour, 138-40, 174, 246
Combination Acts, 169
Commerce and Industry, 95-106
Commonwealth Arbitration Court, 158, 159
Commonwealth Bank, 164
Commonwealth government, 177-8
Commonwealth of Australia Act, 249
Conciliation and Arbitration, see Arbitration Courts
Constitution Act (1855), 244

Convicts, 3, 6, 34, 43, 46-50, 58, 166-9, 231; barracks, 11, 14, 16 (map); system, 15
Cook, James, 3, 194
Cooper's Creek, 32, 38
Cort, Henry, 146-7
Cumberland County Council, 190-1
Cunningham, Allan, 33-4; map of explorations, 35

Dairy industry, 135-7; Dairies Supervision Act (1901), 136
Dampier, William, 194
Darby, Abraham, 146
Darling Downs, 37
Darling, Governor, 25, 34
Darling River, 23, 28, 30, 33-4
Defence, 242
Delprat, Guillaume Daniel, 158-165
Democracy, 230, 232
Depressions (1841), 61; (1893), 128; (1929-33), 178
Desert, 32, 126-7
Dickens, Charles, 90
Diggers, gold, 77-82
Disease, 60, 202-3
Donaldson, Stuart Alexander, 226
Dorman, Long and Company, 155
Droughts, 14, 23-4, 33, 43-4
Durham, Lord, 220

East India Company, 10, 61
Edison, T. A., 104
Education, 86-8, 92; primary, 238
Eight-Hour Day, 170-2
Electricity, 102-6, 204-6; Electric Lighting Bill, 104; Sydney's supply, 191-2; use in Australia, 104, 106
Emancipists, 7, 14, 216, 221
Entertainment, 189
Erosion, 126-7
Eureka stockade, 80

Experiment Farm, 8, 114
Exploration, 21-9
Eyre, Edward John, 30, 37

Factories' and Shops' Act (Victoria, 1873), 175
Factory Acts, 87, 88, 90, 170
Family Colonization Loan Society, 63
Faraday, Michael, 102
Farm Cove, 131
Farming, 4, 5, 7, 8, 9, 14, 19-20, 57, 112-31; first, 112-14; on Sydney Plain, 115-16; problems of, 126-8; science and mechanics in, 120-1
Farrer, William James, 124-6
Fashions, in the eighteenth century, 196
Federation, 241-9; achievement of, 249; conventions, 245-6; reasons for in the 1890s, 246-7; various viewpoints on, 247-9
Film, 104
First Fleet, 107
First settlement in Australia, 3
Flinders, Matthew, 25
Food, demand after gold rushes, 81; in the eighteenth century, 196-7; of early squatters, 42; prices in 1826, 199; scarcity, 95-6
Foreign policy, 242
France, 4; French explorers, 65
Franchise, 91, 219, 222, 228-30; for women, 230
Free trade, 244
Fry, Elizabeth, 90

Gas light, 203-4
Gawler, George, 71-2
Gilbert, Sir Henry, 120-1
Gipps, Governor, 21, 61-2, 74
Glenelg River, 36
Gold, 74-82, 119; consequences of, 81; discovery, 74; Gold Discovery Committee, 75; in

Gold (contd)
California, 74; miners' grievances, 79; rushes, 174; Victoria, 76
Government and welfare in the nineteenth century, 232-3
Governors, early, 215-16; limits to power, 216, 222
Goulburn River Valley irrigation, 133
Graziers, 122-3
Greenway, Francis, 183
Great Britain, relations with Australia, 243-4
Grey, George, 72-3

Habeas corpus, 332
Hargraves, Edward, 74-5
Harris, Alexander, 43, 49, 56, 166-7, 168
Health services, 95, 202-3; Public Health Act (1896), 232
Henty Brothers, 36
Higgins, Henry Bournes, 177-8
Hindmarsh, Governor, 71
Hotham, Sir Charles, 80
House of Representatives, 223
Housing, 194-210, 239; diagrams of Australian houses, 208; English homes in the eighteenth century, 194-7; in Sydney, 188, 197-200; plan and design, 207-10
Howard, John, 89
Hudson Brothers, 188
Hughes, William Morris, 153
Humanitarians, 89-91; in Australia, 90-1
Hyde Park Barracks, Sydney, 16
Hydro-electric power, 103
Hygiene, 197, 202-3

Immigration, 21, 51-60, 234-5; Act, 174; policies, 173-4; problems, 56-7; results, 57-60
Individual citizen, the, 231-7; early restrictions, 231; rights

Individual citizen (contd)
of, 232; social advance, 235-7; standard of living, 234-5
Industrial Revolution, 51, 92, 120, 145-7, 170
Interior, the, 30-9
Internal combustion engine, 106
International Exhibition (1879), 187-8
Ireland, 51; potato famine, 95
Iron and steel industry, 146-65
Irrigation, 133-4

Jury, trial by, 58, 221, 232

Kanakas—see coloured labour
King, Governor, 6, 7
Kwinana, 156

Labour Party, 152, 173, 174, 175, 248, 249
Laissez-faire, 231
Land Acts, 170
Land tenure, 40, 57
La Trobe, Charles, 45, 76-7
Lawes, Sir John Bennet, 120-1
Legislative Assembly of New South Wales, 104, 224, 226-8
Legislative Council, 58, 183, 217, 218, 219; New South Wales, 224; setting up of, 58; work of in New South Wales, 221, 222, 223
Leichhardt, 37; map of explorations, 38
Lewis, Essington, 155-6
Liebig, Justus, 120
Light, William, 71
Lister, Lord, 202
Literature, 243-4
Living standards, 178-9, 234-5
London, 52, 181
Lord, Simeon, 183
Lowrie, William, 124
Lysaght, John, Pty Ltd, 154

Macarthur, John, 8-10, 19-20; ambitions, 8-9; and rebellion,

Macarthur, John (*contd*) 9-10; and wool trade, 18-19, 116-17; farm, 114-15
McKay, Hugh Victor, 123-4
Macquarie, Lachlan, 8-20, 216; achievements, 17-18; and pastoral expansion, 19-20; hopes of, 11; map showing influence in Sydney, 12; plan of Sydney, 183; Sydney under, 11-12
Macquarie River, 23-4
Manners and culture, nineteenth century, 237-8
Marsden, *Rev.* Samuel, 117
Masters and Servants Act (1828), 59, 167
Melba, *Dame* Nellie, 238
Melbourne, 58, 60, 75, 81, 185, 186
Melville, *Captain*, 48-50
Metropolitan Water, Sewerage and Drainage Board, 203
Mines Act, 88, 90
Miners, licence, 79-80; grievances on goldfields, 79-80
Mitchell, *Major* Thomas, 34-9; map of explorations, 35, 38
Mort, Thomas Sutcliffe, 121, 136, 142-4
Municipal Reform Act (Great Britain), 170
Munitions, 156
Murray River, 25, 26, 27, 28, 29, 30, 34, 107, 134
Murrumbidgee River, 25, 27, 28, 37, 107, 133-4
Myxomatosis, 127

National Welfare Fund, 179
Nationalism, Australian, 242-4
Neilson, J. B., 149
Newcastle, 14, 154, 155, 156
Newcomen, Thomas, 96-8
New South Wales Corps, 8-10, 114
Norfolk Island, 50, 65
Otto, Nikolaus, 106

Overland Telegraph Line, 204; map, 105

Pacific Islands Labourers' Act, 174
Papin, Denis, 97
Parkes, *Sir* Henry, 244
Parliament, British, 226; New South Wales, 226-30; diagram of houses of, 229
Parramatta, 8, 13, 107; Fair, 20
Parsons, Charles, 102-3
Pasteur, Louis, 202
Pasteurization, 136
Pensions, old age, 175
Phillip, Captain Arthur, 3, 112, 113, 180, 181, 215
Police, 11, 17, 72, 77; mounted, 49
Poor Laws, 170
Population, 60, 81, 82, 95; English, 187; Sydney, 183
Port Jackson, 3, 180, 235
Port Kembla, 154-7
Port Pirie, 159
Press, censorship of, 58, 231; freedom of, 221-2; law of libel, 232
Prisons, 89-90
Primary industry, 112-32; achievements of, 131-2; farms, 112-16; graph of, 131; graziers, 122-3; problems of, 126-8; science and mechanics in, 120-21; wheat, 117-20, 123-6
Public Health Act (1896), 233

Queensland, cattle industry, 121; exploration of, 37-9; federation, 247; sugar industry, 138-41

Rabbit, as pest, 127; Destruction Act, 122
Railways, 96, 100-1, 104, 108, 109-11, 186, 189, 204; map of in the 1890s, 111

Reform Act of 1832, 91, 219, 222

Reid, *Sir* George, 248

Responsible government, 215-230; Canada, 220-1; citizens' rights in penal colony, 216; demands for, 222-3; diagram of evolution in New South Wales, 225; granting of, 222, 224-6; reform of in Great Britain, 219-20; representation claimed, 217-18

Ridley, John, 118-19; diagram of stripping machine, 119

Rights of Australian citizens, 231-2

Rivers, exploring the, 21-9

Roads, 13-14, 57, 64, 107, 109-10, 186, 206

Rocks, the (Sydney), 62, 198

Roebuck, J., 146

Rose Hill, 113

Rum, 6, 9-10

Ruse, James, 8, 114

Schools, 17, 87-8, 92, 231; grammar, 87; primary, 89

Science and technology, in agriculture, 120-1, 124; in industry, 149, 203-4

Scotland, 51

Secondary industry, 142-4, 145-65; in Australia, 147-8, 158-65; iron and steel, 146-57

Settlers, first, 3, 83; free, 51; problems of, 56-7

Sewerage, 206

Shaftesbury, *Lord*, 90

Sheep farming, 9, 14, 19-20, 41, 42, 46, 122-3, 129

Shipping, 95-6, 107, 108-9, 136

Shops Act (1899), 233

Slavery, abolition of, 89

Smallpox, inoculation, 95

Snowy River Scheme, 134 (map)

Social advance, 235-7

Social classes, 5, 84; Australian colonial society, 83-92; con-

Social Classes (*contd*) victs, 6; emancipists, 7; gentry, 84-5; hierarchical arrangement, 84-5; officials, 5; traders and merchants, 6

Social life in the nineteenth century, 185-7

South Australia, 29, 30, 67-73; Company, 68-9, 71; compulsory arbitration in, 233; iron and steel industry, 155-6, wheat industry, 117-19

Squatters, 21, 40-50

Staple commodity, 8, 18

Steam power, 96-8; boat, 101-2; first engine in Australia, 100; train, 100-1

Steamships, 108-9

Steam turbine, 102, 103

Steel, *see* iron and steel

Stephenson, George, 101

Stirling, *Sir* James, 66, 219

Strikes, 173, 175, 178; (1890-91), 233

Stripper, Ridley's (diagram), 118-19

Sturt, Charles, 22-33; first journey of, 22-5; map of explorations, 22, 31; second journey of, 25-9; third expedition, 30-3

Sugar industry, 138-41; map, 140; Colonial Sugar Refining Co, 140-1

Supreme Court, 216

Superphosphates, 124, 159

Sydney, 180-93; colonial, 181-3; expansion (present day), 192-3; (1788-1950), map, 193; modern buildings, 192; plan of in Macquarie's time, 12; planning growth of, 190-2; services and amenities, 188-9; twentieth century, 189-90; under Macquarie, 11-12

Sydney Harbour Bridge, 154, 191, 192

Sydney Municipal Council, 185

Tank Stream, 180, 181, 183
Tariffs, 177; problem, 244-5
Tasmania, 50, 65, 82, 223
Telephone and telegraph, 104
Tench, Watkin, 114
Ticket-of-leave, 47
Towns, 6-7, 52
Trade unions, 168-79; struggles of, 172-3; Shearers', 172
Transport, 189; steam, 107-111
Transportation, 15, 47-8, 50, 58-9, 74
Tull, Jethro, 113
Turbine, steam, 103-4

Unemployment, 15, 72-3, 178
University, 87, 98, 186
United Kingdom, conditions in, 51-2
Utilitarians, 91

Van Diemen's Land, 21, 36, 48, 50, 57-8, 65, 88, 217, 218
Victoria, 223; goldfields, 75-7, 79
Victoria, *Queen*, 224
Voting, for women, 230; qualifications, 219, 222; rights, 228-30

Wage, 36, 52, 53, 56, 81, 120, 236; basic, 177-8

Warragamba Dam, 191
Water supply, 206
Watt, James, 98, 99, 100; beam engine, 99
Wells Fargo, 107
Wentworth, William Charles, 92, 197
Western Australia, 65-7, 156, 219, 247
Whaling industry, 6, 19, 36, 70
Wheat industry, 117-19, 123-6, 131-2
White Australia Policy, 174, 235
Whyalla, 155, 160
Wilberforce, William, 89
Wilkinson, John, 99-100
Wireless, 104
Wool, 14, 19, 21; and Macarthur, 116-17, 122-3, 131-2; industry, 96
Workers, Australia's need for, 53-5
Working conditions, 166-79, 232-3
World War I, 153
World War II, and industry, 153-7, 178-9; and social welfare, 178-9
Wright, Wilbur, 106

Yampi Sound, 156